CROSSI
THE STAGE

Redesigning Senior Year

Nancy Faust Sizer

HEINEMANN ■ Portsmouth, NH

Heinemann
A division of Reed Elsevier Inc.
361 Hanover Street
Portsmouth, NH 03801–3912
www.heinemann.com

Offices and agents throughout the world

Library of Congress Cataloging-in-Publication Data
Sizer, Nancy Faust.
Crossing the stage : redesigning senior year / Nancy Faust Sizer.
p. cm.
Includes bibliographical references and index.
ISBN 0-325-00412-9
1. Twelfth grade (Education)—United States.
2. High school students—United States. I. Title.
LB1629. 7 12th .S59 2002
373.238—dc21 2002004064

Editors: Leigh Peake and Alan Huisman
Production: Elizabeth Valway
Cover design: Joni Doherty
Typesetter: Technologies 'N Typography, Inc.
Manufacturing: Steve Bernier

Printed in the United States of America on acid-free paper
06 05 04 03 02 VP 1 2 3 4 5

For Ted

who has lived with me, but also with this book, for many years.

Foreword

Reading *Crossing the Stage,* voices echo down the years from my own past.

"We're in charge now!" from my best friend, when we were high school seniors forty years ago.

"They remembered every play in every game, and every movie we went to on Saturday nights," Jimmy said thirty years ago, speaking of his high school buddies when I asked why he returned to the small college in Ohio where I was an assistant coach. He had left school at the end of his sophomore year, discouraged at the financial and academic struggles he faced, not expecting to return. "They were my best friends in high school, and they stayed home and went to work in the mills. I realized senior year was likely to be the high point of their lives, and it wasn't all that great. I want something more."

"That job has taken over my life!" Melissa reported twenty Aprils ago. A most talented and sensitive writer, and a model student—hard working, enthusiastic, reliable, helpful to her classmates, generous in her critique of teachers—Melissa was explaining her virtual disappearance from school over the past four weeks. She'd taken a job waitressing at a local diner in the evenings. "The people there aren't all that interesting and the work is routine, but it's the only place in my life where people actually depend on me, so I look forward to it every day, and don't like days off. It's the most seductive thing that's ever happened to me."

Two days before graduation fifteen years ago, Joy came into my office laughing through her sobs. "I've wanted this year to end for months, and now I can't bear to leave here . . . it's been the best year of my life."

Ten years ago, a mother of a June graduate (the first of three sons) called in August: "I didn't believe you in October when you said I'd be relieved to have Jeff out of the house. Not him—he's been so special—and not me, I thought. But I want you to know that I'm counting the days until he leaves for college, even if he's not, and it can't come fast enough."

At dinner with friends ten days ago, we were discussing senior year from the perspective of parents. "I decided," Alice, whose son had graduated from high school in the last decade, reported, "that if you're the mother of a son, your only real job is to keep him alive during his senior year. They're so reckless! If they make it through graduation, you've done your job."

Nancy Sizer captures the senior year in a way no one has before in *Crossing the Stage*. Her careful and extensive research, joined with her own experience with seniors—in her words, as one herself, as a mother, as a teacher of seniors—and with her thoughtful analysis give her writing a power and authenticity found only in the very best books about kids and schools.

For most of us of a certain age, the senior year was a genuine marking point. We expected to work harder as seniors than we had in earlier years. For many (or even most) of us, it was the end of formal education, and no stigma was attached to not going on to college. We joined an adult workforce in which a high school diploma marked us as educated, and we had a more than reasonable chance financially to become or remain a part of the growing middle class. Some, but not most of us, would leave our communities to go elsewhere seeking our fortunes, or more education. If our senior years were never as warm and happy and saccharine as the Andy Hardy movies made it out to be, it was loaded nonetheless with enormous genuine as well as symbolic importance.

Using an ingenious design, Sizer takes us chronologically and thematically through the senior year, using seniors' own words to bring the year vibrantly and achingly alive. She lets them talk us through their relationships with their teachers, their friends, and their families, through the college application process, the second semester and the infamous and now passively and almost universally accepted senioritis.

Somewhere over the past quarter century, as Sizer points out, high school has become "a way station" for our children. While most of us, in various ways—parents, teachers and administrators, employers, college admissions officers and legislators—have made our own largely unwitting contributions to this sea change, we also find ourselves peculiarly mystified at how it happened. Sizer helps us understand what has happened by describing with acute sensitivity what the senior year is like for those who are adolescents today in our nation's schools.

It is the voices of these seniors that give the book its power. We hear the confusion and bravado and occasional insights, the hypocrisy and opportunism, and the resignation and disappointment that characterize so many of our students' senior years. While she doesn't let these seniors off the hook, Sizer wisely doesn't shake them until they come to their senses, as many readers will want to do. Her greatest gift is that she helps us to understand that these seniors, in their various and mostly honest ways, are simply trying to negotiate an honorable way through a system that we have built for them.

Student voices may give the book its power, but it is Sizer's careful analysis that helps us understand what they say. If the careful researcher gathered the data, it is the passionate and wise teacher in Sizer who makes visible what we have created. She helps us to see unmistakably that the convergence of expectations, mythologies, transitions, responsibilities, fantasies, and consequences over several decades have made the senior year untenable. It serves no one well, neither the larger society nor each year's crop of seniors. Reading *Crossing the Stage,* no one can be proud of this passage as it now exists.

Fortunately, Sizer also provides us with a description of a way out of this mess. Some recommendations can be implemented unilaterally by schools, colleges, and parents and some of each will no doubt do so. Because her recommendations are thoughtfully sensible rather than flashy, require adults to trust one another as well as cooperate, and to work toward a common good rather than individual advantage, they may well be beyond our ability to achieve. For all of us who care about public schools, and especially for our seniors, we can hope that enough of us will heed Nancy Sizer's call for change.

—Rick Lear
Center on Reinventing Public Education
University of Washington

Preface

I have been a senior, the mother of four seniors, and the teacher of hundreds more over twenty-five years. During that time I watched the quality of the senior year decline, especially its purpose. I was convinced that the seniors themselves perceived this decline and had ideas about it. I also knew that since any plans for reform had best be made with their thoughts in mind, someone should find out what they were.

That someone turned out to be me. In 1994–95, enjoying my first year out of the classroom but missing it acutely, I conducted tape-recorded interviews with more than 150 seniors in twenty-six diverse schools all over the country. I talked with them as individuals and in small groups. I did follow-up interviews at two schools to mark attitude changes over the year. (I did not interview dropouts.) This book derives in part from the story these students told me about their senior year as they saw it. The students' names in the stories at the beginning of the first six chapters are pseudonyms and, in some cases, I used sentences from different sources to build a narrative with greater depth.

Since I had taught mostly in middle- and upper-middle-class high schools, I complemented my own experience by seeking out students with more diverse backgrounds. Many of my most memorable interviews took place in inner cities, alternative learning programs, and technical high schools.

There is much talk about "going to college" in this book. In the fall, most seniors, even those who said they had little money and hated school, insisted they intended to continue their formal education after high school. However, in the spring a measurable number of students admitted they were not going to college or training programs—at least not for a while. Later I learned that this pattern—a near-universal expectation that college is ahead, at least in the beginning of the senior year—is remarkably common.

To an amazing extent, the seniors I talked with felt they were on a momentous and recordable journey. They were not surprised that I wanted to interview them. They were eager to describe their experiences, and they were able to tell their story not only in words but also by the way they sat, in their tone of voice, and with the look on their face. I have relied heavily on their own language in this retelling, since they were impressively insightful, mostly honest, and sometimes poignant narrators of their story. (I should mention here that although the portraits I present in this book are straight from the students' mouths, a few are composites—for the obvious reasons of conciseness and readability.) It was fun talking to seniors who didn't owe me papers or who weren't going to ask me to write recommendations. They were refreshingly straightforward. I liked them, and when you meet them in these pages, I think you will too.

I am concentrating here on seniors' public life, on the ways in which they and the high school intersect. Although the story they told in our interviews was complex, I am aware that it was not complete. There were important parts of their private lives which they were not likely to share with a stranger and about which I chose not to ask any questions. However, a few made statements about and allusions to those more personal areas that yielded clues to their lives as a whole during this challenging period.

As for questions, I needed to ask very few. I usually started by observing that most students looked forward to being seniors. Had they? And how was it going now that they were? They took it from there, spinning the details of their lives into themes of clarity, irony, transition, tradition, expectations, and disillusionment.

I might, I suppose, have been able to identify these themes even if I had never talked with seniors face-to-face. And I suppose I could have collected the written stories of hundreds of seniors whom I never met. But my hands-on research suited a teacher who still wanted to be of help. By way of these conversations, I was able to meet some fascinating people; hear and record their stories at considerable length; and offer them respect, sympathy, and perhaps perspective.

Later, at home, gathering their sentences off the tape recorder brought their voices and even their faces back, a rich harvest. Still later, as the transition counselor in a small public school, I was able to test my emerging perceptions against another crop of students.

And finally, by writing about the seniors' experience beginning with the way they perceived it, I can bring to seniors, teachers, parents, and the policy community a richer analysis of what the senior year in high school is like these days and what we can all do to improve it.

Acknowledgments

Over the years, when people asked me about this book and I told them I was writing about seniors, many took a look at my graying hair and assumed that I was writing about *those* seniors. But although the two groups earned their titles because they have the poignant prospect of leave-taking in common, it is the seniors in high school who have fascinated me the most, and over many years. I am grateful to the many teachers and parents who helped me see senior year as a particularly important but also confusing and demanding time in a person's life. Their stories, their critiques, their explanations and regrets—as well as my own—motivated me to find out what seniors themselves thought about life just before they "crossed the stage."

And so I added more stories to my growing body of lore. I am grateful to the adults who allowed me to arrange interviews and to the students who participated so eagerly and articulately in the following high schools: The Alternate Diploma Program, Newport, Rhode Island; Barris High School, Muncie, Indiana; The Bromfield School, Harvard, Massachusetts; Chicago Vocational School, Chicago, Illinois; Classical High School, Providence, Rhode Island; Cooley High School, Detroit, Michigan; Croton Harmon High School, Croton-on-Hudson, New York; Jefferson Davis High School, Houston, Texas; Eastlake High School, Redmond, Washington; Gig Harbor High School, Gig Harbor, Washington; Grass Lake High School, Grass Lake, Michigan; Hanover High School, Hanover, New Hampshire; Homestead High School, Cupertino, California; Hope High School, Providence, Rhode Island; Indiana School of Math and Science, Muncie, Indiana; Kirkwood High School, Kirkwood, Missouri; Minute Man Science and Technology Center, Lexington, Massachusetts; Montachusett Technical School, Fitchburg, Massachusetts; Mt. Pleasant High School, Providence, Rhode Island; Oceana High School, Pacifica, California; Phillips

Academy, Andover, Massachusetts; Pueblo High School, Pueblo, Colorado; Rogers High School, Newport, Rhode Island; Vandercook Lake High School, Vandercook Lake, Michigan; Westbury High School, Houston, Texas; The Wheeler School, Providence, Rhode Island.

With the seniors' voices still buzzing in my head, it was time for analysis. What inevitably and even preferably will stay the same in the senior year? What must change? What improvements are the wisest and most feasible? Many helped me answer those questions. Besides the books cited in the references, work on transition to adulthood by Robert Kegan, Fred Newmann, and Kathy Simon was especially useful. Two experiences in Washington, D.C., were helpful. One was my work in the Leader Schools initiative of the Corporation for National Service, through which I learned much about how service learning can help a high school student connect with his or her future; this greatly influenced my thinking about senior projects. The other was my membership in the National Commission on the High School Senior Year. Through its readings, its speakers, and its discussions over a year, as well as the shaping of its reports and the interviews with the press that followed their publication, I not only broadened and deepened my concerns but learned how to express my own ideas more concisely. I thank the atmosphere "inside the Beltway" for its insistence on focus and results. It's not all we need, but we do need it at times, jointly (as a country) and individually (for me, as a writer who is loaded down with details and needs to get her message out).

Although I cast my net widely through these meetings and readings, my instinct as a career teacher was to stay close to the high schools, and it was in them that I learned the most. I am particularly grateful for the work of the seniors' teachers (and their valiant colleagues, their principals) in Bromfield High School, Harvard, Massachusetts; Eastlake High School, Redmond, Washington; Jericho High School, Jericho, New York; Maryville High School, Maryville, Tennessee; Francis W. Parker Charter Essential School, Devens, Massachusetts; and Souhegan High School, Amherst, New Hampshire. Through conferences, exhibitions, visits, and letters, I learned much about what these teachers thought, what they did, and what they thought about what they had done. Lots of people these days use the word *reflection:* these teachers embody it. Their examples and their thinking lend vitality and authenticity to the last section of this book.

But not just my ideas about senior year needed shaping; so did my book. How to cast my findings? As a description of a culture or as a polemic? A call for help or an action plan? Hundreds of conversations with family, friends, and colleagues have helped me find the place in between these poles where I can comfortably stand. Jim Cullen, Andy Hrycyna, Betsy Lerner, and Carole Saltz also read the book in various iterations and gave valued specific advice. And at Heinemann I am especially grateful for the substantial help of Alan Huisman, Leigh Peake, and Bill Varner. I was more stubborn as an author than I expected to be, but all these people believed in the book and helped me bring it to a conclusion.

And then there is Ted Sizer. Besides being my number one fan, an excellent quality in a husband, he served this project in nearly every capacity. Although he has always made it abundantly clear that he respected my career as a classroom teacher, nearest to where the real action is, he kept me grounded in the broader world of high school reform partly by what he suggested that I read, partly by what he and his colleagues said and did. He acted as a model to me in every book he ever wrote, especially the most recent one, *The Students Are Watching: Schools and the Moral Contract,* which we wrote together. It was he who first suggested further work on the senior year (among dozens of other worthwhile projects that frequently occur to his fertile imagination) without realizing, I suspect, that I would be interested in doing it. When it turned out that I was, his contributions were large and small, self-conscious and serendipitous. Besides helping me shape both the ideas *and* the book, he funded my research trips, introduced me to many of the schools in which I conducted interviews, talked over several versions of the book's structure, critiqued key ideas, read drafts, marveled at the seniors' statements, and even, when necessary, advised me on whether to phone or email the editor (pretty small potatoes as a dilemma, but not to me at the time) and then instructed me on how to send attachments! I was sometimes stubborn with him, too, a situation he always handled beautifully. He is the wisest and most gracious person I know, and it is an honor to dedicate my book to him.

Introduction

America's high school seniors are in such trouble that a national commission was created to analyze the problems inherent in the senior year and come up with solutions. I welcome their work—I served on the commission—but having been a high school teacher for twenty-five years, I don't need outsiders to tell me something is amiss. The experience of being a senior has grown more and more confusing and, for too many, meaningless. Senior year is seen as a kind of holding tank, a way station on the road to somewhere else. That "somewhere else," the object of so much of the seniors' focus, takes on enormous, even disproportionate, importance in the seniors' minds. However, though the seniors' minds are elsewhere, their bodies are still in high school, and work must be found for them to do there.

The institutions that ought to support the seniors—high schools, colleges, the workplace—seem isolated from one another. High schools charge ahead with the same old schedule and the same old program, seemingly uninterested in the number of new challenges that have been added to the seniors' lives, only marginally willing to help them cope. More and more colleges are admitting students on the basis of tests taken and grades earned during the junior year; the senior year is thus no longer a period when important accomplishments and growth are expected. Workplaces are notorious for being uninterested in high school transcripts, attendance records, or the work that was done there.

The result is emotional chaos, which seniors try to simplify by calling it stress. There is too much to do; seniors are living at least two lives at once, and in neither can they do as well as they would like. Should I finish this paper or check out the website of that college? Should I master this skill needed for a job in the local factory or that skill needed to pass chemistry? Can I do both? Neither? Maybe I'll just go out with my friends and clear my head.

Academic rigor is defined in new ways in the final year of high school. Seniors face "ultimate tracking" as they prepare themselves to operate effectively in a wide variety of environments. Some students cripple themselves on the hurdles, while others slip serenely under the bar. And as they do, they watch one another—disapprovingly. After years together, they are preparing for the big breakup. Expectations are so broad and competition so fierce that there is little time to reflect on and manage the experience. As a result, a senior year is often handled unwisely—and is more unhappy than most seniors feel able to admit.

For years, while I was teaching them, I blamed individual seniors for hysteria or laziness or for not being able to resist the cynicism and manipulation that crept into so many of their attitudes. Getting away from the classroom, I have been able to see more clearly that for teachers and students alike, senior year is a cultural and political challenge at least as much as it is a personal one. And that's good news, because it means there are concrete steps we can take.

What's Being a Senior Really Like?

Step one is to understand what the senior year really is in the mind of someone who is going through it. Being a senior is a pervasive American cultural experience, ranking up there with being married, having children, holding a job, attending church, and going to baseball games. Between 80 and 90 percent of our teenagers finish high school. They build up expectations for their senior year, live through it self-consciously, and remember it clearly for years. These are—or are meant to be—their "glory days." More young women may wear a prom dress than a wedding dress. High school graduation is a milestone.

Senior years everywhere have strikingly common features. Despite tremendous differences among schools, the experience of going to and then leaving high school is a unifying one. One will be part of "the class of 2005" whether one is rich or poor, northerner or southerner, boy or girl, black or white. The spotlight shown on seniors captures the imagination of far more people than just the seniors and their parents and teachers. The experience is full of fascination and mythology for us all.

The way the year is spent—or misspent—is significant. Other nations have high schools, and their young people experience many of the same transitions and rituals. But in most other nations, seniors expect to take an important exam at the end of the year. Their future depends on how well they do on it: they will not have time to be school politicians, varsity athletes, and homecoming queens. In the United States, for a variety of good and bad reasons, the senior year is perceived to be not as rigorously academic as the earlier high school years. It is both a kind of apogee and moratorium at once, and our young people turn their prodigious energy toward other things. "Being a senior" is far more important than any specific piece of schoolwork a senior might do or any specific qualification a senior might earn. Status outweighs performance, at least academic performance.

And ceremony outweighs achievement. The pomp and circumstance of the typical American graduation ceremony has taken on a meaning of its own. The function of high school may have been forgotten or even spurned months before. But for seniors, the form—participation in a joyous and proud ceremony—still carries a lot of clout. Underneath all the posturing lies the conviction that they will be different people once they have walked across that auditorium stage. Since the prospect both delights and terrifies them, it absorbs a great deal of energy.

The Senior's Cultural Imperatives

When faced with personal challenges like this one, we often turn to culture for guidance. But what is culture? Anna Quindlen, in *One True Thing,* writes, "Everyone makes up their little stories and then they wonder why their own lives aren't like that" (1998). I think of culture as those "little stories," those voices in our head that tell us what is good and bad, beautiful and ugly, natural and unnatural.

When we older folk meet a senior in high school, few of us can resist telling an anecdote from our own senior year. Some of these memories dwell on our triumphs and some on our troubles, but all reinforce the idea that it was a vibrant and crucial time, one dominated by bonding and ritual. And even if our stories begin with an acknowledgment of how scared we were, they usually end with the message that a newfound energy and maturity were somehow found to deal with tremendous new challenges. The math course was passed. The application was filled out. The winning point was made. The prom was well organized. The yearbook came out on time. The emphasis here is on "somehow." In our memories, the transformation was magical. It could happen to these seniors too. Hence the assumptions that surround the experience of the senior year.

Seniors in high school have dozens of these "little stories," these insistent voices, in and outside their head, telling them what, as seniors, they will be like, what they must do, even what they will feel like. It is a year filled with cultural imperatives.

Seniors in high school have dozens of these "little stories," these insistent voices, in and outside their head, telling them what, as seniors, they will be like, what they must do, even what they will feel like. It is a year filled with cultural imperatives. Talking with seniors, I heard so many "supposed to's," so many "should's," so many "since I am a senior's," it seemed as if all the seniors in the country had been handed the same piece of music and were distinguished from one another only in the way they chose to sing. Nearly every senior agreed with at least a few of these cultural imperatives:

- Transition dominates the senior year. It is present in what the students do, what they think about, how they relate to adults and to one another, what they think of themselves. And transition is harder work than many of us remember.
- Senior year is meant to be a rite of passage between childhood and adulthood. A young woman I spoke with had been bringing her mother home from bars since she was nine, but she did not feel she would really be considered an adult until she graduated from high school. Another senior, a young man, said, "I'm not just leaving high school; I'm leaving the first eighteen years of my life. It's kind of a morbid thought, but you almost want to have all your affairs in order before you move on."
- Seniors have a daunting job to do: leave a less selective, less expensive institution that has in most cases become very familiar and strike out in a new direction. "You want to take as much of the intensity as you can, before you need to start all

over again. It's your best year, because after that you have to go through life."

- Seniors expect to be honored as leaders. They will be—and belong—in the spotlight. "Seniors," one of them stated, half-shy, half-boasting, "are the hottest of hot stuff. I can express myself as a senior. I'm admired more. My voice can be heard with more emphasis." Another felt that experiencing senior year was like being the bride at a wedding: "Everyone wants to be you, not literally, of course, but that's what they aspire to." "Senior year," one student confided, "you're up there. You're the tallest. You're the high ones in the school, the ones in the front, in the middle of the pictures. You're supposed to be at the peak of your form, in school and in sports"; as the oldest students in the school, they are "coteachers, almost." Theirs are the days of being prom queen—or at least, as one young woman put it (poignantly, since she was not), "in the running for prom queen." This is the year to catch the touchdown pass.
- "Your senior year is the last chance to enjoy the only real friendships you'll ever have." Though the seniors have no direct evidence, they have been told this so often they believe it. Friends are not only to enjoy, however. Senior year, they are convinced, is when these friendships need to be cemented, "so that you will always have them."
- The glorious nature of senior year will trump personal attributes and personal circumstances. "The high school years are the best in your life, and senior year is the best year in high school," said a young woman in a large and dreary high school, in between a litany of specific complaints. Another senior, mired in extraordinary family problems, nevertheless asserted, "I'm a senior. I'm at the top now. This is going to be the pinnacle and it's supposed to be the finest year of my life." Later, changes will be catalogued. Later, issues of power, responsibility, reputation, may be analyzed in terms of what they meant about a person's life. Each individual story can be weighed and measured. But first, there is the simple issue of status, and the change in status happens to every senior.

"I'm a senior. I'm at the top now. This is going to be the pinnacle and it's supposed to be the finest year of my life."

- Life for seniors ought to be easy—at least in school. "Senior year is like a payoff for all the hard work you did in your first three years." One student told me that he had first heard that senior year would be "your party year" when he was in sixth grade. "It sounded like a *great* idea," even to an eleven-year-old, "but then I didn't turn out to be much of a partier."
- Seniors live in three time dimensions at once. They are reaping the rewards—or bitter fruits—of the past; they are living in a complicated, stressful ("hyperefficient or maybe just hyper") present; and they are "creating memories for the future," so that some day they can be as nostalgic as Bruce Springsteen (who wrote "Glory Days" well after his senior year in high school) and their parents and their parents' friends. Living in the present while planning for the future can test the mettle of even the oldest and wisest of us.
- Great changes are anticipated. "I can remember the day the old seniors left and we all had a celebration. We kept saying, 'I can't believe I'm going to be a senior!' Essentially it was as if we were a different person." It is a year full of snapshots, but it is still a whole year long. It is a year when "the weeks go by *so* fast, but the hours go by *so* slowly." Seniors need money, although they won't have the time to earn it if they are to do everything else well. They also need to sleep enough, eat right, help around the house, be nice to the neighbors, just as if they were not living through the most eventful and crucial year of their lives.
- All these achievements, all these transitions, are meant to be, or at least to look, effortless. That's what the culture demands—being "cool." Seniors' and their families' dreams are exposed for all to see. But they mustn't look nervous. They need to be considered ready for the next step. They need to achieve but make it all look easy. They need to be beautiful but without make-up. They need to stay idealistic yet take part in a college admissions and job procurement process that is, in some respects, dishonest and unjust. They need to deal—really deal—with the issue of money and how much of it they have or haven't got. They need to be hopeful but not arrogant, proud but not entitled.

The Down Side of Expectations

Expectations are the baggage on the senior train: necessary but also burdensome. So many of the students I listened to seemed calm, hopeful, sure that they had "earned" their status. But in every case, there were also pockets of almost desperate darkness. "I expected a lot. Nobody really said anything about the pressures that would come with it." Senior year, they said, was "supposed to be perfect."

Perfect? For whom? These cultural imperatives are not only numerous and extravagant but also at cross-purposes with one another. Looking "cool" is not the same as taking "down time," and looking like an achiever sometimes gets in the way of being one. Too many seniors are warped and defeated by the sheer bulk of these "little stories," so that they end up wondering "why their own lives aren't like that." "This is fantasy-to-reality year," one of them told me in midwinter, and for him the "reality" had already been painful.

Several students I talked with described senior year as "a year full of compromises." No matter how hard they might try not to show it, they all had one or another deep disappointment. One "model student" in Michigan slid easily into a number of colleges, hardly breaking a sweat, but then found that she had a terrible time making the decision of where to go. She had followed directions beautifully, but would she be able to act on her own? What had high school taught her, anyway? A young Texan had caught that touchdown pass and been wonderfully celebrated by the newspapers, his school, and his family, only to find that without better work in math he might not graduate.

Senior year is nearly as hard on parents and teachers as it is on the seniors. Much of the emotional turmoil in seniors and in the people who work with them is understandable. There is no point in grieving unduly about the natural process of growing up. We adults must be honest, however, about our own challenge: the next phase of life for people we have come to treasure will have to be somewhere else. Indeed, their departure has already begun. There are many other dynamics in the senior year, but the central pair are these: the students are facing considerable change, and the people in their lives who would normally help them cope are facing considerable change themselves.

Shifting Into Neutral

Step two is to identify and understand the aspects of high school that have taken an undesirable form, almost without our noticing. "Senior year," I was told again and again, "is blow-off time." For many students, the work is not meaningful. Most believe that because they have collected the bulk of the credits they need for graduation by the time they end junior year, senior year is not designed for academic growth. They have "permission to coast." This is true even in schools where the seniors' skills are inadequate for a good job or the entry-level courses in the local college. A certain amount of treading water will be tolerated.

How can that be?

Progress through high school has become almost automatic, which puts less emphasis on the careful demonstration of increasing proficiency in necessary skills and increasing sophistication about important content. Students may know how many credits they still lack, but they do not know how much they know and are able to do in order to perform well, in whatever arena, after high school. They know they passed algebra in the ninth grade; they don't know how much they still remember or whether it might be needed in a job or whether they will be able to use what they know—and learn more—once they are elsewhere. The same uncertainty exists regarding reading and writing. Even though they are tested constantly, the format of the tests—rushed, high-stakes, external, standardized, crammed into a room with a lot of other nervous people—makes them doubt the results. They don't know whether they will be able to do the close reading that will matter to them. Without knowing what they still need to learn, they carry around a lot of subliminal nervousness, but they are not sufficiently alert to the dangers of a year of "coasting."

Sensing no real emergency in a failure to make much academic progress, the seniors put their energy into the transition and to making whatever progress they have made look as impressive as possible. They also attend to the many other cultural imperatives related to senior year, many of which require a lot of time. As a result, the academic purposes of high school are further shortchanged. Since students and teachers relate mostly on that academic dimension, their relationships suffer.

Too many seniors limp away from high school, ashamed of their last few months there, no longer as respected by themselves, their peers, and their teachers as they were just months earlier. Too many parents and teachers are angry as well as hurt as they watch them go. Parents may have a chance to repair these frayed relationships. But many teachers do not, and it affects the way they feel about their work. Perhaps a wealthy nation can afford to give a year of "retirement" to its eighteen-year-olds, can let the prom replace intellectual development as the focus of school. Perhaps—or perhaps not.

Not With a Bang But a Whimper

In most cases, senior year does not live up to the hopes that the seniors, their families, and their teachers have for it. It is a year in which confusion, dishonesty, fear, risk taking, cynicism, and malingering have come to play too large a part. Not every student succumbs to behavior like this, of course. But for too many of them, the culture seems to be there, ready to pounce. "She tried to keep her balance," one senior said, describing her older sister's senior year. "But in the end, she slipped down." It was a struggle she too was about to undertake and which she feared, because she already sensed that she would lose it.

Seniors are dealing with more than just a sense of foreboding. They have a disease named after them: *senioritis.* A student in Michigan described it this way: "I have a friend who's gotten A's and B's her whole life. And ever since spring break she's not there any more. She just doesn't—it's just not easy for her to do what she has to do any more."

"I have a friend who's gotten A's and B's her whole life. And ever since spring break she's not there any more. She just doesn't—it's just not easy for her to do what she has to do any more."

There are many reasons the seniors seem to fade away. Many, in fact, lose their ability to fully engage in their work long before spring break. Some reasons are more general, as in the case of the student who had heard for years that during senior year, he "wouldn't have to work"—essentially, that he would get something for nothing. He never seemed to doubt that "right." Other reasons are more specific. Unreasonable time demands in junior year and in the fall of senior year inevitably lead even the "best" seniors first to taking efficiency measures, then to cutting corners. Juggling a number of deadlines leads to procrastination and in time to simply not meeting one or more of them.

Finally, there is the widespread feeling that once the last high school grades have been sent to the college or the job, there is no longer any need to do one's best. Learning has not been for a larger goal but "just to get the grades." Once the grades do not matter, schoolwork doesn't matter. This is the cultural expectation that most clearly demeans the high school, yet it is overwhelmingly endorsed by seniors and even many of their parents; even some teachers reluctantly accept it as if it were as inevitable as the tide. "I'm definitely not typical, because I'm still working," one senior admitted, somewhat apologetically. Resisting her classmates' posture of edgy, even belligerent lassitude took real energy on her part, energy that might have been used elsewhere. And she was ostracized.

By spring term, most seniors declare that they are "worn out." The 70 percent who are still expecting to go to college are tired of "playing the game." The endless conversations about who got accepted where, the primacy of standardized testing, the way they pumped up their credentials in order to compete, have all undermined their most honest picture of themselves, the one they confront in the middle of the night. They have become dispirited by the exigencies of what others call the "real world," by the number of questionable practices in which they have taken part, by the number of thorny problems they have tried to resolve. They stop doing homework, act out via pranks that are sometimes funny, sometimes just angry, or withdraw physically and emotionally. They threaten perfectly healthy relationships that, earlier, they had taken some care to build, and the only reason they can find for doing so leads them to express a cynicism about their school, their town, their families, and their teachers that they may not want to feel.

For years I taught seniors and was involved in those relationships. I expected the students I knew to withstand the destructive culture that had grown up around the spring term. When they could not, I was disappointed, hurt; I blamed them and myself. I considered "senioritis" a collection of individual failures, including my own.

What Can We Do About It?

Experiencing the senior culture more broadly has lent perspective. It has given me a chance once again to recognize senior year as a multidimensional challenge for them as well as a frustration for us. Even though we adults may have been seniors in high school once, we need both a reminder and an update. The far-flung and anonymous seniors whom I interviewed, their words and their stories, may help us find the excitement, confusion, and sensitivity—perhaps even the charm—that still resides in the youngsters we ourselves deal with. Seeing the experience and the culture of the senior year for what it has become may help us understand and appreciate the individuals who are caught up in it.

But we need more than just sympathy and adjustment. We need change, and this is step three. There are not going to be any cheap or quick fixes. We have to solve our problem as Americans, not just as competitors in a world economy. A terrifying national exam would change some aspects of the experience for high school seniors and the adults who care for them. It would provide a certain motivation and end some of the malingering. But it would not necessarily improve the seniors as learners or as people.

Holding on to the structure of senior year but jamming it with a panoply of watered-down courses is more than a failure of imagination; it is a failure of purpose. Sending students away from high school without making an effort to shape their experiences or evaluate what they are learning is just as irresponsible, at least for those who intend to award a meaningful high school degree.

We can't abdicate the senior year; we need, instead, to redesign it. With the seniors' help, we need to examine the senior year for what should stay the same and what can be altered in small and even big ways. Perhaps we teachers should recognize that the academic growth that has been our worthy stock in trade for many years must be not abandoned, not cheapened, but altered to suit the seniors' changed circumstances. We need to treat high school seniors like adults nearly ready to become competent and fulfilled workers at real jobs, rather than as children out at recess for a whole year. But we need to decide these questions, high school by high school, by looking at the experience full in the face, as an expression of our personal but also of our national values.

We need new, more authentic, more impressive academic hurdles and rituals. We need to define academic growth differently, with skills, habits, and attitudes taking on more importance, "carnegie units" and memorization somewhat less. We need more fully to acknowledge—and learn how to assess—other kinds of growth. A change in the seniors' routines and expectations does not necessarily mean a decline in academic challenge. Taking stock, reflection, synthesis, a senior seminar, a capstone senior project, immersion into a demanding workplace, and the intelligent assembling of the material needed to make good decisions about their own future would be worthy ways for seniors to spend their time. There would still be room in the senior program for making up for lost ground where it is needed and for offering demanding courses where they are called for. There is much we could do.

And there is much we must do. Most of all, we need to bring about a more graceful transition between high school and what follows it. Our goal is to leave all the participants feeling that the senior year was a glory time but also one of permanent usefulness, one to feel proud of after all. High school seniors need to live productively in the present even as they prepare intelligently for the future. It is a tall order, but they are up to it. And we parents and teachers need to understand and help them at the same time we prepare to let them go.

A school principal recently told me, "*We* failed our students' senior year, because we didn't help them become sturdy enough to thrive—or even survive—in the first year after high school." He and his faculty are completely redesigning the experience they are offering, concentrating on the special challenges seniors face, helping each one develop the appropriate academic and emotional skills. I really admire that principal and faculty for their willingness to accept responsibility and to get to work. I hope this book will help them do so.

PART ONE

1 Seniors and Their Teachers

Michael wasn't sure what to make of his senior year. It was supposed to be so different, but he had the same schedule as the year before, the same friends, the same extracurricular activities. His courses still followed the pattern he had experienced all through high school: two weeks of information dispersed to the student, one hour of information relayed back to the teacher. And he took the same subjects. He had to take English, of course—he needed four years of English to graduate—and government was a senior requirement. He was advised to continue French and math, because if he dropped them now, he'd forget things and never be able to get back to where he was. He should probably take a science too—"that would look good on my transcript"—and it would be nice to tuck in one more photography course before he graduated.

It felt as rushed as ever, except that he was determined to be far-sighted about it. This was his last chance. "You absolutely have to do well, because colleges really do look at your senior year to see how hard the classes you're taking are and how well you're doing in them." He resolved to start the year right, with an outstanding effort on each of the first big assignments. "The first paper of the year makes an important statement," he believed. "When you turn in your first project you set your standards for the whole year. After you set that standard, the teachers expect it. They think of you as an A student. Even though later you might not live up to their expectations." All his papers had to be typed, spell-checked, put in binders. He needed to do his job on the newspaper in a way that would show what he had learned about being a leader. It was important to get into shape quickly so he could hit the ground running in soccer. And when he got a chance, he would send away for some more college catalogues.

Although school seemed mostly the same, there were subtle, welcome differences. "I can chat with a few of my teachers about a lot of things. Before senior year, they were so separate from the students." Teachers of seniors seemed to have first names, nicknames, kids of their own, and other personal attributes. They went to the market late at night in their blue jeans. They had gone to college themselves and told personal anecdotes about how they got there. "They were not always as serious as they are now. They tell us what they went through when they were kids and more about what they think."

Classes had more variety. "The teacher can act a little wacky without losing discipline." For example, Michael's English teacher threw a piece of string on the floor and then demanded: is it art? When the students gave the predictable responses and were ready to move on, she insisted that they go deeper. Though only a minority of the class was still engaged after a while, the others were tolerant and polite enough to let the conversation continue. Michael came to appreciate not just what his teachers knew but also the fact that "they value *your* ideas more." He also enjoyed learning from his peers. He was amazed at the first papers presented by his classmates, even the ones he had considered "goof-offs." He had been in class with them for years but "never realized how much they knew. The way they think is incredible!"

The teachers seemed more trusting; some didn't collect homework and assigned papers rather than quizzes. There were longer-term assignments and fewer internal deadlines. In English they learned less grammar and discussed more literature. In Spanish they acted out plays. In physics they designed solar houses. Michael welcomed the new format and took part enthusiastically, although at the end of the day he wasn't really certain what he had learned.

He felt as if his "brain had had a workout—and that's good, isn't it," but there wasn't time to record his thoughts so that later he might assemble them into coherent observations. It was time, instead, to rush to chemistry—just like all the other years in high school.

As the grades on his first round of papers came back, he was gratified by his good start. "All that typing helped. I'm working harder. Sundays are pretty much spent writing papers, at least lately, but I'm getting used to it. All the kids in my class get together and work together, which we never used to do." His teachers encouraged collaboration, as long as in the end they wrote their papers separately. For Michael, the new method of working had proven fruitful. "I've learned more in this half year than in all the others. All through my life I was preparing to be somewhere else. But this year I realized that high school has an existence of its own. This is what I'm doing now. It's important to me and so I want to make the best of it, which is why I get involved in things." He was a senior, as effective as he would ever be in this school.

"I've learned more in this half year than in all the others. All through my life I was preparing to be somewhere else. But this year I realized that high school has an existence of its own. This is what I'm doing now. It's important to me and so I want to make the best of it, which is why I get involved in things."

By the time he got his first cold, Michael wondered if he could keep up the pace. After all, he was not superhuman. There were only twenty-four hours in a day, even during the crucial period—junior year, summer, first half of the senior year—when he felt he was being watched most carefully. If he took hard courses, he might not get A's. If he wanted to maintain his impressive academic record, he might not be able to spend as much time on sports. All through high school, he had been learning his limits: how much sleep he needed, how much stress he could take, which classes challenged him to grow and which only intimidated him. But now, he felt, his courses and his grades had to reflect what was being asked of him rather than what he could produce over the long haul. "There is just so much to do that I can't work ahead," he complained. He wasn't able to handle long-term assignments well. Planning ahead required a measure of serenity, and "hyper" was his dominant mode. "My procrastinating is actually pathetic. I need to set priorities and not try to do the government reading on the night before a math test. Because tests are key." Since French consisted of literary criticism rather than the translations or questions and answers of earlier years, he could afford to hang back sometimes. His photography teacher could probably be talked into giving an extension. And any preparing for his future would have to wait until the next vacation.

He regretted the arduous schedule he had elected at the beginning of the year. He was even sorry about the standards he had set for himself by doing so well at first. Now, any less effort would be considered a "slump." "I feel like I am turning into an automaton," he fretted. "You shouldn't even take a minute off." Getting a job, doing family chores, having relationships with kids who weren't going on to college, all had to be put on hold. Habits were disrupted; movies weren't seen; trips weren't taken; newspapers weren't read. "This isn't going to last forever," he apologized to his friends and family, but at times, he felt as if it would.

He wanted to turn to his teachers for help with reordering his priorities, but all they did was pile on more work. As new concerns competed for his time and attention, his teachers—at least those teachers who were not also counselors—became less important. Michael could sense this happening, but he was too polite—or too shrewd—to let on.

He felt trapped. He had expected so much from his senior year, but how could he really learn when there was no time to reflect? How could he gather information about and consider options for his future? When would he ever get the chance to talk with anyone about what he wanted to do with his life? More and more, he felt that such talks would have to wait for the second semester, when his record as a high school student would be sent somewhere else for others to evaluate. But without time now, he was afraid he would not be able to decide where that "somewhere else" or who those "others" ought to be. There was just too much on his mind for him to do anything well.

* * *

The most important aspect of life in the classroom in senior year is that from the beginning it is increasingly dominated by life outside the classroom. Yet the connection between teachers and seniors is fantastic at first. Ambition and energy walk in the schoolhouse door in September. These kids seem superhuman! There is health in their faces, swagger in their walk. Students' dreams concern the future, but many of their responsibilities are to be met in the present. Their teachers' minds grow wonderfully busy, thinking up suitable projects for them.

Teachers have always needed a lot of their students' time; why should teachers of seniors be different? Students who want to do well in a certain course spend time not only in class but also doing homework. Time is not the only factor in a student's progress, but it is a big one, and teachers are like farmers: they measure their success by the amount of growth that occurs on their watch. Besides time, teachers need the sense that they and their work are at the center of a child's life. "Nothing is as important as a good education" is what a number of seniors told me in the fall, and teachers are society's recognized stewards of that education. They stand at the crucial crossroads of the universal and the particular. On the universal side, they know, from study and from experience (their own and that of their students over the years), what learning is needed to accomplish a certain stage of schooling honorably. On the particular side, teachers know an individual student well enough to assess and accelerate his progress. This has been their role in a child's life ever since kindergarten.

The seniors who spoke with me in the first few weeks of the school year all acknowledged this expertise. One described a teacher who really knew how to get his students to think like logical, imaginative chemists. Another mentioned a teacher who facilitated a debate that brought out an array of facts and opinions in an atmosphere of intensity yet courtesy. A third singled out a teacher who helped her students find meaning in a piece of art, and perhaps also excitement or solace, that had eluded them before. These were important activities, leading to the development of human qualities that ought to buy the favor of that all-important judge, "the real world." These pursuits, the seniors attested, were worth taking the time of busy people. Since so many seniors start the year like Michael, motivated to do well, their teachers might get a little cocky. Indeed, some teachers may never have felt more important to their students.

The match is potentially brilliant. The students and their teachers both want the same thing: for the student to demonstrate progress. And many seniors have fascinating intellects. They are able and willing candidates for discussion courses: able because they have more skill, knowledge, and confidence than they once had, and willing because they are eager to have their voices heard. In many respects their whole life is a discussion course. They are struggling to determine their political and social identity: what they think about the issues of the day, and why. Some teachers may not enjoy this endless questioning. They may not like listening to what can be quite pompous speeches. But other teachers revel in it. "I've been waiting all these years to take Mr. Y's upper-level course," one senior told me. A room full of that kind of student is a teacher's dream.

The New Equality

For seniors, some of the rigid boundaries of high school are softening. The line between the generations is blurring. In subjects such as mathematics and languages, the classes get smaller and the students get the impression that they are favorites. "Because I'm at a higher level of math," one said, "they treat us with more respect." Another described her Spanish teacher as a person who was ushering her students through some much more mature texts in a particularly sensitive way. "Over the years," she said, "we've built a relationship with her." Senior year is payoff time.

"You have a lot more influence in the school," a number of students told me. "You interact with teachers and they rely on you." The student conductor of the band and the newspaper editor in the journalism class are acting like teachers. So are the facilitators in small groups in English class. In technical schools, shop classes are often organized so that freshmen and juniors, sophomores and seniors, work together, the older students introducing the younger ones to ideas, information, machinery, and the ways of the shop. Much of the machinery is dangerous and the teachers count on the seniors to keep a watchful eye, to protect people and resources. The result, as one student put it, is that "instead of teacher-student, it's more equal."

Many seniors in technical schools feel particularly close to their shop teachers, partly because there is more one-on-one conversation, but also because they plan to have quite similar lives. They are master and apprentice, and the students appreciate it, not only for themselves but also on behalf of their teachers. One young woman remarked, "It must be a psychological thing when they know that what they're teaching is really worthwhile to the student in the trade area. The teacher must think, If they get really good at this, they'll make a lot of money, and they'll remember the person who taught them what they're doing."

The seniors I talked to realized that "shop teachers want to share what they know about their trade." All teachers want to do that, but sharing seems more helpful, more generous, in this near-work setting. The seniors can use not only the knowledge but also the contacts. They listen when recent graduates return to the shop to fill their former teachers in with details from their lives and their work. Alumni don't visit as many academic classes; that would be disruptive. But the shop teacher is glad to see a person in the trade—and so are the seniors, who appreciate their teacher as the magnet who draws alumni back, who might welcome them back some day.

Choosing Courses

Seniors are more self-defined; they're getting to know themselves as learners. Part of this stems from the upcoming choice of college or work. "My interests have broadened this year, because I knew I'd have to come up with a major sometime." But even more immediate is the choice of senior courses. Most students feel they finally have some time in school that they themselves can plan. "I was just signing up for classes because it was the next step and that's what you had to do." But now their choices are wider, more exciting, momentous. They can choose subjects, levels of subjects, and sometimes even teaching styles. Only English is still required in most schools, and even in English there is still so much tracking that most students can influence their schedule and thus the teachers they will have. For the rest of the curriculum, if one has met the basic graduation requirements, one can continue—or abandon—math, languages, history, or science.

By senior year, most students believe they know their school, and many of their decisions about what to take are based on these expectations. Their explanations vary nearly as much as their decisions and are very personal. "This teacher really believes in me." "I'm sure I would never be able to understand that stuff." "Because of who the teachers are, the regular class is actually harder than the honors class." "I dislike a read-learn pattern. I prefer a read-think. I need to find that kind of course, now that I can." A teacher is hard, but he is lenient on due dates, and "that means I can probably manage" or else "that just tells me that I don't respect him as much." Armed with all this increasing knowledge of their options, their high school, and themselves, the seniors plan their programs. Almost everything is an elective by now, but they don't see it that way. In their minds, there are the courses they ought to take, and then there are the others.

Many of the courses seniors ought to take are also the ones they want to take. They've come a long way and want to take advantage of it. Advanced math, advanced-placement history, honors English, are potentially exciting classes. The students in them "like school more," the subjects are important, the teachers "up for it." Students need permission to take these upper-level courses. Usually one's past record decides things, though in some cases a student can get in by sheer will power. These high-status courses vary more than most people think. Some are more prescribed and others leave more discretion to the teacher; some are more thought provoking and others more loaded down with facts. Whatever the hurdles that have to be jumped, for the students there is a certain amount of prestige in just being there. An external exam at the end of an advanced course is like the dangerous equipment in a technical school. Teachers are viewed more as helpful coaches than as stern judges. All these factors tend to improve the morale in these tough classes.

More-general electives have many of the same qualities. They too involve selection, though it is based more on student interests, less on previous performance. These electives also presume engagement—perhaps more so, because there has been such a clear choice on the student's part. They too are often designed so that as a class, the students and teacher become close. Electives are a chance for a student to learn about an unfamiliar subject or to dig more deeply into a subject of particular interest. Instead of AP biology, one may take ecology, or anatomy and physiology, or animal behavior. Instead of AP history, one may choose twentieth-century Africa, or women's history, or current events.

Senior electives are good for many students, but they may be even more popular with teachers, who like the idea that they can teach a subject about which they feel passionate and who feel sure that such passion will affect the students and will do them good. Because electives are designed for and assessed in relation to the students who are taking them, teachers are not as predictably caught up in relaying information. They are freer to concentrate on projects that will help students think, question, present, argue, do. If you define academic work broadly, electives ought to offer the richest experiences in the curriculum. All over the country, the seniors I interviewed described electives as being well subscribed, interesting, and challenging at the same time. When one of these courses was "hot," it was discussed, written about, celebrated, and remembered. The government seminar in one school, the architecture project in another, stood for something in the seniors' minds. "I'm at the stage where I can handle the freedom wisely," many insisted. Even with all the distractions, they believed that if they could choose to study what was most compelling to them, they would be engaged in their schoolwork.

Nonetheless, in spite of choice, variety, and the high hopes that most teachers have for their electives, the genre has a bad reputation. Many students tell their teachers they don't expect to work very hard in a certain course because "it's only an elective." Honors courses are also chosen freely—elected—and often carry the same number of credits. But they are more highly regarded by parents, admissions offices, and even some teachers and students. Why?

The seniors I talked with offered a number of reasons. Some courses feel risky and too independent. "He's asking for way more work than he should in an elective." Or, "It was a lot of fun, but I'm not sure what it added up to." Teachers design them on their own, rarely asking for help. Whom would they ask? Others in their department may never have taught the subject. Some electives are on very discrete topics, and teachers may feel they need to provide a dramatic impression rather than a careful evolution. Electives are often not sequential and can be taken at several grade levels, so they lose "selective" status. A sophomore whiz in a computer class may intimidate the senior who is plodding along at the next desk. A bunch of friends may sign up together and essentially dominate a class. One senior described a new teacher who was handed a senior elective and told to "do what you can." The implication was: not much.

Electives are also the school's first real market-based product in an otherwise "command" economy. The students are the consumers, and they are excited but not particularly knowledgeable. Rumors abound. Deals are, or are rumored to be, struck. Yet teachers judge themselves, and one another, on how many students they have attracted to their electives. Twenty? They are "good teachers." Ten? They are not.

Three considerations seem to be in conflict here: academic standards, broadly or narrowly defined; the number of students who sign up for the class; and truth in advertising. Does one of them need to be sacrificed? Most teachers come to think so, especially during the second half of the senior year and especially if they fear that students do not plan to put out much effort. If class size is sacrificed, a teacher may not have enough students to generate a real discussion. If truth in advertising or academic standards are sacrificed, at least some students will be disappointed. Whatever the teachers sacrifice, they are not likely to speak openly about it but are sure to feel a little shabby.

Seniors sense the change in their ability to intimidate, please, or influence their teachers. Teachers are not used to having to pander, but in this situation, many of them come to the reluctant conclusion that they must. This is how electives in so many schools come to be pejoratively—and with self-fulfilling prophecy—called "fluff courses." An otherwise astute and serious young woman told me that her senior history teacher "didn't know what he had to do, because it's just an elective." Asked to define an elective, she said, "Basically it's a class that is, to me, nothing, because we don't do anything." Her definition of high school was a narrow one, and what she had seen of electives did not persuade her that they belonged in it. "After all, what are they good for? Really?"

Hanging over senior year is precisely this dilemma: how broadly or narrowly to define high school? What should electives be "good for"? Do they exist only to amuse students who have grown tired of high school? Is a course "soft" just because its content or its methods are out of the mainstream? On the one hand, seniors are pressured to follow a safer route: the prestigious options that may not reflect their real interests or style. On the other hand, they are urged to make considered choices that will reveal them to the world, and a strong collection of electives can help them to do that.

"I'm Working My Head Off"

How hard should seniors work in their academic classes? Their own ability to do better work reinforces their new status. Still, they are torn between their responsibilities for leadership, their determination to show what they can do, and what they have heard about senior year as "your slacking year." The dark cloud of imminent selection—or rejection—by anonymous admissions officers also plays an amorphous but definite part in nearly every one of their decisions. "Since it's my final year," said one earnest young man, "I intend to do it the best. But teachers need to keep you at it."

Most teachers welcome that challenge. There is probably nothing more fun in teaching than seeing a student's grasp catch up with his reach, watching him accomplish something he did not think he could. Rare is the teacher who can resist it. "The questions are more cosmic than they used to be," one student boasted, and a teacher's comments on a paper are likely to center around the strength of the argument or the grace of the prose rather than on spelling and grammar. Seniors feel that the work they are being asked to do has been jacked up sharply but that they are up to the task. Some students told me proudly, "Now we have to really *know* what they were telling us for the last three years. I know how to do all the things I was only introduced to earlier."

One young woman was sure she knew what was in her teachers' minds: "Teachers want you to realize that this is your last chance to get free education and to get all this put into you. They just want to do the best they can to get you ready for the next step, because the next step is college, which is very different, from what I have heard. So I think teachers want to prepare you as much as they

"Teachers want you to realize that this is your last chance to get free education and to get all this put into you. They just want to do the best they can to get you ready for the next step, because the next step is college. . . . So I think teachers want to prepare you as much as they possibly can, and cram as much into you as they possibly can—although, of course, *you* want to coast through!"

possibly can, and cram as much into you as they possibly can—although, of course, *you* want to coast through!" She gave a sympathetic but embarrassed laugh. "They want to get you to learn at the next level, not just doing the busy work and worksheets, but at a level where you're doing the critical thinking and writing the big papers."

Most students appreciate being at the next level. "Details are important but they can get cumbersome," one senior explained to me. He liked teachers who "can go beyond them," and he found that more of his courses in senior year "can be related to abstract concepts." Even a straightforward subject such as biology was related to the math that might be behind it. College, he believed, would take him even further in that direction. He also noticed when new methods were introduced to help him grapple with tougher assignments. Before senior year, he just listened to the teacher explain the books they read if he did not understand them already. But his senior English class was broken into study groups "like college," in order to help them read difficult books. "Senior year you're in the middle," he observed. "You can't just say what the teacher said. The small group forces you to work out what *you* think. My classes are the hardest they've ever been. Those who think senior year is easy aren't taking very challenging classes. Seniors may think classes are easy. But that's because we've had four years to learn time management, what our abilities are, how to study. We know how much leeway to give ourselves. We know how much time things take."

Most seniors I spoke with agreed that greater skill made it possible to be more efficient in their work. They could make it look easy when it really was not. But others admitted that after three years in high school, they had also learned the tricks of surviving there. They knew more about what was expected. One young man told me that all his troubles in school up to then had stemmed from his inability to understand his assignments. Under the gun in senior year, "I totally had to change. I learned to adapt to teachers. I adjust to what they want. That's how it really works." He admitted that others might see him as manipulative, but he believed that was "just part of school" and anyway such efficiency would be "required in life."

Students like Michael, whose story began this chapter, set newer, tougher standards for themselves in the first flush of being seniors. Having set higher standards, however, they want to be able to reach them on their first try. It's much too risky otherwise. And they measure their progress primarily through grades. "I'm really disappointed in myself," one admitted, "when I don't get the grade I deserve." Although *deserve* is not the right word, he went on. He had "messed up. I could do better. I know I didn't earn the grade I wanted."

Presenioritis Syndrome

Any teacher, of course, is likely to be pleased by all this energy and ambition, but it is then that the teacher's reach starts to exceed her grasp. The result is what I have come to call *presenioritis syndrome*. It occurs during the first half of the senior year, before the final record is assembled for colleges or other future programs. Teachers, sensing that their students' motivation will not last, feel they need to assign a lot of work while they can. If the students read one chapter per assignment last year, have them read two chapters this year. After all, next year, they will have to read a whole book! If these students tackled battles last year, let them tackle war this year. If they read Hemingway last year, let them read Faulkner this year. If they performed scientific experiments from their textbook last year, this year they ought to design their own. Even though so many other aspects of the seniors' lives have grown more complicated, fall-term courses are a little harder than they ought to be. Somewhere in their mind, teachers think this will make up for the upcoming spring-term courses, which, they tacitly acknowledge, will be easier than they ought to be.

The extra workload makes enormous sense for seniors who are staking their claim to being a good student primarily on the work they do in a particular course. If they plan to do more science in college or the workplace, it makes sense for them to undertake a thorough and extensive experiment. If they are fascinated by art, it makes sense for them to prepare a portfolio. If they are intending to pursue the study of French, they had better read, write, and speak knowledgeably about Camus. Serious high school students *can* do work at this level.

But in how many different areas at once, and for how long? Certain students may be able to perform astonishing feats. One may play Lady Macbeth and construct a telephone during the same month. Another may read Cervantes and do his calculus. They have the talent, and they can find the motivation. Seniors are at their broadest and most amazing as individuals, and they know and glory in it. But most teachers do not have the luxury of dealing with individuals when they plan their class projects. They deal with groups. So everybody reads Shakespeare or nobody does. Everybody does a research paper or nobody does. This is one reason so many teachers like homogenous classes, but even in them the students' abilities and motivations differ tremendously. The would-be scientist will be tackling the same work as the class poet, and both of them feel that this term of all terms they have to earn an A.

I was certainly guilty of presenioritis syndrome, and the college-bound students whom I taught seemed willing to play along, to accept my definition of what seniors could do. I assigned more books but still expected my students to be attentive readers. I asked my students to construct a "multimedia presentation" even though very few of them knew how to draw, or interview, or splice tapes. I assigned more papers but still expected them to be polished. I asked the students to write, and rewrite, every kind of essay I thought they might be assigned in college. I even told them I wanted their college teachers to write me fan letters. They thought I was kidding, but I was not. I really believed that I was doing it "for their own good."

And I was, for certain individuals. But for most seniors, by the middle of the fall their schoolwork seems overwhelming. All these demands come from people who are seemingly unaware of one another. "Everybody thinks I have assignments for nobody but them!" All high school students say that, but for seniors it seems especially true.

As the pressures build up in the other parts of their lives as well, they hit a kind of wall. They run out of time. They get less and less sleep, and their good judgment suffers accordingly. They start by "being efficient," something the world condones, something their various taskmasters even presume about them. But being efficient is not just reading faster or getting down to work more swiftly. Being efficient is letting their improved listening skills in class take the place of work they do outside class. There is much overlap anyway; many high school classes, even for seniors, follow the pattern of "going over" the homework. Once is enough for many of the seniors, they told me, and knowing what techniques will help you learn something is part of growing up.

Several seniors told me why they had given up doing homework in certain classes. "I don't do my physics," one said, "because the teacher says what the test will be about and he also says what the book says anyway. So what's the point?" The teacher, he implied, did not really care whether the students did the work. "All he does is talk." This teacher did not listen to what the students said as long as they learned the material. He was not particularly interested in the way their minds worked. The senior felt a little wistful about it. But he believed this teacher felt he was a success if his class was orderly and if the students did well on tests.

Seniors can appreciate these priorities. During senior year, realism demands a certain respect for tests. Tests are to be given often, corrected quickly, "so I can learn what my problems are faster." Reading a substantial book and writing many drafts of a paper on it may be more appropriate as students grow older, but "papers take too much time, and I need those grades." Feedback is important in any year, but in the senior year it seems crucial. Perhaps test grades are not as sensitive as other kinds of feedback would be, but at least they are there: frequent and consistent. And at least there are numbers, even if nobody quite knows what the numbers are supposed to mean.

Seniors are proud that they have grown more "test wise." Unfortunately, tests have begun to influence the academic courses of which they are meant to be only a part. As a student comes to know himself well, he knows the best way for him to prepare for them. This may not be the same way other students do it; it may not be the procedure the teacher has advised. I remember one of my students telling me he never read the assignment before the class on the subject, he read it before the test. All my protests—that he should contribute to class, that he should take notes to review for tests, that this style was not going to work once he got to college—were unconvincing. Doing it my way would lead to richer class participation, more time for synthesis, with benefits for him and for the rest of us. Doing it his way would lead to his doing a better job on tests, because the class discussion would help him focus and the material would be fresh in his mind. There was not enough time for both. Tests were important now. Privately and grudgingly, I had to agree that from his point of view, he was right.

Since time as well as tests are so important, seniors try to use their time as carefully as they can. But at some point, for most of them, efficiency morphs into cutting corners. They take part in a class discussion without having done any of the reading. There are hurried consultations with friends in the hallway about the plot. Details are lost, but, as one senior explained, "the essentials are what are important anyway." Unprepared in class, this senior—more and more self-consciously—"fudged it," either throwing out the fancy phrases that had become a little more comfortable lately or staying alertly quiet. Sometimes she even nodded her head in mock-agreement with other people's statements. But "by the time you're doing that," she admitted, "you know it's become kind of a charade."

Another, late at night, decided to write the assigned paper even though he had only read half of the book. "I probably got the main points of it, from all that time in class." Writing it seemed preferable to missing a deadline. Missing deadlines looked childish, and anyway, he would have to take the time to read the book if he asked for an extension. And time was what he did not have: not now, not this weekend, not next week. There was no exam at the end of the course in which details of the second half of the book might be required again. He decided simply to do his best, "retire that project," and try to keep up better with the next one.

The pattern that develops is not the one teachers mean to design. An alumnus came back to school once to tell me that the really demanding course he took in our department had prepared him well for college. As I puffed out my chest, ready for compliments—was it the sophistication? the abstraction? the level of the writing we demanded?—he continued his explanation. He said that most college courses were "entirely out of line," with teachers piling up books in their reading lists "only to impress their colleagues. No one could possibly do all that work; one had to make choices." Our course in high school, for whatever reasons, had been "also much too tough." He could not do all the work assigned; he could not admit it; so what our course had taught him to do was to "make choices." Making choices sounds pretty benign—at least to students. The college man was all smiles, and I smiled too, because I realized that he did not mean to upset me. But inside I was devastated, because I could see that what we had facilitated, at least for him, was a pattern of deception.

High school seniors' careers as dishonest academics begin in such small ways. They begin because of genuinely tight spots they have been put in, at least partly by the very teachers who wish them well. And they begin earlier than one might have thought, because on the surface seniors are still trying to look like serious and engaged students. Younger students cut corners, too, of course, but they are more closely monitored, so the wall they hit is not as hard or as high. Their assignments tend to be short-term, with more internal deadlines. The homework they do is more likely to be handed in. And, though they do not realize it, their world has more time for school, so they can meet their responsibilities better. What you see is more likely to be what you get.

All over the school, there are bad days when the teacher suspects that he is carrying way too much of the class. There are polls by the exasperated teacher: "How many of you actually did this homework?" But in senior classes, even in the fall, there will be fewer hands raised when that question is asked. The culture of the class has subtly changed, from the informed speculation that seemed so valuable in the early weeks to limp and unspecific discussion. The seniors' excuses for their lassitude are serious ones; it's too early, they know, for them to express a sense of entitlement—at least with their teachers—so they plead fatigue. They can't do all of the work assigned, yet the stakes are as high as ever.

This leaves too many teachers out in the cold, confused about their mission. Should they attend to their students' future or to their present? Should they charge ahead, assigning lots of demanding work, hopeful that the seniors' basic maturity and seriousness of purpose will somehow help them find extra energy and take time away from more frivolous things? Should they plan classes that require participation and concentration when they know that their students are not sleeping well? Should they count on the kids who *did* the homework—all five of them—or have a big showdown with the other fifteen?

Assessments

Most painful of all, what about assessment? It has always been central, but now it's "make-or-break time." Teachers of seniors know that fall-term grades will be watched carefully. Should they grade seniors more leniently so that their students are not punished as they struggle to adjust to a heavier load?

"I appreciate honesty from my teachers when they don't like my work," said a highly successful senior. "I can see myself not writing a paper as well as I could, just to get it done or if I'm sick of the class or if I didn't like the book or even if I didn't have time to read because I was out playing. But if I were to do that, I'd like the teacher to come to me and say, 'I've had you before. I've read your paper; this is not your best paper. You could do so much better and I'd like you to write another one for me.' And I think this would be the best thing to do, since it shows that the teacher respects me, respects my intelligence, and knows that I can do better than this." He wanted a second chance—one that might not be offered to others—but he did not want the teacher to pretend that he did better work than he really did.

Honesty and criticism are also desired in the technical schools. In the shop classes, "Most of the teachers don't yell unless you really mess up," one senior explained. "Even then, they'll tell you what you should have done." Students appreciate the face-to-face nature of the explanation, are glad the teacher takes the time to "go through it step by step." It feels authentic to them, like what they hope for from the workplace they are shortly to enter. They are sure that it helps more than remarks on the bottom of a paper, no matter how sympathetic or elaborate those remarks might be.

Seniors' reactions to honest grading, however, depend on their personal confidence and their trust in their teachers' judgment. Some feel they will be able to rewrite a paper or respond to constructive criticism in time to get a good report by the end of the term. Others feel on shakier ground and are more likely to give their teachers a hard time when their grades are low. Resentment creeps in: "It was awful, being that dependent on doing well in his course." Their sense of equality and close connection is being erased.

The obsession with "looking good" undermines the relationship on the other side as well. The Chinese history I taught was fine, because it "sounded hard," although my students assured me that it didn't need to *be* as hard as it sounded. (I was also advised by a colleague that a course in current events was likely to be harder than it sounded, so its title should probably be changed to reflect that reality.) Some seniors even marched into my classroom and told me the grade they would "need to get" there. Although they may never have performed at that standard before, I was certainly willing to help them try, but their statements carried more than a whiff of intimidation.

Yet even as the gap widens, students often turn to these same teachers to help them with their larger transition—the one out of high school. They want their teachers to assess their abilities more broadly and give some advice. Teachers want to help, but there are a variety of factors in their way. Some feel they may not know the student well enough, and with the loads most teachers carry, they are probably right. Others realize that their knowledge of the workplace, training programs, or particular colleges may be out of date. Teachers have learned over the years that guessing who will get into which college is nearly impossible, but every new generation of seniors comes to them demanding certainty. Some teachers are afraid that if they express doubts about a student's suggestions, he may take offense. Is it really honesty the student wants, or is it a more precise discussion of his strengths but not his weaknesses? Will too much realism make students—or their parents—fall apart?

Even harder to predict is how well a student will do in a given future environment. The teacher-student relationship is based on daily contact; it is intense in some ways, but limited to one time, one place. A teacher who can predict what a student will be like in high school may feel completely inadequate when trying to imagine what the student will be like somewhere else. Yet some students interpret their teacher's caution as laziness. "When I ask for advice about a college," one told me, "I want honest feedback, not just, Oh, everything will be fine." Things won't always be "fine," of course; there are problems everywhere, in colleges and in jobs. But what those problems will be and how the student will handle them is difficult to predict. That's the honest answer.

Besides sensitive grades and cautious advice, there is another form of teacher feedback: the recommendation. A new aspect of the teacher-student relationship in senior year, these recommendations, which dominate the fall and winter, are among the reasons teachers feel important. For a while, the process brings the teacher and the student closer. The affirmation goes both ways, since students usually request one from a teacher they like. They also may have done well in the teacher's courses, and it helps if the courses have the reputation of being demanding. But even more often, the teacher chosen will be seen as someone who is sympathetic. One student, whose parents had not gone to college, described the painstaking process he went through in choosing the teachers he would ask. He specifically wanted people who had watched him grow up, from a rather "happy-go-lucky" freshman to a more serious senior. "They know me pretty well," he explained. This seemed to be the most important factor in his decision. "I can go up to them and they'd be happy to do it."

He was right: most teachers are happy to help. It is a lot of extra work, and they know it; many are the winter vacations sacrificed to this cause, but the teachers keep it up year after year. They may grumble a bit to their families or their colleagues, but it is a proud complaint. They are doing what they are supposed to do: they are connecting with kids. They are helping the seniors get on with their lives. I came to recognize the look in a student's eyes as she was about to ask me if I would write her a recommendation. The posture of the self-confident senior was belied by a few moments of hesitation. The conversation was desultory at first, usually centering around how my elective was going (seniors were rarely interested in what I might be teaching to underclassmen). I learned to let it stay awkward until the student was ready to blurt it out. It was fun to tell her I would be honored to write her recommendation, to see the relief in her face as she realized she would have an advocate. In the course of writing a recommendation, a teacher is likely to talk more with the student about her interests and choices. The two of them are usually quite close to begin with. By the end of the process, they are closer still.

But there are difficult aspects. Some teachers just do not do this particular job well. They may look, or even be, disorganized. "Their intentions are good but they don't really help you," grumbled one senior. "You have to remind them over and over again to write your recommendations. I feel like they're backing me in their words but they're not backing me in their actions." A teacher, by writing poorly, ungrammatically, vaguely, or—heaven forbid!—unenthusiastically, can harm the senior's chances. How can that happen? It is awkward to say you cannot write a positive recommendation, so

"[Teachers'] intentions are good but they don't really help you. You have to remind them over and over again to write your recommendations. I feel like they're backing me in their words but they're not backing me in their actions."

very few teachers admit it. Instead, they indicate that they support the senior's candidacy when deep in their hearts they do not, at least for certain colleges. They may not yet know the list of places to which the student will apply. By the time they know what they are up against, most decide just to plunge ahead.

The potential dishonesty in the relationship now goes both ways. The teachers are tempted to lie, to gloss over problems, to fail to discriminate. Sissela Bok, in her book *Lying: Moral Choice in Public and Private Life* (1999), writes that end-of-high-school recommendations are notoriously dishonest. After I read her book, I made it a practice to say one mildly disparaging thing about each candidate, just to show that I could discriminate and was willing to admit that nobody's perfect. But I felt I needed to explain myself first, because so few teachers do that. And then I feared that I was drawing attention to myself instead of the seniors. After a while, I gave it up.

Some students notice the ambivalence in a teacher who wants to be an advocate but is asked to be a judge at the same time. "I was just talking with my mom about this last night," said one perceptive young woman. "What does a teacher do if they're writing a recommendation? The thing is to be honest, but what if a student struggles in a certain area and they're asked to comment on it? The teacher doesn't want to send off a comment that's going to discourage the student from getting admitted. How does the teacher deal with that? I'd think that would be so hard. Even though they love the kid to death."

Another complication is that the teachers are often writing about an ongoing relationship. Should they write glowing college recommendations about a student who performed well last year but who is distracted, overwhelmed, and simply "not there" this year? Seniors are understandably wary of this possibility. Recommendations tend to indicate a talent and industriousness they are not sure they can sustain. "The whole thing makes me nervous. I mean, what if she stops liking me?" One student told me he had refused when his teacher offered to let him read the recommendation she'd written. He couldn't figure out why the teacher wanted him to read it. There was too much potential embarrassment if the teacher wrote something "nice," too much pain if she didn't.

Could there be a hint of blackmail here? Much is said, much is left unsaid, and both sides know it. It is uncomfortable and corrosive. Some teachers regard college or job recommendations as a kind of money in the bank. They assume that the student, feeling beholden, will behave himself, at least in this class, for the rest of the year. The admiration in the student's eyes when he asks, the admiration in the teacher's eyes when she accepts, will last. It will lead to great things. A continuing supportive relationship. Admission. A student who is forever grateful. Well, maybe.

High schools that have enough counselors may be able to steer individual students toward the most reliable and effective teachers for writing recommendations. They know that Ms. X is respected in certain colleges, that Mr. Y writes well, that Mr. Z frequently misses the deadlines. They can have this delicate conversation with a single senior in their office. However, in yet another example of the inequity among American high schools, high schools without enough money in their counseling budgets have to give out their advice in all-purpose lectures, a venue in which names will not be named. Essentially, they have to let their students fend for themselves or get specific advice only from last year's seniors. And the disgraceful irony is that the most poorly funded schools for this and other purposes are usually those serving the children of the poor, whose families are least likely to be able to offer direct experience and advice.

Ideas on how the teacher recommendation can become a better form of communication are presented in the chapters of Part 3. However flawed, teacher recommendations bear a crucial message: colleges and workplaces do need to know their candidates in the ways that teachers can best provide. Still, because of the sheer number of challenges seniors face, even teacher recommendations are a kind of camouflage for how marginal seniors' teachers are becoming.

Seniors and Their Friends

"When I woke up the first day of school, I wanted it to be so beautiful," said Suzanna. "I thought about what I was going to wear, how I was going to look." As she lay in her bed, she replayed the decisions she had made weeks before. She started with her hairdo, and worked down to the blouse, the skirt, the belt, finally the shoes. She wanted everything to be perfect, since she knew she would be noticed in a way she had never been before. She was a senior.

She had once been a freshman like those who would be watching her so carefully. But the journey she was thinking about was even longer than that. "I thought, Twelve years and I'm finally here now." She was at her prime, her destination. "I put my nose in the air," she confessed with a twinkle. "By senior year a lot of people know you and you don't even *know* they know you." She wondered if they would have bothered if she were a sophomore. The fact that they knew her name was a source of great satisfaction, even if they knew nothing else.

"Everybody was always older, but now they aren't. We're the people everybody wants to hang out with because there's nobody else higher. They could hang out with lower, but that's not really satisfying. But I figure we must look younger than other senior classes." How could she really deserve her status? Surely she and her friends were less mature than other seniors, than the seniors she remembered from her freshman year, than seniors elsewhere in the country.

She felt as if she had changed during the summer, even more than most years. She worked as a counselor in a settlement house day camp, as usual, but there was more responsibility in her job this year, since she had other kids working for her. That unsettled her at first, but she was proud that she found ways to carry it off. Teaching photography to the little kids made her feel older—her own maturity was definitely on her mind—and she liked learning how to present lessons. Having students with the right attitude certainly was important! It made her feel more empathy with her own teachers.

After camp, instead of a family vacation, she went off to look at colleges. She got to know her father better by having him to herself and by watching the way he dealt with being in a new place. And all those new places! This was not just a tour; this was an attempt to determine what it would be like to live and work in a different environment. She even found a couple of colleges she could imagine herself attending. But could she ever call it home? The mere thought shook her up.

She looked carefully at her classmates when she got back to school, noticing what they were wearing, of course, but also anticipating that they would sense big changes in her and wondering whether they too were different after the summer. From what she could see, they were not; all the conversations were about parties, the trig class, the prospects for the boys' soccer team. Still, she sensed a new bravado in her friends as they strutted around being seniors; it made her reluctant to share any vulnerabilities. There wasn't time for lengthy talks anyway, but she was grateful to still have people whom she knew, glad that they could go through the momentous senior year together.

A few weeks later, Suzanna chuckled at her excitement and naïveté on that first morning of her final year in high school. She had definitely returned to jeans and sweaters. Senior year was not the end of the line; it was the beginning of the next leg of the journey. There was little time to enjoy "here." Instead, one had to prepare for "there," whether or not one had really thought about it. New friends, new directions, new interests and competition, all affected her relationships at a time when she needed both stability and flexibility.

Still, she was no less determined to make her senior year "so beautiful." In spite of all her personal doubts, she would put her "nose in the air," act the part, live up to the challenge of both the notoriety and the transition.

"The Best Friends You'll Ever Have"

"I enjoy being a senior," one student told me. "You have more freedom, a better choice of classes, and it seems as if all of the different cliques in the school are coming together and everyone is friends." During the senior year in high school, friendship is special in a number of ways. For seniors, "class unity" is a big part of friendship and, if achieved, is considered a good thing. Beyond just being recognized by acquaintances, however, they are ready to attach more meaning to some of their relationships. Much time is set aside for friends, especially in the second half of the year, at least partly because they are constantly alert to their impending separation. Social life more often involves secrecy and risk, dangerous activities and new love affairs, as students grow readier to define their own values and spend time away from their families. However, their experiences can strain their friendships, which is even more disappointing because it is unexpected.

Adults tend to approve of the need for senior bonding—as long as it doesn't take too much time. Privileges are offered to seniors with the justification that being able to attend this exclusive event or enroll in that special section will increase their knowledge and appreciation of one another in their last year. "Our class is huge," said a young woman in a multicultural high school, "more than four hundred, but we pretty much get along." It is as if a psychological cordon has been set around the senior class, setting them apart in a way that has never been true before. A sense of superiority is widespread—even inevitable, partly because they compare themselves not with freshmen but with themselves when they were freshmen. Socially, being a senior is like being on a rising tide: it lifts all boats. Even for the unprepossessing, there is an advantage.

"When I was a freshman I was really nobody," one student admitted. "It seemed like it would take forever to get to my senior year. I looked up to seniors without their even demanding it, and I didn't think I'd ever be big enough to have people want to hang out with me. Freshman year was unbearable. Sophomore year was unbearable. Junior year was—well, it was that much closer to being a senior." The lyrics in a senior song were etched into her brain, and she sang it for me: "We've shared laughter, we've shared tears. Sorry, freshmen, three more years!" Now that she was a senior herself, she didn't know how she felt about singing the song to the freshmen. She definitely agreed that one's senior year is when one has the deepest relationships. But like Suzanna, she was not sure that the laughter and tears she and her friends had shared were as significant as the song implied. And she worried about the "Sorry, freshmen" part: it felt like a put-down to her. Status, however welcome, was confusing and even cumbersome. "We've worked very hard and have earned authority," another young man told me, "but we're not going to push on little kids."

> "When I was a freshman I was really nobody. It seemed like it would take forever to get to my senior year. I looked up to seniors without their even demanding it, and I didn't think I'd ever be big enough to have people want to hang out with me."

Out of notoriety comes a new sense of closeness. Within the class, very few make radical social changes: the "in" crowd stays in, dominating things as it always has, and the "outs" feel nearly as shy and alienated, although they have often found one another by senior year. Within the broadest groupings, however, there are adjustments, and they seem noteworthy to seniors because they will be the final high school social decisions. "I talk to people I haven't talked with since eighth grade," one senior said. They might have drifted apart, or never have been close, but now that they were about to split up, they might as well know what they had missed. "I want to get to know some of the people I never got to know before we leave." Within this wider perspective, social groupings, once so crucial, begin to look a little silly. "There's only five months left. Why hate that person?" one senior asked.

Very few seniors change schools; a "home base" from which to launch into postsecondary life seems crucial. Seniors recognize one another, know one another's names, finally feel comfortable in the halls that are such a large part of social life in high school. However, the line between friends and acquaintances is not sharply drawn; the familiarity will be missed, not treasured friends. The briefest of social interactions can seem significant. When asked what she would miss about high school, one senior said, "You have a lot more people to say hi to, and you're not scared to look people in the face. You don't necessarily have to be close to people. I'll miss walking down the hall and seeing someone and saying, 'Oh, hey, Andrew. What's up?'" It did not seem as important that Andrew reply to her question.

Appreciation of the present mingles with fears about the future. "Seniors are there to know things and to make you laugh," said one quiet young man. "And now it's our turn." The value of familiarity, of feeling smart and funny, is a large part of what makes seniors comfortable and happy among their peers. "I'll miss casual conversation and being able to be recognized, because next year I'll be in this strange new world where no one knows me." And where he knows nobody. "You feel like you'll be alone, whereas in high school, everybody's right there."

Some seniors do describe their friendships as increasing in depth, however. "In senior year, you do more than know their names. You hang out with them, get closer, get to know what they're like," one young man insisted. His friend agreed: "You don't really know them until your senior year." Seniors feel that only other seniors can understand the experience of trying to decide, and negotiate, what comes next. "You chat about applications, and help each other out, remind each other of deadlines. Things like that." Again the friend chimed in: "Earlier, we had classes with each other but we never talked with each other. Now there's more of a bond."

All kinds of seniors feel they are less shy than they used to be, but they also feel they are better at reading others. "I'm noticing things about people that I've never noticed before," said one young woman in the heady days of early autumn, when one of the best aspects of her life was simply that she had finally become a senior. "Last year I might have thought that this is not a person that I want to talk to, but this year she seems sweet. That's interesting, you know. It's strange!"

Well, not so strange, as it turns out. As seniors' interests develop, so do their circle of friends. An African American senior who hung around only with other African Americans during her first two years in high school realized that she wanted to be a dancer. It was likely she would make new friends in the dance club, even more likely that she would widen her definition of friendship. For her, friendship was now based on more than having something in common; it was based on doing things together, especially the supremely binding experience of being in a musical. "Just being African American" began to seem too passive as a basis for friendship; the other basis, dance, was active, absorbing—preferable. Working on projects in class also deepens seniors' friendships. "All the kids in my history class get together and work together, which we never used to do," said one young man. "I feel like I know the smart kids better this year."

Besides having the maturity to define friendship differently and to make new friends, seniors feel as if they can hold on to their old ones more gracefully than before. "Bad behavior used to really upset me," one somewhat abashed student admitted. "Now I realize that that's just the way people are sometimes. There's only so much I can do, besides act properly myself. I think you become more adult when you become a senior, because you can accept other people's personalities for what they are. Because you know they're not going to be able to change." And because they realize they are not happy when other people try to change *them*.

On the one hand, the members of the senior class seem determined to achieve unity, to meet historic challenges together, and to create a common reputation. On the other hand, they feel they need to respect individuality, they must not be too judgmental about idiosyncrasy. Like so many other aspects of being a senior, this social challenge pulls them in two directions at once.

Widening the Circle

High schools are packed places. One senior described what it was like to go through the crowds. "It's weird to walk in the halls now because it seems like everybody is really loud and obnoxious. It seems like there's so much immaturity at our school. People can't just walk to class. There's people singing or screaming or throwing things around. All I want is to get to the other end, and so much is blocking it. I just need to get through it." The halls are filled with underclassmen, people who are just beginning to establish themselves socially and who need a lot of time in school to do so. In most schools, however, a rushed lunch is the only time set aside for them to see one another. This senior could not believe she had ever been that loud, though she did remember the time when nearly all the social life she had was between classes at school. Things were different now. She tried to use her time well during the day—she *needed* to get to the library at the end of the hall—so that she could dispatch her homework with efficiency and move on to other things. "You separate your times. You have time for schoolwork, and then you go out and have fun."

"Seniors don't fool around in school as much as freshmen do," said another senior. "We know when to stop wasting time." The amount of time spent on friendships—"wasted" or not—is still substantial, but much more social life during the senior year takes place away from school. Seniors are quick to make the distinction that they see their acquaintances during the school day but their friends after it. This is possible because they are less reliant on their parents for transportation. In their households the telephone has become available for the first time in years, but the car is gone.

It is also a mark of maturity to have outside friends. Many of the seniors' friends, particularly their boyfriends and girlfriends, are already high school graduates. "I spend the week in high school, but on the weekend I head for college," one senior explained. Her high school boyfriend had graduated, moved on, and it was natural that socially at least, she was ready to move with him. Having friends outside high school is also a sign that one can make friends in new places, which insulates seniors from their worst fears about transition. "I have several friends in other states because of camps and other things I've done in my life," one young man commented proudly. Friends from work, league athletic friends, or friends from nearby towns: these mysterious "others" lend a certain spice to what one senior described as the "same old same old" of romance during the senior year. But even when romance is not involved, a wider circle seems desirable.

There are more parties on weekends, bigger and more open. "Senior year, it's your friends who are throwing the parties, so you tend to go," said a young man. "During your senior year," he counseled me, generously overlooking the difference in our ages, "you shouldn't stay away from parties because your friends won't be there. You have to 'make' the party."

"Next year, we'll be in college parties," I was often told. Family rules, seniors believe, are less and less relevant, and too much supervision implies a lack of trust. Temptation overcome is preferable to no temptation at all. With more parties tucked into less time, senior parties have a reputation for somewhat wild behavior. "You may have to party harder," one senior admitted, "because you have only two hours to do it in." Pleasure has to be considered as deliberately as everything else. "You really take it seriously when you're having fun, because you only get to do that twenty percent or thirty percent of the time."

The verb *to party* often implies alcohol and drug abuse; according to recent statistics, as many as one third of high school seniors admit to at least occasional binge drinking. When they use *party* as a noun, however, seniors describe it in various ways. They spend a lot of time together after school, often spontaneously, sometimes in planned ways. Some groups regularly "catch" certain TV shows together, or go on charity walks, or have sleepovers after basketball games. I even heard about a group that began meeting once a week for breakfast before school during their senior year. "Everybody kind of parties," one young woman explained, "but they party in their own way."

Being together is the important thing. "I felt like I needed to go with them," one student declared, "partially because it's the last year. We're going through the same points in life together. And we always have." As graduation approaches, seniors take themselves more seriously, and since friendship is such a big part of life, especially for teenagers, that means they take their friendships more seriously too. If they have had certain friends for a long time, they are likely to say they've "grown up together."

Nostalgia is already creeping in. "I was at a friend's house the other night, on a school night, until eleven o'clock," one young woman told me, sounding surprised at her own behavior. "We started talking about kindergarten. We'd never done that before."

Laughing at how silly they used to be, they were able to look back on themselves fondly. As juniors, she implied, they might have been frightened to admit to such immaturity, but vital changes had occurred during senior year. "I wish I could be really close with all of them," said a young woman in a rural high school. "That way I could still hold on to my memories." But she did not sound hopeful. "We're going our separate ways." The drifting apart that is beginning to occur in so many friendships seems less wrenching than the dramatic rupture they are about to face.

Growing Apart

Despite the rhetoric, despite the real closeness that has been achieved by some seniors, there are also special new strains on their friendships during this last year together. A senior class never achieves the much touted "unity"; its cliques seem as divisive and cruel as ever; competition sharpens and grows more crucial; students begin to accept their impending separation; exotic liaisons formed outside school threaten the longstanding friendships within it—these scenarios and a dozen more create confusion and anxiety. And guilt, because seniors believe these fractures should not be happening. These are supposed to be "the best friends you'll ever have."

The events that cause these strains vary, of course, nearly as much as the seniors, but a good number of them are related to the selectivity of postsecondary placements. One young woman described the strains in her relationships this way: "You're competing against all your friends. I don't know you! Get away from me! You're going to take my spot!" Another senior told me that he had realized during the fall that his friends had "started cheating again." He considered cheating an activity, rampant in middle school, that was shed like other bad childhood habits as one grew older. Faced with the cheating of his friends during senior year, he was caught in a web of contradictory emotions: disapproval of an activity he considered dishonest and therefore wrong, anxiety that his friends would get into college and he would not, anger at a system that "forced" people to show themselves off at others' expense, fear that his friends would—or would not—get caught. For months he was paralyzed with indecision, with obsession, with jealousy. And for months he was isolated. "For me, socially, it was a lousy senior year."

As seniors mentally line up before their favorite choices—colleges, jobs—they scrutinize each other in new ways. Even those who have always been considered good students look to the right and left. They ask themselves, What if this college values qualities that I do not have but he does? And if a traditional academic rival is applying to a different school, a brand new set of rivalries is likely to develop, even among longstanding friends.

The fact that these jealousies are predictable does not make them less painful. Ranking causes some students to dislike one another, sometimes intensely. "Let's face it: his class ranking is higher than mine," one senior said, explaining his troubles with another senior. It is easy to assume that someone has an unfair advantage. It may not have mattered earlier, but what will it mean now? The seniors' conviction that a college will take a specific number from their school no matter who applies also intensifies competition. "I just hope I get in," said one young woman. "I mean, I want my friends to get in too, but. . . ." In this kind of environment, individualism takes precedence over the welfare of the group, though many seniors can't assume this shift in values lightly. "After a while, I just wanted to find my own college to apply to," one told me. "I was just so tired of going up against my friends." Being apart next year seems preferable to painful rivalries this year.

"After a while, I just wanted to find my own college to apply to. I was just so tired of going up against my friends."

Money—and the lack of it—also disrupts friendships more than it ever has before. Students who need scholarships are sure their options will be narrower than those of their more wealthy friends, and they are right. Yet it is not only the poorer students who are troubled by the issue of money and the advantage it bestows. One young woman explained why she had resisted her parents' suggestions that she take an SAT prep course, and why she was angry at her friends who were taking it. In her mind, it was very clear: "Some people can afford these courses, but others can't." The way she saw it, the people who had money could literally buy access to the colleges that would "help them earn more money so then *their* kids will be able to get into college. I just don't think that's fair at all." Her critique then took a slightly different tack—away from money, but still focused on justice. "All these people cramming: it doesn't seem a very accurate judge of a person's ability." In those test-prep courses, she believed, "you actually learn ways to cheat." Her insistence on considering overall justice rather than personal advancement was unusual. What also seemed painful, however, was that her principles were isolating her from her friends.

Money differences during senior year also surfaced between a young man and his friends in a tough urban high school. He was almost afraid of money. "I had a job, but it was making me get off track," he hinted darkly. "I was getting in trouble, coming home late, doing a lot of things." He solved his problem by quitting his job and intensifying his efforts in school. Now he felt he had a good chance to win a scholarship to college and later to medical school. His friends, especially as the end of high school approached, were different. Some of them had done well in high school, but even they could not make themselves go on to college. "All their attention is on money right now. Getting money is a big thing to them, is like their life." He pointed through the windows of the high school to the street. "They want to be like those people: driving by in their own cars, having the good life, on the street, wearing good clothes, selling marijuana."

It was quite an indictment, and his voice sounded disgusted, yet worried. "They have no focus," he said, and he admitted that he was afraid he would lose his as well. He too wanted "the good life," he knew, but he thought he could wait until he was a doctor to get it. "Money is easier to get than an education," he acknowledged, at least for him and for his friends. "But the way they are getting it is risky, against the law. I try to talk to them, but they won't listen."

Competition and differences over money are not the only threats to longstanding friendships during senior year. Despite the seniors' rhetoric and good intentions, some of the gaps between people prove too hard to cross. "High school is when people start to try new things and experiment and choose their paths," one insisted. It seems preordained. Many cliques—especially those built around illegal drug use, which require extraordinary loyalty from their members—remain rigid and socially divisive. One young woman said that the groups that had dominated her class all through high school—the smart kids and the athletes and the "druggies and underachievers that trash things on weekends"—were stronger than ever. "I'm not really a partier at all," she claimed. Her identity in this and other respects was surer in her mind now. "The result is, I don't see my classmates on weekends." She counted on college to be different.

Planning for the future also prompts changes in the way seniors want to spend their social time. One senior told me about the group of five girls whose closeness had been very valuable to her throughout her sophomore and junior years. During senior year she was surprised that one of them had pretty much given up hanging out as often. She was not sure why and she seemed afraid to discuss it; "probably, it was all that work." As they headed off "to *very* different colleges," however, they were discovering how varied the paths they were choosing in life were likely to be. And she had to admit that during senior year, boyfriends seemed to take more time than they had taken earlier. At least hers did.

The social fallout and resulting loneliness are uneven. More girls than boys feel abandoned when their older friends, especially romantic ones, graduate. It is hard to stay close to older friends, even when the graduates come back for visits, because, as one senior observed, "We're on totally different levels now. I miss them, but I'm glad they are gone because I think I need time." The massive, complicated job of getting through the passage out of high school is still ahead. Alumni give the impression they are better off. "They're in college and I'm in high school. They are there and I'm not. We're on different planes—almost different planets. My mother tells me this all the time."

It is a volatile environment for romance. "I feel I have the time for one last fling," one student said. "It's almost inevitable to fall in love during the senior year, especially during the spring. For one thing, you want to go with someone to the prom." In his case, however, his longstanding buddy had already asked his new girlfriend. "It's sticky. I don't know what's going to happen," he admitted, but the romance was "definitely worth it." Unlike the girls in his class, he was not looking forward to the college scene. "It's back to the low man on the totem pole, socially," or so he had heard. "I'd rather have a girlfriend from high school." Maybe even the one he had just acquired. He would see.

Some couples stay together for the sake of the senior festivities. "I suppose we should call it quits," one young man declared, "but it doesn't seem like a good time. So it goes back and forth. There's no intermediate." It would be easier to break up during the summer, when he would not have to see her every day. And it was definitely too late to get another date for the prom. So he was staying put, but devoting a lot of energy to his decision, and he was somewhat resentful that he was not as happy as he had imagined he would be. (Or as he should be. Expectations and imperatives are never far apart.)

Though they still talk about unity, seniors are beginning to distance themselves from one another. During the spring, they criticize one another's decisions. Those who are not going to college claim that some of their college-bound classmates are not prepared to work hard enough to succeed there. They are "only using it as an excuse to get away from home and party all they want. Just because they want to leave doesn't mean they're ready." Those who are going to college are just as critical. "You have to stay in practice with school," one senior believed. Inactivity of any kind seems offensive after the rushed nature of high school. "A lot of kids don't know what they want to be or what they want to do," said one young woman. "It's like reality hit them in the face and they don't want to live up to it. They just want to live at home and be a bum and not work." She described a friend who had no plans for college or work and who even resisted her advice to "go to City Year [a community service program]! Just do *something*!!" She feared her friend would just "add to the problems in the streets."

Quite a few seniors criticize their friends for refusing to adapt to meet their new challenges. "A lot of seniors are afraid to grow during senior year," one senior observed wryly. "They're afraid of becoming nerds." They need to look spectacular but also to keep "that all-round image." This juggling act does not leave enough energy for a real friendship. "It's pretty lonely when you've grown up and your friends haven't." Their imminent separation hangs over them. "I look at my friends differently now. I put all of them, consciously or unconsciously, through a test of friendship. It sounds really weird, but I've been making a note of everything they've done to me and what I've done to them. And if I find out that I've been treated rudely by them when I think I've treated them nicely, well then, I just think I'm not going to put forth the effort to keep in touch with them next year. So I have my mental lists. In a way I feel guilty for doing that. Maybe I should just let what happens happen."

But senior year is much too self-conscious a time just to let "what happens happen." Many seniors seem to keep these "little lists," and like the Lord High Executioner in *The Mikado,* to be convinced "they'll none of them be missed." As one senior confided, "There are days when I go to school determined to get closer to my friends, and then there are other days when I think, Oh, why should I bother to talk to her? I'm not going to see her next year."

"There are days when I go to school determined to get closer to my friends, and then there are other days when I think, Oh, why should I bother to talk to her? I'm not going to see her next year."

Seniors are looking at the whole subject of high school friendship more critically now that they are about to leave. "High school can be a very cruel place at times, making fun of other kids," one senior said in the spring. "We've been together all these years but no one really knows me here." Others, equally critical, feel they know each other too well. "You spend so much time with the same people," one senior explained to me. "By the end of the four years, all of us just want to get away from each other. It's like, I already know everything there is to know about you."

It is time to move on. They are ready to change themselves, but they believe that in order to do so, they need to get away from the personalities of people in their class. One girl who was very reserved confessed that she definitely planned to speak up more in college. But in high school "there are people who talk just to hear their own voices," and as long as she was with those people, she was not going to make the effort to change. It would be too hard to get any airtime. The routines were set; even the teachers expected a certain pattern. "So I just sit back. I'm glad I don't know anyone at the college I'm going to. I think it'll just be nice to have a fresh start."

Another girl had a different personality change in mind. "I think I'm a college person," she said. "I'm not in the running for prom queen. I was a cheerleader my freshman and sophomore years, but it wasn't something I basked in. It was just something to keep me fit. I love my close friends, but I don't like the socializing aspect of high school. I look forward to being in a place where everyone can be an individual and not worry about fitting in. When I went to the college for a visit, I saw such great individualists like I can see myself being and being respected for. Other than being here and being looked at as kind of weird."

"Up until this point," one young man observed, "we've always been defined by our friends: who we hang around with, what we do, what activities we're involved in. And now we're not doing that any more. We'll have to start over, like when we first came to school." His voice hesitated. "Like the first day of school." He was remembering himself as a ninth-grader, or perhaps even a first-grader. His sense of vulnerability was palpable, and he wanted to get started, to prove that he could make friends again. But he was less sure that he wanted to be defined by who his friends were, and most of all he was not sure what to do with his high school friends while he waited to get to the new place.

The Prom

She was a class leader, usually in charge of making sure the class dances were fun for everybody else. And she was not normally the sort to have romantic prom fantasies. She had very few idle moments for indulging fantasies; when she did, they were usually spent considering the idea of becoming a writer and living in southern France. This year would be different. "I'm looking forward to the prom. The guy I'm going with asked me in a real creative way." Her escort to the prom was more than a buddy; he was a "real date." She had handed over her leadership duties; she was not going to have to decorate or deal with musicians or lecture her classmates about their behavior. She had "found the prettiest dress," and she thought she would just give her sensible self up to the notion that this was going to be *the* night. "Every chance I get, I go out now. This is my last chance. I just know things change drastically when you stop going to high school. It doesn't matter how many times you say, 'Oh, things will stay the same.' They will change! We'll have the memories and that will be great, but friendships do change. So I'm just taking advantage of it while it is here."

The limelight that has been part of the senior experience is especially strong in the final days of the year. Adults who attend high school proms are usually amazed by how the kids they see every day, especially the girls, look when they get dressed up. The focus is on perfection. A perfect dress, a perfect tan, perfect hair and nails: these young women are the best version of themselves they can possibly be. Their tastes may vary from what others think is beauty, but for that night beauty is the ideal.

Get behind a bunch of these young princesses in the ladies room of the local hotel in May, however, and you will see that the goal of perfection is limited to the visual. It may be a feast for the eyes, but it's a famine for the ears. While they anxiously scrutinize themselves in the mirror, hunting down infinitesimal flaws, the cacophony is striking, full of screams, snarls, shouts. When their talk is intelligible, it is laced with swearing, bad grammar, and harsh put-downs of just about everyone. It is like watching a Walt Disney movie with a Stanley Kubrick soundtrack.

Yet it is not to be missed. Other formal dances in other years may be expendable, but this one is a rite of passage for all but the most resistant. If there is no one to go with, one young woman assured me, "you might even let your mother fix you up with the son of one of her friends—as long as she doesn't try to give you advice about what to wear." The significance attached to the ritual is intergenerational, even by those "boomer" parents who refused to have proms themselves.

The subject of the prom, however, is not an easy one in high school. Along with the starry-eyed Cinderella-type expectations of beauty, adventure, and romance are conversations about money, sex, and drinking. Every year, parents and teachers try to arrange things so that expenses are contained and there is nothing but fun for all. And every year, some seniors insist that it's their prom, so they should be the ones who define what fun is. If that means continuing the party in more private settings where they set—or abandon—the rules, so be it. These seniors may not be in the majority, but they are loud and powerful, and the rest don't dispute their version of the truth. After the prom, those who end it by going home have the feeling they have not had the whole experience after all.

The Yearbook

Another aspect of crossing the stage is leaving behind a record. The printed words, the photographs, lend a final and memorable feeling. "The yearbook establishes our place in history," one editor claimed. "It's an indelible record of who we are at this stage of our life, of our place in history." At the same time, and especially in the smaller schools, it is a vehicle for individual expression—"my life," a page or half a page offered to each senior. Besides individually chosen photos, there are quotes (mostly lyrics from their favorite music), lists of their accomplishments, and messages to favorite people. It is an opportunity to bring into focus exactly who they are and all the growing up they have done. The finality of it, however, can also make it a burden.

One senior described the evolution he endured. "For the past three years I've been saying, 'Wow, my senior page is going to be the best one that this school has ever seen!' And until the first day of my senior year I couldn't wait for my senior page. And then they started talking about it and I wondered what other people were going to do. Other things came along, and I got distracted. When I was putting it together it was exciting, but I was trying to look for the best quotes and the best pictures and everybody kept reminding me of the deadline. And when I finished putting it together and gave it to the editor, she just put it in the folder without even looking at it. So now I look back on it and say I could have used this other picture instead and I could have used that other quote and I don't need the quote I used. I'm still interested to see how it will look. But once it's down, you can't change it. It's in the yearbook and everyone's going to see it and that's that."

His story illustrates a far too familiar experience in the senior year. Seniors are evolving persons who are asked to present a flattering snapshot of themselves—and then stick by it. All their anticipation has been built around confidence that they can capture not only who they are but also who they are about to become. This confidence ebbs away as they see how difficult—how impossible—a task it is. The senior page as a mirror of essential character is no more or less accurate than the college essay or the job interview. It implies a permanence that is the very opposite of what the students feel themselves to be. They want to find a different quotation, choose a different photo, almost as soon as they've completed the tasks. "Getting it right" will never mean as much to the yearbook editor or the college admissions officer or the job interviewer as it does to them. These others are doing a job. For the senior, each step is a milestone.

Or not. "You know, I wanted everything to be great, and now . . ." This senior's voice trailed off. "It was not the best senior page," he knew. To dwell on his lost chance obsessively, however, would be too painful. And so, he explained to me, he "didn't take it seriously. It's just a yearbook—full of kids."

Others, offered less scope and perhaps for that reason suffering less disappointment, disagree. This was not "just a yearbook," another senior assured me. Her school could not afford a senior page for each student, but she still believed "this is *the* book. No matter how many times I move, I will never, *ever* donate it to a yard sale. Shakespeare, maybe. Not this book! And this is the way to look back on our high school years. If my kids go to this high school, they will say, 'Mommy was in that yearbook.'" Although she had talked about her desire to move, I saw that perhaps she expected to end up in her hometown, with kids who would be grateful for the institutional connection between her generation and theirs. This was the first time I had heard her talk that way.

Certain aspects of the yearbook experience are common in high schools all over this country. Nearly everyone starts the year with high hopes, not only for quality but also innovation. The group preparing the yearbook shrinks during the year, as the less committed seniors realize how much work is involved and begin to miss meetings. Those who persist stay because they have been given responsible positions or because they are excited about creating something lasting. Some are determined to influence "their" book in one or another way, in ways the faculty does or does not appreciate. In every staff meeting, there are discussions about what others are likely to think about their decisions. And when. Will the joke inserted into the senior history still seem funny after twenty-five years? Will the insult still hurt? Will the oblique threat seem benign?

Taste matters. In some schools there is a second "unofficial" yearbook that the seniors prepare without any supervision. With regard to the official yearbook, however, the issue of censorship comes up often. "There is one senior memory section, but they are pretty careful with us," one senior admitted. "No abbreviations or initials or secrets are allowed. Of course we try to sneak a few in." Authority is there to be challenged, even this late in their career. Strict teachers, and students perceived as the teachers' favorites, are likely to become the butt of secret jokes. "But only a few people in the class really get it. The result is that it's just a book."

What is a yearbook? A history or a memoir? Artistic expression or the last senior prank? "We are only graduating once. This is our final say. It is how we want to be remembered," one editor insisted. "It's hard to deny someone that last little bit of expression." The faculty had taken offense at two of her staff's decisions. They insisted that the book had to reflect the overall values of the school as well as the artistic sensibilities of the staff. She understood their reasoning in one instance, but not in the other. She also felt that the faculty should understand how hard everyone had worked. Surely a little slack could be offered them for that reason? Still, she realized that the seniors on the staff were not likely to learn from their mistakes. Feelings might well be hurt, but accountability for any fallout in the community would disappear when they did. "Basically, the yearbook comes out and we're out of here."

"We are only graduating once. This is our final say. It is how we want to be remembered. It's hard to deny someone that last little bit of expression."

Money is also often an issue. One yearbook staff was told that if the seniors insisted on color, they would have to raise the money separately, because the school would not allow them to raise the price of the yearbook. The yearbook had to be available to all, not just the wealthier members of the class. This led to a lot of talk about social class and artistic value. The yearbook staff, for the most part the seniors who could participate in extracurricular activities instead of holding down a job, had little understanding of why the cost had to be contained. The students who would have trouble coming up with the extra money were not comfortable saying so. They retreated into a who-cares-about-this-high-school-anyway attitude, leaving only the faculty to insist that they would buy a yearbook if the price was right.

As in every other aspect of American education, available funds determine what the yearbook offers. In most schools, the seniors' faces are jammed onto the pages. "I've seen the yearbooks in other schools," one senior told me. "They are so cool. But our class is so big that all we get in the yearbook is just one tiny little corner. All we get is lists of who's most popular and that leaves just about all of us out." In another large school, the practice, endorsed by the students I talked with, was to allow ten outstanding members of the senior class—"outstanding" defined mostly by grades but also by leadership positions—each to have her or his own senior page at the beginning of the book. The others, twenty to a page, with names but no other information, followed. As one might imagine, competition was fierce for those ten pages. One of the young women in contention was a member of a group I spoke with, and she was making no friends as she insisted on her credentials for the coveted position. But as she told me later, "I don't really care whether they like me. I'm moving away after this year, and I won't see them again. And this is something that I have earned—definitely."

Some yearbooks have dedications, histories, and predictions. Great precision is taken over every word. Class wills reflect, as one senior put it, "the fact that we will be as good as dead to this place after we go away." Some yearbooks emphasize photography rather than words. "Since I am a photographer," one editor explained, "I am more comfortable with the whole notion of freezing something in time."

There is always the worry, often deserved, that if the responsibility for the individual senior photo is left to the senior, there will be students who never produce one. These lapses lead some schools to insist that all the photographs be the same size and be taken by the same photographer, with everyone wearing similar clothes and facing front. When asked their opinion of this practice, the yearbook editors in one such school just shrugged their shoulders. They did not like the system, but they had dealt with those particular classmates for years. "A yearbook has to include everyone, even those who don't care. We don't have the energy to round up all that stuff." Displaying the photos in that way may look like conformity, but students have lots of stories demonstrating that the kids in their high school are a varied lot. Reminded by these photos, they will remember their classmates, and thus their stories, for decades. "Once I get out of here, the chances of ever seeing these people again are pretty slim. What you take with you is what you have left." The relationships are pretty much over. The memories, however, will always be important.

Managing nostalgia, which grows more necessary as the year passes, finally dominates almost everything they do. The yearbook makes it worse—and better. Its finite words and images contain the experience of high school and their senior year in a way that makes it manageable. Now that the facts have been gathered, they can allow themselves to come to conclusions. This event, that person, can be characterized. These conclusions allow them to move on and gather new experiences, new insights, and new friends in other places. Later, with the benefit of time and perspective, they may review and revise these opinions—if they still feel like thinking about high school.

One of the most startling aspects of the yearbook is the effect it has on the school once it comes out. As if responding to primeval habits developed over centuries, the behavior of nearly every student and quite a few members of the faculty changes. First, the book has to be read, with an intensity startling to behold. Next, messages are written all over it, obscuring the photographs, altering the design. While the students perform this important ritual, studies are abandoned, shopping trips are postponed, halls and courtyards clog up, attention wanders during classes, meetings, and games, and parties turn into silent writing sessions. Students feel strongly that they have to get these last thoughts right, but they also have to write quickly so that the book's owner can pass it on to someone else. Some students want as many people to write in their book as possible; others are more choosy.

They are saying goodbye, but also memorializing a period of time they have spent together: describing incidents, reinforcing admirable qualities. Sometimes they tease, but gently. This writing, more than any other they have done, is meant to be reinforcing, positive. "Of course, it needs to be flattering," one senior explained. "People are going to be reading it for years."

Last Rites

As they grow nearer and nearer to graduation, frightened by new thoughts about the future, all seniors can think to do is to spend time together. They expect all the rituals at the end of the year to make them feel closer to one another than ever. "It's happened to other classes," the students I spoke with claimed.

Or has it? So many expectations about senior year have not been met; perhaps this one will not be met either. "We want to end on a good note. We're trying to keep together but it's not really meant to be," one senior realized. He didn't dare to admit it. "We're pretending to be close but there's a lot of tension between us." Behind the tension are those "little lists." Which people will continue as my friends? Seniors have a new realization of the importance of context. What will they have to talk about when they are not on the team or in the play? When they no longer walk the same halls and gripe about the same teachers? Can their friendship survive the big change that lies just ahead?

To answer—or perhaps to avoid—such questions, most high schools organize a number of formal and informal occasions to honor accomplishments but also to give their seniors the chance to spend time together as a class. "This is when the seniors get closer," one young woman told me. "I just feel like I have to take it all in and make the most I can of it while I am still here." She showed me her schedule. Her class was planning to prepare and to celebrate during the late spring with the following activities and events, in this order:

Coronation nominations begin for the senior king and senior queen

Meeting to decide the class motto

Senior BBQ

Candy sale for graduation scholarships

Senior girls night out

Class gift committee meeting

Senior trip (two or three choices)

Senior parent involvement day

Last day to submit a senior poem

Last day to order graduation announcements

Last day to order caps and gowns

Pictures taken in caps and gowns

Senior prom

Senior dress-up day

School dance
Ceremonies for the honor society
Senior week
Senior banquet
Senior awards ceremony
Graduation practice
Senior talent night
Senior party
Graduation breakfast
Graduation

I was staggered by the length of this list. And these were just the celebrations; concerts, art shows, and senior project exhibitions also brought people together, but they were part of the curriculum. In this school, the SATs were offered every three weeks all spring, for seniors whose college admission depended on improving their scores. There was also a last chance to take the state achievement test, which was a graduation requirement no matter what the school thought of a senior's work. All this partying cannot be conducive to last-minute study, but a certain number of seniors are faced with this double agenda. "I need to graduate," one senior assured me, "but I would never forgive myself if I stayed home and missed out on these parties." The events surrounding the milestone are as important as the milestone itself.

Mixed messages about how to spend the last few weeks are present in every high school. "You can't let up, or you'll forget how to work," one senior believed, right up until graduation day. Much attention is devoted to the few seniors who are in danger of not graduating for either academic or social reasons. In some schools, seniors are excused from taking final exams if their averages are high enough, an incentive to keep them working during the spring term, but also an acknowledgment that the grade point average is likely to slip otherwise. There is the universal fear that if the seniors have nothing to do except party, they will only get into trouble. The tragic accidents that occur too often at the end of high school have been personally experienced by most teachers and many students.

On the other hand, all the adults interacting with the seniors know they need to acknowledge what is an important transition. Getting a new outfit, having their grandparents come, inviting their parents' friends to a party is very nice—maybe even their due—but it is not enough. The seniors want to celebrate with one another, and many feel they need to have their parties while school is still in session so that everyone can be invited.

So the senior events and traditions take place, with waxing and waning enthusiasm on the participants' parts. "I'm killing time," one senior admitted. He knew he was supposed to be excited, but he could not summon the energy he had expected to feel. He had been to a few of the senior events, but he didn't feel closer to any of his classmates. Underneath the pseudoexcitement, the parties seemed lame. The way he saw it, there was the I-know-where-I'm-going club and there was the leave-me-alone club, and they were having trouble relating to each other. He didn't think it would improve after graduation either, even though the reputed iron hand of high school discipline might be lifted. "No matter how much they drink, they still won't really be friends. Everyone is saying that we should have this big party, but it probably won't happen, because half of the class will be partying with people from other towns." And he was not going to get involved if it started getting too emotional. "My sister's graduation party was pathetic. A bunch of girls crying." He shook his head as if to banish the unpleasant memory, then returned to his own sense of what his responsibilities were. "I'll go to a few of the parties, but not to stay. Just to say it's been great going to high school. I've got to say goodbye some time and that will be as good a place as any."

As graduation approaches, class unity is still talked about, but it seems a more elusive goal. The process of separation has already begun. "I'll miss my class" was a common statement in the fall. This became "I'll miss some of them" in the winter. In the spring, as the seniors rushed from event to event, I was surprised to hear, in a number of private conversations, "I'm not losing anybody that I really care about." But this was said in such troubled voices that I didn't know whether to believe the speakers or not.

Senior events, planned with pride and anticipation, are, for some, as much fun as they are supposed to be. For most, however, they are just a way to get through a time that is beginning to feel extremely confusing. Seniors are still carrying around inside them the questions they asked themselves on the first day of school. Are they mature enough to be going through all this? Are they letting themselves and other people down because they still don't know what to do? "We don't know how to say goodbye, so we just try to brush it off, just fade away. We don't mean to be rude about it." However, they're afraid they probably are.

Seniors and Their Families

When Peter was accepted into an Ivy League university in December, he prepared to "enjoy the rest of the senior year stress free." However, he never withdrew his application to his second-choice college. In March, his second choice admitted him as well and invited him to fly there for a visit, all expenses paid. Besides looking around and having fun, he would be asked to take a special test; if he did well in it, he would be awarded a large scholarship and special status in the university. He would be admitted to limited-enrollment courses and would have first chance at working with certain professors. "At first, this offer seemed like a monkey wrench—something to worry about." He had done a lot of visiting, reading, and thinking when deciding on his first choice, and he wasn't sure he wanted to change his mind. "Most of my year had been comfortable, and I had enjoyed being in the know about next year," unlike so many of his classmates. This put him back in a vulnerable position, wanting something he might not get.

Still, he admitted, he had not been quite as serene as he had tried to look. "Just before this scholarship came up, I had been concerned about money. Not the fact that money wouldn't be there, but just the idea of going off to college and being so much indebted to my parents in terms of financial support. And on the other hand, this emerging independence. Two conflicting feelings." He shrugged his shoulders. His parents valued education as much as he did, and they had saved money for it. But he was not sure his younger siblings would be offered this kind of scholarship. Did bright children owe it to their parents to take all the financial help they could get? "You're taking on responsibility in other ways, but you know you're very far from supporting yourself," he continued after a few moments' thought. Since he was already admitted to both places, he figured he couldn't lose, and it would be a lark.

So he went for the weekend, "got the hard sell," liked the people, and took the test. When he returned home, he went through some fretful weeks waiting for the news; when he won the scholarship, he went through more anxious days trying to decide whether to give up his place in the Ivy League university. His friends and family took sides, of course. How far away was this new possibility? Could he give up his earlier preference? Would he jeopardize his chances for graduate school by going to a college that was not an "Ivy"? His parents were very circumspect, but he felt he was on to them. "Even though my parents aren't putting pressure on me, I can see where saving—I don't know. It's just a huge amount of money. It's a big chunk of money that you can see." All the money that had been spent on his behalf for the first eighteen years of his life was somehow easier to accept. It was spent on the mortgage or in the supermarket, spread among them all, part of his parents' decision to have a family. The taxes that paid for his elementary and high schools were similarly dispersed. When his parents sat down to write this tuition check, however, it would be about *his* present and *his* future. It would be very clear what they were doing and for whom they were doing it.

Peter was also aware, though he didn't like to talk about it, that other seniors had parents who didn't have as much money as his parents did. And they probably weren't going to be offered scholarships when they "didn't really need the money," although they too might have liked to rely less on their parents. As he prepared for his future, he felt isolated from these friends even before high school was over. The feeling grew so uncomfortable that he didn't enjoy their company as much as he had thought he would at this time in their lives. Why did all of these changes have to be so complicated?

"It's a big hole that you can't fill yourself," he acknowledged ruefully. He meant the money hole, but he realized that other things were missing too: a way to pay for college that is recognized as fair, enough opportunity for all who can use it, even the knowledge of what would be best for him. But now he could fill one of those holes by accepting this scholarship.

* * *

Peter's story illustrates the ironies in the changing nature of parent-child relationships during the senior year. At a time when seniors need to feel independent, they also need to accept an increased level of support, both emotional and financial. At a time when they should be thinking about the service they can render and the work they can do in their whole life, they are consumed by the need for quick cash, which is most often provided by time-consuming, dead-end "teenage jobs." These facts of life must be accepted, and that's hard enough; managing one's emotions so that one can weather these changes gracefully is harder still.

Another irony: seniors are mostly at their full height; they drive; they take care of other people's children. Most of them expect their senior year in high school to be their last year under their parents' roof, subject to their parents' rules. Most parents acknowledge the need to let their teenagers move on, build a new relationship with them based on respect and acceptance. But during this hectic last year, much needs to be done before the seniors can be sent on their way. And at least some of what needs to be done will be handled—directly or subtly, smoothly or awkwardly—by the seniors' parents. The imminent changes in the seniors' lives, especially the complications of college admissions, have a way of making parents return to an earlier, more protective mode. "My parents know I'm growing up," one senior told me, "but they're in my face so much more than they used to be!" For parents of seniors, the whole year is drenched in this dichotomy, and its strangeness is not lost on their children. The double agenda is the source of much of the tension between them.

Still at Home

After those first all-consuming days with their newborns, parents expect to play less and less of a role in their children's lives as they grow older. This is especially true in high school, when adolescents steadily gain experience and autonomy. The kids may not yet be growing up, but they are certainly growing out. They are away from home more, learning how to do things that their parents cannot do or even understand. By the time they are seniors, they have made decisions and lived with them, taken up with suitable and unsuitable friends, broken up with boyfriends or girlfriends whom their parents liked. Many have jobs, often in another town; they have cars and pay some of their own bills; they have friends whom their parents have never met. As one senior analyzed it, "My parents are definitely treating me differently; I don't have to explain as much."

Teenagers' zones of privacy grow larger and larger, until their parents conclude they may learn more about their children's lives in a weekly email or ten-minute phone call once they move away than in the little snippets of information they get while the kids are still at home. They're usually wrong: parents learn quite a lot about their teenagers just by seeing them every day. And during senior year, most still retain broad supervision or at least the right to cede it self-consciously. "I've noticed that at about eighteen, the parents say you can do this and you can do that, but that it's still the parents who are giving permission," one young woman remarked. She believed that her mother was keeping her on much too short a leash, grounding her whenever her grades went down, even blaming her for having a boyfriend. In fact, several people besides her mother—her teachers, her coach, even the honor society adviser—were telling her what to do. But she had developed a strategy: "I need to have a life, but a lot of fights would ruin my senior year. So I pretend to listen to the naggers, and just go ahead with my own life on basically my own terms."

For other families, however, many of the rules and habits that have governed the relations between the generations are loosening up. "I tell him where I'm going to be and, if possible, when I'll be home," said a senior about her relationship with her father. She no longer asked permission to go where she liked. Telling her father when she would be home was a matter of courtesy on her part rather than control on his. She got along well with him and was offended by the students who had become "more rebellious in their senior year. They even swear right at their parents sometimes! I have a higher level of respect for my father," she said, though she was fiercely determined not to take a penny of his money for college, even if it meant she couldn't go. On the edge of adulthood, she was suddenly aware of all that he had already given to her; she could not stand the thought of being even further in his debt. She planned to go into the army.

Having a parent nearby is not all bad: many seniors acknowledge that this is their last year to have their parents as a useful cover. But no matter how many compliments the seniors' parents get for acknowledging their children's new status as near-adults, they are still parents. Issues of safety, of what and how decisions are made, and of how things are to be paid for continue to concern them.

Moving On

Parents help their children through the initiation rite of leaving high school and finding a berth out in the world, an age-old process for both animals and humans. The activities and responsibilities of the senior year are therefore of special importance. A certain course will be set; it can be reset, but it will never again be unset. The parents, simply because they have lived longer, realize this, and during the year, more and more of the seniors come to see it too. The two generations are also likely to agree that there is too much for the seniors to do in a few short months. These agreements, however, often lead to disagreements: how much time should seniors "waste"? Are they going about their lives in the most efficient way? How much help do they need to accept? Should this help come from their parents or from someone else?

Of course, parents have already helped in many ways. They've established the context, by example and explanation, in which teenagers can earn credentials as adults. They've talked about various jobs or colleges for years: what they're like and why they're important. They've connected the qualities of their child with the qualities needed in various segments of the workplace. Since so many of today's parents started but did not finish college, they know the pitfalls to avoid when choosing one to attend. The lessons may be informal, but most parents act as the coaches whom their children, the players, need in order to function well. Like coaches, they build on their children's strengths. "Once they heard my interests," one senior acknowledged, "my parents helped me find good choices."

Even when parents' participation in the college application process is not necessary, it is often helpful. Some parents approach the college tours with competitiveness and/or trepidation, loading their children with apprehension, but most manage to make it fun. In many households, a parent sends away for catalogues, remembers deadlines, and reminds the child about the applications. "I have a mom who nags me," said one senior cheerfully. "That's why I got my applications in." Of course, this arrangement would help him only in the short term—"I know I have to become a little more organized"—but shortterm was what he was dealing with during this hectic year. "I've talked more with my dad this year than I ever did before," another young man exulted. "We just sat down and discussed *me*." Still, it turned into a tense discussion, because although the son was talking, he had the feeling that his father was not listening, and all the examples his father brought up were from his own family. "These are the stories I have heard for years!"—stories permeated with strong emotions, especially blame and guilt centering around lost chances. From the father's vantage point, this senior realized, there was wisdom to be gained from other people's experiences, and he needed to consider all of the particulars to see what he might learn from them. "But the bottom line is: I'm not a bit like my uncles!"

"I've talked more with my dad this year than I ever did before. We just sat down and discussed *me*."

Realizing that parents are giving good advice doesn't necessarily make things easier. As the deadline approached for a special program that both she and her mother felt would be a good one for her, one senior told me she couldn't stand the way her mother handled her. "I just broke down. And what I thought about it was, Fine! I won't do my homework! I won't get any sleep! To make *you* happy!" She realized she needed the option the program represented, but she could not cope with the day-to-day aspects of applying for it. The way she saw it, "My mother didn't have enough to do, so she sat around all day thinking up things for *me* to do! She was right. I did have to get it in. But the college gave me only two weeks to do it, which at that point in my life was absolutely *insane* because of the work I had. *No way*!" What she remembered best about the episode was how mad she had been at her mother. Looking back, she didn't judge her unreasonable self too harshly. Slack had to be cut sometimes. Her mother needed to understand the strain she had been under and would be under again. She was a senior.

Seniors need advice—and patience—more than ever before in their lives, but they often find it difficult to take from their own families. One athlete who wished that his college counselor would "get on my case more than he does" nevertheless found it difficult to talk to his father. "My dad is helping me a little bit," he admitted, "at getting my list together. But my father gives me hassle when I suggest things. He'll say, 'Oh, that's not a good enough college for your grades.'" His most recent grades had been B's, but he wasn't sure why, and "I don't think I should count too much on their staying *that* good." His father, he feared, was suddenly seeing him as a new person, with more academic ability than he really had.

This father and son also disagreed when it came to athletics: the son depended on them as a lever into college more than his father thought he should. Since the role of athletic prowess in college admissions is uncertain and changing, the two generations had rather different slants on it. Neither one knew who was "right," but the father sounded so sure of himself that the son translated this as "bossiness. And especially in your senior year you shouldn't have to put up with that. In some things, I guess, his sights are just higher and in some, lower." As a senior it was the son's job to get through all this, so he compared himself with his father as if they were two friendly sightseers taking in the view.

The High Road and the Low

All seniors experience these differences between their ambitions and those of their parents. These differences are responsible for much of what they learn about each other, but also for many of their disagreements and regrets. Parents are often accused of setting their sights too high. "Parents just sit there and they make standards," an indignant young woman complained. "When the kids meet them, all of a sudden they raise another standard." In my interviews, however, more seniors complained about other seniors' parents and about parents in general than about their own. It was as if they felt they had to protect their own parents from such stereotypical accusations but at the same time share powerful stories that would reinforce parents' bad reputations and explain the pressure students felt.

"All parents care about is the name," one senior claimed. "I have friends who are applying to schools they don't want to go to, just because their parents want them to go there." Her own parents had been understanding and helpful. She had looked for a college that would reflect her interests and personality and was putting prestige on the back burner. Her friends' parents, however, had been "ridiculous. My friends say, 'Gee, I wish I could have done what you did,' but it's just not possible for them. They could never even take a year off to think about it because it would disappoint their parents."

Another senior told a story about the parents of his best friend, an all-state football player who had decided he did not want to play football in college and felt he ought to be up front about this decision. His friend's mother had been livid and insisted her son had to "keep his options open." This meant his friend had to pretend he would play football so that he could be accepted by a more prestigious place. Besides the deception actively encouraged by the older generation, there was the matter of who was making the decisions. "I see the pressure on him from his parents," his friend commiserated. "Whose life is this anyway?" The story was his friend's, but the question was his as well.

Another student told me about a household, again not his own, in which "the only topic of conversation for months and months and *months* was college. My friend got crazy. He was always working on an application. Some he did for his father, some for his mother, some for himself. He couldn't go out, couldn't even hang around after school. He finally applied to about fifteen places." Did his friend want to fill out all those applications? "I suppose so. He couldn't decide what he wanted to do. And this was one way to keep the peace."

"My family think highly of me, and they look forward to seeing me succeed even though that feels like pressure. I'm the oldest. They put a lot of emphasis on how I'll turn out, because my younger sisters are going to follow my lead."

When seniors complain about their own parents, they try harder to understand motives. "My family think highly of me, and they look forward to seeing me succeed," one working-class young woman conceded, "even though that feels like pressure. I'm the oldest. They put a lot of emphasis on how I'll turn out, because my younger sisters are going to follow my lead." Her parents wanted to offer their kids hope, and she realized that with her good record so far, she was their best bet. These dynamics had been governing relations in her family for years and were now being applied to the decisions of senior year. Another young woman was the hard-working younger sibling of a disappointing son. She had watched her parents' pain all through her childhood, and though she suffered from their concentration on her academic record, especially during her senior year—she was tense and clearly anorexic—she did not really resent them for it. She felt she was their last chance to have a child they could be proud of and, all in all, they deserved it.

Birth order is not the only explanation given by seniors for what they consider their parents' unreasonable and obsessive interest in them. Seniors often describe themselves as prisoners of their family's culture. Everybody can imagine what a child whose family "has always gone to Harvard" must feel. More surprising are the strong allegiances to less selective institutions to which the family tie is not nearly as binding—the expectation is just as intense. Other family cultures are based on ethnic identities—New England WASP, Jewish, Asian, to name a few—assumed to be permeated with an expectation of success. Some students describe their cultures proudly, sure their family values have done them good. "If you fail, try again. That's our family motto," one young man told me. But others, like the senior who described himself as "the only bad student in a very smart family," are troubled by the culture clash. They feel their own good qualities are unappreciated, especially during senior year. One young woman was particularly poignant about it. "My parents reflect the Asian culture," she explained. "Because I'm Asian, my parents think I'm supposed to be smart. They're so hung up on my being perfect that they don't really care if I have fun."

"My parents tell me I can go anywhere to college," another student claimed. It must have seemed a simple enough statement on their part. They probably thought they were being supportive. But he interpreted it as a signal that they thought the whole world was open to him. It was a nice thought, but he was a senior now. It was time to get serious, to get realistic, to narrow things down, to face the fact that some things could never be. Were his parents afraid to get on with that job because they did not want to hurt him? Did they think they would anger him by seeming to sell him short? Did they even know him well enough to help him take on such a demanding and sensitive process? "I almost cracked up," he admitted. "No college list was good enough. They kept asking me why I didn't apply to places I had never even heard of." Seniors all over the country feel pulled between the cautionary tales of their college counselors and their parents' grandiose dreams.

Other sights set by parents for their children seem to be too low. There are parents who tell their children to adjust their aspirations. Some warn their soon-to-graduate offspring they are not likely to do well in certain trades, or in college, or in a more demanding college, or in a large college, or in one that is far away. A number of seniors give up lifelong plans after these conversations with their parents.

A student I talked with described this process. "I would have figured that I would have been one of the students who was writing a lot of essays and trying to get in to a lot of private colleges," she said. "But I ended up just deciding that I'll go to the state university that is nearby." Had she changed? Not really. She still wanted to do well in college, maybe go to graduate school. She was still ambitious, but she "had to get a little more practical. I'm kind of a momma's girl, and my parents—well, me too, I guess—want me to be nearer. I think that will be better. My family is a big part of my life." She had been going out more and was starting her summer job early, so "it's not that I'm not old enough to go away." She was definitely making the break with them, but she didn't "want it to be too final." Also, her older brother's college was costing a lot. Instinctively, she felt hers should be less expensive. And "anyway, in my family, I'm the peacemaker, and I always try to accommodate. So I suppose it will be better this way."

Another student also felt he had altered his picture of who he was—and, in his mind, lowered his sights—after talking with his parents. All his life, he said, he had expected to go away to a private college. "The other coast" was a kind of mirror for him. He wanted to hold it up so he could see himself more clearly. He was the biggest man on campus in his high school. He could be admitted to his state's most competitive university. But how would he stack up nationally? For as long as he could remember, he had intended to use college to find out. The East Coast was "a beacon." It had helped him negotiate the stormy seas of adolescence safely, encouraging him to take the hardest courses, get the highest grades. Travel had become a metaphor for self-improvement. "I thought college might be my one chance to live on the East Coast for a while. When you have a family and stuff, you might not be able to do that. So it was a chance to try something new."

During his senior year, however, he learned that his fantasy was unrealistic. When he told his parents about how he had planned out his life, they were unable to see his point. "We talked about it a lot, and they said, 'If you can get in, and wherever you want to go, we will find a way to pay for you to go there.'" He suddenly saw his lifelong plan in a new light: he was being selfish. Both the parents and the child were determined to be considerate of each other. "They definitely said I have the option to go East. And I wasn't as concerned with my parents' dreams as with my own. But they'd like me to go to the state university, and they believe it's as good an education in my field as any." As state university graduates, they also knew more than he did about the requirements for medical school, which he considered his goal. When he looked harder at the whole picture, he saw their logic. "It is wonderful support, but I didn't want to put that strain on our family. I decided to stay closer to home, and I knew that's where they wanted me to go.

"My parents didn't want to say, 'We're not going to help you with your dream,'" he insisted. But it was his dream, and had never been theirs, for themselves or for him. And he suddenly saw the importance, to a certain extent, of parents and children sharing dreams. He was staying home. If the East Coast was to be a mirror or a beacon for him, it would have to be later. He even told me a story about a kid who had tried an eastern college and "wasted a lot of money being lonely and dealing with the weather." Anecdotes like this were the emotional armor he needed, and I believed him when he said he had accepted that his parents were right. If only he had not come back, again and again, to the word *dream*.

Straining Family Relationships

The turbulence of working out life plans is a strain on both generations, made more so by the feeling on both their parts that their very identities are on the line and by their fears that they will let each other down. Some seniors feel their parents are uniquely qualified to handle the difficulties of transition. "It all depends on personality," said one student. "My mother's been relaxed about my decisions, and I take that as a sign of her confidence in me. It gives me the opportunity to think about other options." Much soul-searching had to be done, and it was going to take some time. "But my mother doesn't seem to be as worried about time as some parents are."

Another had a different experience. "I'm finally getting some serious respect from my parents," he boasted after he got into college. For years, his parents' fretting, nagging, and constant oversight—even their vigilant advocacy—had convinced him they were never going to trust him to be successful on his own. Now a faceless committee hundreds of miles away had given him the status in his own family that he had feared he would never earn. But was this about his future or their bragging rights? He almost resented their jubilation. "I tried my best for myself, but not for them."

"My parents always argue about my senior year," another senior told me, but she believed the arguments were really about unresolved questions in their own lives. "My mom conformed. She married very young and that was the end of her education. She wants me to accomplish everything she never did but always wanted. That's how I see it. I always did." These ruminations were tied up with her questions about how ambitious women should be. How could she respect the job parents do when some parents themselves didn't seem to respect it? She did not want to ask her parents' advice, because she could already sense that she wanted a sharply different model and she was afraid she would hurt them if she "brought it all out in the open." Still, she felt she needed to sort all this out before she decided where to go to college.

It is not only her mother's dreams a daughter is expected to carry out; in some cases, it is her father's. In one young woman's family, the mother had been a successful student, had finished high school, and was fairly relaxed about senior year. "She realizes I'm not going to be eighteen forever," her daughter claimed, and so her mother was more casual and trusting about her social life. In fact, having had a senior year herself, her mother enjoyed talking about all the events and parties. Her father, however, was cautious and controlling. This, his daughter believed, was because he had dropped out of high school. Her father had made a lot of money since then, but her senior year seemed to have reawakened a sense of vulnerability in him. "He takes it out on me, thinking I'm going to do the same thing. I'm so tired of his complaining that I don't do well in school, that I'm relaxing more now just to rebel against him. He doesn't realize that compared to a lot of kids, I'm just about perfect. I don't smoke or drink—I don't do anything!" Bad behavior was the threat she potentially—but unconsciously—held over her parents' heads. "And I do my work, but I want to get a job." The young woman tried to understand her position as a high school senior in terms of this family history. She admitted that she argued with her father more than she ever had before and that she tried to get her mother to take her side against her father, at least on these issues. As behavior, this was not mature; it was, she knew, hardly "perfect," and she felt bad about it. "But I can't take the blame just because he got a job and then dropped out when he was a kid." And she believed her father was asking her to do exactly that—make up for the decisions he had made in his life by letting him make the decisions in hers.

Although most seniors realize that their parents mean well, they are afraid their parents are becoming too invested in what should be the seniors' own lives and the seniors' own prospects. "It's been so hard to get along with my parents," said one senior, speaking for many, "because I want to make my own decisions." Although she believed that her parents had "done an awful lot for me, way more than most parents" and were "basically good people," she was angered by her parents' anxiety after she came back from visiting a college that had accepted her. She had had a wonderful time, but it was far away. There were so many factors to consider that she could not be sure. "I don't know," said this model student and model daughter. "My parents have been driving me nuts." Parents, she had noticed, always seem to think there's a "right" decision. "I guess it's a big deal to them, but I don't understand why." It wasn't their lives that were going to be tremendously changed by whatever it was that she worked out. It was she, after all, who would be living in one place or another, participating in gymnastics on one level or another, studying certain subjects or others. She was trying to face these decisions rationally, but her parents were not helping her stay calm with their insistence that she be certain. "They worry about it a lot more than I do. I wish they'd kind of calm down a little bit, is all."

Students have each other to complain to, but parents may feel isolated from other parents during senior year. "Sometimes I feel sorry for my parents," one senior told me. He realized that in an effort to avoid tension, his parents were backing off. But he wondered "how much they really mind that I'm not as close to them any more. They seem kind of tired." Another realized she had not lived up to her parents' hopes. She was aware that she was still a burden to them, just as her parents were to her. "It's not just my parents," she said. "I let my whole family down. In the beginning of the school year, I had my parents and my family backing me one hundred percent. But then I started slacking off and doing badly." Working and boyfriends had been diversions for years, but she had always been able to keep up with school. She had gone further in high school than anyone else in her family, and she believed that she was "still going to graduate." If she did, she would take pride in that, but she had run out of steam during her senior year.

Other flare-ups between parents and their children during this period seem even more serious. "I've had to raise myself and I've had to raise my mother," one claimed. "Now I can be on my own and I can live my life. I don't have to worry about living someone else's too." She and her boyfriend, she said, were "both running away from our families. We've been the neglected child in the background for so long, and now we want to care about ourselves." She was eager to leave, but her mother was even more eager to have her go. Right around graduation, her mother informed her that since her eighteenth birthday was approaching, she would have to "get out of the house right away. I was expected suddenly to be completely responsible for myself." The sudden rupture was unnerving. She had to move away from her boyfriend in order to get help from relatives. Her college plans evaporated.

Another student told me she couldn't finish high school if she had to live at home. "I think that I could make it better in life if I weren't fighting with my mom so much." She moved out of the family home to live with some other teenagers even though her graduation was still a few weeks away. It was hardly a glorious senior spring for her. Shopping for a prom dress was the last thing in the world she would—or could—do, and she felt that she had very little in common with most of her classmates. But she was determined to hold on, to get through graduation. She was working hard, trying to keep house, show up at her job, and do her schoolwork. The kids she was living with were far less reliable. To her, however, moving out had been a constructive move, one designed to "get myself together so I can make it better in life."

Many seniors express this desire to stand on their own. "I need to leave home," another senior said. His home life was not troubled, and he summarized the convictions of many other relatively happy students. "As long as mom and dad are there, they'll take care of everything." His voice was tolerant, even empathetic. Parents' natural desire to "handle things" is often seen as manipulation by their young, especially during the last months before they go away.

Money Matters

One of the most shocking aspects of senior year for those going through it is how much more often money needs to be considered. "Suddenly, I'm a much more expensive person," one student confessed. "This year," one young man said with a touch of surprise, "we have things that I need to pay for." In some schools, senior privileges cost students more than they expect. Open campus policies encourage them to spend money in local eateries. "Dues for high school clubs get awfully expensive once you're a senior," but the seniors can't just quit. They feel they need a long list of clubs to get into college and, after that, to get local scholarships.

Then there are the same traditional expenses—the yearbook, the class ring, the prom—many parents and teachers remember from their senior year. This list of necessities, however, has grown, as have the prices. Outfitting a senior is a proud and sentimental tradition, but it has also become a lucrative and elaborate business, with invitations, rings, hats, t-shirts, class gifts, and caps and gowns all adding up to a considerable sum of money. Furthermore, yearbook photos are not taken by the senior's little brother with his Brownie camera anymore. The prom dress is not a simple hand-me-down. A hotel has replaced the school gym as the prom venue; a limousine has replaced the family car as a way to get there. The class trip is not likely to be to the local state park. So there is tradition, but there is also change.

Applications to college are expensive too. Most seniors don't understand why they cost so much. Some students are not able to apply to as many colleges as they would like because they or their families can't afford the application fees. Working-class students, many of whom assume these costs themselves, feel especially squeezed.

Who pays for all these extra expenses? It varies by family, of course, not only according to family income but also according to whether the family considers the expense a necessity or a luxury. The "necessity" tends to be the college application; the "luxury" is the limousine to the senior prom. The "necessity" is something the whole family thinks is important; the "luxury" is something the senior thinks is important. The family's circumstances help shape these definitions. Once the distinction between a necessity and a luxury is clear, seniors know what to do. "I pay for lots of my own expenses," one girl claimed, but when I asked what they were, she said, "Oh, hair conditioner and stuff."

Most seniors talk about their budgets in worried tones. "I haven't been saving as much as I thought I would," one lamented, "and I'm always about to go broke." The future is what they need to save for, yet they feel they should assume at least some of their own senior expenses. Why? "Because it is my expense, and because I do have the money—just not enough." It's one more dichotomy to figure out: I have money, so I need money.

Paying for the Future

Money is hard for seniors to talk about, even with their families. "I hate having to revolve around money, but you have to, in order to move on. Money is important now." They do not want their parents to feel embarrassed or pressured or guilty—nor do they want to feel those uncomfortable emotions themselves—so they keep quiet. But the costs of living away from home have to be computed. It is one thing to be aware that going to college is expensive; it is another to look at all those zeros. Suddenly, rooms have rent attached to them; a bowl of cereal is part of a "meal plan." Thousand-dollar decisions often get confused with hundred-dollar decisions, and short-term purchases get confused with long-term commitments, mostly because the seniors are so often alone with their thoughts.

One young woman seated on the floor in her guidance counselor's office was surrounded by this year's books and notebooks but also next year's scholarship brochures. It was a colorful display, and she tried to stay cheerful about it, but her joke was a rueful one. "School isn't going to be free ever again. I can't believe how much I'm going to have to pay just to keep on doing homework and sitting in class."

Most seniors and even most parents are like her; they can't believe how much it is going to cost to go to college. It is the biggest expense most parents expect to take on for their kids, the one they've thought about even before they had kids. In nearly every case, savings will have to be used to meet the college-education bills, and families expect to curtail their lifestyle during these years.

Many other nations do not put such a large burden on parents of college-bound students, providing substantial government scholarships for nearly all college students, even those who can pay. These other nations, however, do not offer the option of college to nearly as large a percentage of their population. In these countries, the privilege of further education is offered only to the academic elite, mostly as defined by national examinations. So the range of opportunities is greater for American eighteen-year-olds, but they and their parents—and all kinds of other benefactors—have to figure out a way to pay for it.

One of the first lessons seniors learn is that expenses for college and training programs vary tremendously. Seniors know the price tags associated with various colleges and believe the more expensive ones are better. However inappropriately, their voices take on a somewhat ashamed tone when they explain why they are choosing a cheaper option. One senior I talked with had not enjoyed his high-powered suburban high school and had done very poorly there. I expected him to tell me he was glad he was not going to college and to extol the job he would try to get instead. But even he did not close off the college option; he told me of career plans that would involve not just college but graduate school. Not now, of course—he "had a monetary situation," so he would "pick up some kind of work" after he graduated from high school. As he saw it, it was his lack of money rather than his academic difficulties that held him back. The local community college would eventually be a good fit for him, but not because it might be less selective, appropriately paced, part-time, "more hands-on," or more receptive to older students. The difference as he described it was entirely financial. "That way," he explained, "I will get the basic credits out of the way at a cheaper price."

In spite of this kind of dismissive tone, seniors are very grateful for the range of academic as well as financial options that make allowances for their interests and their academic and personal circumstances. It's not "either you go to Yale or you stay home and work" as it was for so many of our ancestors. There is a suitable alternative somewhere in between. It takes time and energy to find it, however. "Are these big schools really worth the money?" one senior asked me. "Of course, when I was a little kid, I rooted for their football teams. But seven-hundred-person lecture halls are not for me." Another senior, thinking in terms of college plus graduate school, decided that he would take the cheapest good option available now, because graduate schools were likely to be rarer and more expensive. "Besides," he admitted, "I might get better grades at the less expensive college, and that would be helpful. My parents could send me anywhere I wanted to go, but I don't know how long they would be paying for it. So I'm going to the state university. Even though it has had lousy press lately, it's likely to get better."

Seniors learn to be cautious before they give away their heart. "I didn't know there would be an out-of-state fee until I started looking into it, so I changed my mind real quick." They are trying to predict exactly how valuable each dollar spent will be. "Why should I ask my parents to send me there when I know that this other place will probably be just about as good? I know one thing. I don't want to have loans to pay back for years and years."

The issue of tuition and living expenses complicates the process of achieving adulthood. I listened as two seniors compared their plans. One, somewhat ashamed of having "messed up" during his senior year, said he would not be able to go off to college the way his friends planned to do. They would have adventure, meet a lot of new people, just get away. And that was growing up, he guessed. "But I have a job and I'm going to move out of my house, away from my parents," he insisted. He wasn't just going to hang around being a kid. "I'm going to support myself—make that transition—right after I graduate." After a considerable silence, the other senior observed wryly, "I may be going to college, but I'm not paying for college. Technically, I'm still under my dad's roof."

Then there are the seniors who are not living under Dad's roof but who are making decisions with implications for Dad's life. All over the country, the complications of divorce exacerbate the complications of college costs—and vice versa. One young man I talked with had been admitted to his favorite college. When he first saw it in the fall, "I liked it right off the bat and I thought, Blast it, I wish I'd get accepted at this stupid school." The school was "stupid," he explained, because as a well-known university, it had no right to tantalize him because it was a long, long shot. When it accepted him, it was by far his most prestigious option but also by far the most expensive.

His parents were divorced. He lived with his mother and she knew how much he wanted the university, but his father was the one who was going to pay for it. His mother did not argue that she knew him better, though many mothers in this situation do. Instead, "My mom has been saying, 'You have to go there. Playing in a more competitive league is what's important.'" She was emphasizing the athletic parts of college over the academic parts, which was new for her. This was fine by the senior—it reflected his priorities—but he thought she secretly wanted him to go to the school because it was more prestigious. Keeping the discussion at a practical level was her way of influencing his decision.

The senior was prepared to make his own case. He went around to the other places that had accepted him, though none of them appealed to him any more. The university was in a city, which he had decided was important. Since it was also near home, and since he had a new girlfriend in the junior class, he threw that into the mix too. His reaction was "mostly visceral," but he had talked to a lot of people about what the university was like. "There's never been a negative comment from anyone—except for the bill." One had to wonder, however, how many negative comments his ears could have picked up at this point.

"I talked with my dad, and he's not happy with the tuition, obviously," he said. "It's a real stretch for him, I know." His college expenses were going to far exceed his sister's. He knew he was not as keen on schoolwork as he ought to be, that he might not spend much time in the famous libraries and science labs that had helped to make the university so expensive. He might not even make the varsity teams in a place that big. It was not really fair, he knew, to ask his father to pay so much when there were cheaper options. But he wanted it so much!

In spite of his conviction that his father could pay for it, he kept coming back again and again to the bill. "He wants what I want. That's the way he is. But it's the most expensive college I applied to." In fact it was one of the most expensive in the country. The next four years were going to be different for these two households. The senior realized his own behavior would be affected by these hard decisions. After a rocky period in his classes, he was determined to pull up his grades in the last weeks of school. He lined up jobs for the summer, and was diligently practicing football. He felt, for the first time, like an investment rather than just a kid. He had to prove worthy of all this commotion, all this sacrifice. "I figure all I have to do now," he concluded, "is to work my butt off."

Another senior was going to be able to go to college, but only the least expensive one. "All my options were open at first," he explained. "But finally money decided it. This is the way real life is. So there was really only one choice." He had come to realize that in the end, he would only be able to go to one college anyway. He was luckier than some people just to be able to do that.

Seniors are up against economic realities related to the role that economic advantage and disadvantage can play in their lives. In many cases, these realities are new; in some cases, they are brutal and unfair. Seniors are exposed to large issues such as opportunity and to whom it should be offered—issues about which their elders have given them weak or even conflicting signals. The issue of money also reinforces seniors' dependence at the moment of their greatest desire for independence. It leads them to curtail their dreams, or to deal with the fact that they can have their dreams but others can not. No matter how beneficial this new realism may eventually turn out to be, it is still relatively sudden—and troubling.

A normally confident young woman spoke for all the others. Money had made her think about her long-range goals, not only in terms of how expensive they would be but of whether she was worth it. "Sometimes I think about all the big bills I'm about to run up," she said. "How am I supposed to do this? I feel like I'm drowning."

Scholarships

"When we first faced the money problems," one student told me, "we just thought, Well, scholarships will help." The word is thrown around by people who have good or bad grades, people who have money or do not. Keeping alive the dreams of its young seems to be a part of American culture; scholarships seem a particularly apt way to do so.

But there are hurdles. The increasing trend toward early admissions exacerbates the gap between richer and poorer students, because college decisions about scholarships are not made as early. Students who are able to pay in full, no matter how stretched their resources, are in a position to make decisions about their future. They are more likely to apply early, indicating they are serious about college, which may help them get admitted. The more places they fill, the fewer places are left for others.

The scholarships seniors apply for are offered by the federal government, by colleges, and by state and local businesses and organizations. They range from full coverage and help with living expenses down to fifty dollars from a local business. The Pell grants offered by the federal government are need-based scholarships. Eligibility is strictly limited to those whose financial resources, including those of their parents, are at the low end of the economic spectrum. Most college scholarships are also designed around that principle. The idea is that if a college education is a commonly recognized and important advantage, each child in the country should theoretically be able to have the greatest possible access to it. The children of those who can afford to pay should pay, so that the children of those who cannot afford to pay will be able to use all the available scholarship money. Even if "access to all" can still not be guaranteed, at least we as a nation will get closer to the goal of greater justice and social cohesion.

Seniors know there are a lot of scholarships available. What is less well known is that many of these scholarships are small, they may be merit based rather than need based, and they will finally not provide as much money as low-income students require in order to take on the expense of college. Seniors need to think through these patterns of eligibility and connect them with their own circumstances. Since scholarships to the more expensive colleges are the most visible and most desirable, some seniors feel there is no point in applying to local community colleges whose reputations are not as good. By the end of the year, however, many of these hopes have been dashed. One lively student was full of hope in February that his good record and his proficiency in chess would win him a fully paid place in the local Ivy League university. He focused on that plan so intensely that when it didn't work out, he was left without any college plans at all. Another student also had high—I thought unrealistic—hopes. She described her after-school job to me, and it was clear that she was earning a considerable amount of money. She said, however, that she was not saving any of it for college. She would need "such a massive scholarship to go to a decent college" that there was no point planning for anything else. She had planned a "safety" for admissions but had no backup plan for financial aid.

Most colleges are reluctant to assume heavy financial loads. One young woman with outstanding credentials had no parents to help her and was in need of total aid. The only college that accepted her and offered her full financial support was one of the most selective and expensive colleges in the nation, where a member of the faculty knew her well. She was turned down cold by fourteen other colleges, including some that were far less selective. It was hard not to conclude that her need for so much money had scared most of them away.

Some expensive colleges accept poor students but offer inadequate aid. "I don't have financial possibilities," said an academically successful young woman who badly wanted to go to college. The admission she had been offered was no longer a source of pride but of poignancy. "People keep telling you what's not true: that you can get a scholarship. I thought I'd get a lot more than what I have. Two or three years' worth would really help me, but right now I've only got the first year covered." She had had a lot of energy and hope in the beginning of the year, but by spring she was worried about her prospects. "There's only one thing I can hope for, that somebody out of the goodness of her heart will say, 'Come on, we'll take you.'"

She felt a little childish admitting that she felt that way. Fairy godmothers did not really exist, she explained. The world did not work that way, at least it was not going to for her. "I have made peace with myself," she declared, improbable though that sounded. "However hard I dream, however much I want to accomplish something, if I do not have that money to pay my way, I am not going to be able to do it. I'm not going. It's not likely." She was seemingly unaware of the subtle differences between her last two statements. Nor did she blame her parents for not having the money now seen as so important. She knew they had already done a lot for her, perhaps more than they should have. "My parents just can't pay for college," she explained. "They said, 'We would give you the money, but we just don't have it any more.'" She knew they were telling the truth. Another similarly disappointed senior could not hide his bitterness. "The colleges want your money," he concluded, "but if you don't have money, they don't want *you*."

More-affluent students have problems too. Scholarship grants can help them achieve personal independence from those who might expect them to be grateful or obedient in return for their generosity. These students, unused to and uneasy talking about income and often unaware of what their parents—let alone anyone else's—earn or have as assets, prefer to avoid the subject of need. "I'd like to help my parents out by trying to get a scholarship," one student told me in March. His football record had not been very good, and he was somewhat indifferent about going to college at all. His parents had told him they had saved money. But a scholarship sounded nice all the same. "Sometimes I wish I were poor," he said. "At least then, I wouldn't have to take money." It seemed easier to "take money" from a scholarship committee than from his parents: it felt earned from the committee and only a gift from his parents. One reinforced the idea of independence, the other of dependence. "I want to go to college but I don't want to rely wholly on my father for financial support," he continued. "I want to do it myself. There has to be a way to do it."

"I want to go to college but I don't want to rely wholly on my father for financial support. I want to do it myself. There has to be a way to do it."

Another senior explained her thinking about the role of scholarships in the culture of senior year this way: "If you get a scholarship, that shows that you've accomplished something." The scholarship branded her as a worthy person, no matter what her financial needs were. It wasn't fair not to get a scholarship just because she did not need the money. "My parents are going to pay for my college," she explained. "They can afford to pay for it. But I get self-satisfaction out of people's acknowledging me for the hard work that I have done and for getting things on my own."

Merit scholarships have been around for a long while. More and more scholarships—from National Merit Scholarships to the $250 given away each year by the local shoe store—are awarded on the basis of merit rather than of need. Athletic scholarships could be called merit scholarships, though so many of them are awarded to low-income students that they might also be called need based. Other institutional scholarships may be designed to beef up the orchestra, the community service program, whatever the personal preference of the donor. Local scholarships of a few hundred dollars dominated the conversation of many of the seniors I talked with, especially those in the South and the West. They seem to be awarded mostly to those who go after them with the most vigor, savvy, and occasionally—at least the way the seniors described it—"connections." Merit is also considered in connection with need-based scholarships when there is not enough money to go around. Since that is nearly always the case, especially with the more expensive colleges, merit is considered by many people—especially high school seniors—to be the primary reason they have gotten a scholarship.

I listened carefully to what seniors were saying about their experiences with money. I also tried to interpret their silences. Nowhere in Peter's or others' very thoughtful summary of the questions they asked and the answers they were trying to find was there any hint that they saw anything wrong with accepting a scholarship they did not strictly need. That particular aspect of the issue isn't adding to the stress of the senior year. Seniors do not seem to be weighing the competing demands of need and merit.

Should they be? It is hard to begrudge their accomplishments, hard to be against merit as a way to distinguish people. Affluent seniors are worthy young Americans, not only because of what they have already done but because of the clear promise they show for fruitful and decent lives. But poorer children without financial backing, without supportive parents, without well-developed talents, also show promise. Perhaps not quite as much promise in certain respects, but more in others. This dilemma permeates the lives of many high school seniors, but they seem only dimly aware of it. What are needs and what are luxuries is a hard-enough question to answer for them as individuals; it seems even harder for their nation.

Who is worth backing? How much merit matters and how it is to be defined depend on how much one cares that opportunity be widespread. The growth in the number and scope of merit scholarships during the last ten years is the outcome of many factors in American society. One is the revolt of the middle class, the taxcappers and the foes of affirmative action, the people who say they are "tired of paying for the poor." Another is the assumption by second-tier colleges that they have to offer financial incentives to the "best students" or they will be permanently lost in the seniors' rush toward more-prestigious colleges. And the steep rise in tuitions during the last twenty years may well persuade any middle-class family that they need the money.

To Work or Not to Work

Even without college to pay for, money has a way of evoking independence problems. As one senior put it, "It's a little tough having big bills come along just when you're ready to get free. I don't want to ask my parents for money, because I like to do things they wouldn't want to pay for." In his mind, money equaled control. As long as he was taking their money, he had to do only what they were willing to pay for—or lie about it. "I got to that stage where I don't like my parents or my brother asking me, 'Well, what do you need the money for?' So I just decided to get my own money, and I know what to do with it." He had to give up sports, which both he and his parents loved: he had loved playing, and they had loved watching him play. He knew they were upset about it, but it could not be helped.

Most seniors are torn by similar conflicting values. During the fall and winter, they have never been more pressed for time. There simply is not enough of it in a day. "My job is to be a student," one said. "I don't have time for anything else." And whatever else working at a job outside of school takes, it surely takes time. Yet most seniors work, and some work a lot.

For the students, a job has benefits besides money. "Since I'm a senior, I might as well take responsibility—learn what it's like."

Some teenagers manage to get work related to their long-term interests. For others, having a job forces them to become more organized. Or the people they work with end up knowing them better than their teachers do and can write them recommendations. They feel reliable, mature, and appreciated when they cover their own expenses and do their work well. Sometimes that contrasts with the way they feel in school, sometimes not.

In most cases, however, their jobs are admittedly boring. They wait on or clean up after other people, with career ladders nowhere in sight. Students expect to start with the worst jobs, since they are young and working part-time. And at first, students appreciate the flexibility. "It's pretty junky work," one senior admitted, "but at least I can get the day off for the senior banquet." These two aspects balanced each other in his mind.

As time goes by, however, even teenagers settle into a job, and demands increase. It's hard to stay on the good side of supervisors unless they take the extra work that's offered. A summer job becomes a winter job. A few hours on the weekend become a steady job after school. Responsibilities are added, and the hours stretch into the evening. One student told me that she was the most longstanding clerical employee in the doctor's office where she worked after school, so she was forced to work longer hours to show the others how things were done. No matter how busy she got at school, she could not consider quitting, because she had to keep her good record and the better-than-minimum wage.

For too many job-holding seniors, schoolwork suffers at a time when it is of utmost importance. They arrive at school late, glassy-eyed, facing the hours of sitting still there with trepidation. He could stay reasonably alert at his job, one senior told me, since he was moving around, taking and fulfilling orders. But he got sleepy in class, and started to blame his teachers for making him feel so embarrassed there. It's not just a matter of supervisors pressuring seniors to take more hours, however; many seniors ask for them. "The bills are tremendous," one senior complained. "We have to work twice as hard to make the money we need." Other seniors might be spending their money on frivolous things, but she wasn't. She needed the money because her father had lost his job, but she did not "feel like explaining all that to my guidance counselor." The personal price turned out to be a high one. Her reputation and relationships at school spiraled downward after she added a job to her other responsibilities. "It's been hard to keep up. Right now I'm so tired of working and going to school and the tests and all the clubs." She had always considered herself and been considered by others to be a diligent student, but now things were different. "Teachers think we aren't working as hard, but I'm working harder than last semester. I work harder at work. I've got more things to do. So they think we slack off, but we're not. We're coming in here, trying to do what we can. I take offense when they don't see that."

More and more, seniors like this young woman are taking matters into their own hands. They are trying to "do what they can" rather than what they have been asked to do. They are deciding what energy can be spared for school, what challenges can be met there, what attention can be paid to it. By the middle of the year, although they often argue with their teachers about the declining quality of their academic work, some of the same students also describe school as "not very challenging. We need to take longer hours at our jobs, just to keep busy."

A young woman also described her feelings about work and independence as a stage, a transition into adulthood. "During senior year," she said, "you're getting closer to being on your own. You start thinking about it. Your own apartment. And how you'll pay the bills." Many seniors believe that financial independence should accompany personal independence, but they feel they have not reached that point. "I'm not leaving home until I'm financially set," a young man in a vocational school told me. "There are too many things to pay for: rent, car insurance, health insurance."

Seniors at the edge of a tremendous expense like college feel they have to approach their parents differently. Parents may try to spare the seniors as they make the arrangements, but most seniors face their financial effect on their family more directly than they have ever done. Slowly the awareness grows on them that their parents' resources are finite, that the choices they are making "might be about to bankrupt the family. I had always thought kind of big about college," one admitted, "and then, this year, things kind of—well, I started thinking more practically as far as, you know, money." He could hardly get the word out.

PART TWO

4 Playing the College Game

"I learned about playing the game mostly last summer, when I went on the college tour," said Elizabeth. "I kept seeing the same people school after school. Some of the mothers—they were like stage mothers prodding their kids to say the right thing. And I applied to a lot of competitive schools and everyone's very aggressive, so. . . ." Her voice trailed off.

One of her school's most successful students and a talented artist, she had always been a high achiever because it seemed the right thing to do. "I've known for a while now that I wanted to go to college," she assured me, "but this is the year I'm doing it. We all realized that next year we'd be out of here, with no place to go." She had found high school to be a cold and difficult place until she started to think about leaving it. At that point, like many seniors, she suddenly realized that the moving van had arrived, that she was loading it with all her baggage (literal and figurative), that in some ways it was already pulling away. It would be nice to invent a fantasy destination—or even to be able to drive around for a while—but she could not. "I didn't think of the year as dominated by college admission. I actually thought of it as a small portion of senior year. And I was wrong—very wrong."

Elizabeth had every reason to be a confident college candidate. Still, she was definitely on the quiet side. Her mother was also shy. They had both felt out of place in the admissions offices among groups of "brilliant-looking" but somewhat unpleasant people. After that experience, Elizabeth resolved that however important it was to *be* good, it was even more important to *look* good. "I'm really kind of modest. But I know you have to do something that will make you stand out because they see so many people." She would have to alter her personality but "only for a while," she insisted, "not forever." She had heard stories about what she called "disasters," in which well-qualified candidates like herself were inexplicably unsuccessful. Thus, she felt she needed to go along with a lot of nonsense, give up valuable time, and accept the irony that she would have to jump around like an extrovert to get the chance to study and learn from the books she loved.

* * *

An outstanding characteristic of the senior year in high school is the sense of transience, even about one's deepest instincts. Choosing and being chosen by "higher" education isn't an easy process anywhere, and I suspect it never will be. Maybe it shouldn't be: the whole country can't be like Lake Woebegon, where "all the children are above average." Since so many Americans are convinced that one's future depends on going to the "right" college, there will never be enough places in those colleges for everyone. And as we all have learned, whether we went to college or not, the scarcer the resource, the higher the "price." Part of the price seniors pay is sacrificing their sense of themselves as valuable persons.

Most students are troubled by this situation, though they try to put it in a favorable light. "You're selling yourself like a product, and that sounds horrible," one of them said, "but the fact is, everybody else is too. So if you don't, then you're putting yourself at a disadvantage. You don't necessarily have to exaggerate or lie, but you have to dig deep and find things that they're going to want from you. That's not necessarily a bad thing."

True enough. Still, from this frantic self-scrutiny and "digging"—these separate but frequent decisions and justifications—is woven a culture of deception so pervasive that a lot of people don't even recognize it. "You're a senior now, and you have to consider the options available to you," said a young man who was the first person in his family to apply to college. "My friends and I basically realized that we had to get our act together—not that our act wasn't together, but. . . ." Students all over the country are newly attentive to their "acts" as they wonder how they add up in other people's minds.

Success in life depends far more on how well a student does in college than on which one he attends. Although teachers and counselors may stress the importance of making a good match rather than putting blind faith in a selective college, it's hard for students to believe it. There are so many mysteries, rumors, and "deals" regarding college admission that it's hard to blame seniors who may prefer to think that a little "luck" now is preferable to the hard work required to do well once they get to college. High school has been given to them. College is something they have to go out and get for themselves. Seniors have to face their prospects squarely: what do they have to offer a college? Many of them aren't sure they like the answer to that question, but they are familiar with advertising, so they get to work. They begin to reinvent themselves, some slightly, some more substantially.

"With all that competition," said a young man in Chicago, "there's a lot of pressure to make yourself look better." Sitting not far from where the nineteenth-century stockyards had been, he agreed that he was "taking on excess water" during his senior year so that he would seem more impressive while he was being "weighed" by the colleges. This dishonesty had been forced on him by the system, he felt, but it was dishonest nonetheless—and he knew it.

High school seniors are never sure they or their records are good enough. Lining up to be chosen, they become more realistic but are also terrified by the numbers, the newness, and the arbitrariness of the system. The proudest and most impressive people in their school, seniors are also at their most vulnerable. They are losing faith in who they really are, in what they have really done. And at the very time of their lives when they are most sensitive to hypocrisy, they have come to believe that recasting oneself is a crucial part of "playing the game."

Why College?

These days going to college is prized by more people than ever before. Most politicians tout it as an option for everyone who wants it. In my fall and winter interviews in a wide variety of high schools, I could not find students who said they did not expect to go to college. They might dislike school, they might have done poorly there, they might have very little money, but they still said that they would go to college. By spring, more were saying that they were going to "take a year off." They would go to college "sometime, but not next year." College is the word on every senior's lips. It is part of the American Dream.

This focus on college is reasonable in some respects. Many employers demand a college degree, and the opportunity to attend college has grown remarkably more available in our time. Changes in funding, transportation, and admissions policies since World War II have opened up college to all kinds of people with a variety of incomes, talents, and interests. Community colleges, which began to appear in the fifties and sixties, have provided even more accessibility. In an increasingly polarized nation, most contemporary college commencements have a classless, multicultural feel not found in churches, neighborhoods, or even grocery stores.

This obsession with college, however, has caused us as a nation to pay less attention to other ways in which a person might prepare himself or herself for productive adulthood. It has also affected the senior year in high school, because it has created the false impression that college admission is the only rite of passage, when in fact there are several. "Everybody builds this up to be the entire culmination of high school existence," one senior grumbled, although he was doing just that. A third of the age group will in fact *not* go on to postsecondary education, but the atmosphere of the high school does not reflect that reality. Each high school is different, of course, largely reflecting the family incomes in the area. In some high schools, the bold posters in the college counselor's office seem misplaced. The building is dirty, the students seem discouraged, and the monitors in the hall treat them more like potential hoodlums than like college material. Seniors in those schools are just proud that they are the first members of their families to get to senior year, to be in line to "cross the stage." As one of them admitted, "I don't need all this talk about college. I'd just like to walk [graduate]. I'd just like to have a reasonable life."

That kind of talk is heresy in other high schools, where the percentage of seniors going on to college is so large that the picture of high school as a kind of way station is justifiable. In one such school, a student who admitted in the fall that she was "not sure about college" led me through her reasoning. Her older brother had gone to college for a few months, "and he just wasted a lot of money." He came home, started to work in a job where "he gets to be outside a lot. He's making a good living. He's done better without college than he could have done with it." She shared her brother's claustrophobia about school buildings, his practical questions about what college was "for." She was offended that so many people in her class were "like sheep about going to college. There's a lot of pressure but I think it should be your own decision." There must be more to life and to the senior year, she reasoned, even in a well-heeled suburban town, than scratching one's way into college.

Another student considered college a backup "in case acting doesn't work out." It was a matter of keeping her priorities straight. "Al Pacino never went to college. I could die without going to college. I can't die without being an actress, at least for a while." Still, her careful listing of various reasons why college might not be a good idea had a defensive tone to it, only reinforcing the impression that college is the most respectable goal for high school seniors. Even technical school students said they would go to college—if they needed to, and if they found the right one. "I'll probably go to college later on, after I've seen how I can do by myself after high school," one told me. "I'll see if I can make it. If I can't make it, then I'll go to college." In his mind, college was the option not of first but of last resort.

Despite exceptions, the overwhelming majority of seniors have a lot to say about why they intend to go to college. First of all, it is expected—practically inevitable. "Even when I was a little person, my whole life was, Oh, yeah, do this high school thing, so I can go to college." College is the reward for surviving high school, the pot of gold at the end of the adolescent rainbow. Yet it also has a serious purpose. "A degree would be good,"

"Even when I was a little person, my whole life was, Oh, yeah, do this high school thing, so I can go to college."

one said, "to get a well-paying job, to keep moving up through the ranks." College will provide not just the necessary credentials but also training and experience. "My parents did not get to go to college, and they both ended up with dead-end jobs. I refuse—I absolutely refuse—to end up like them," said one senior. "I want to be somebody in the future and in order to do that, I need to go to school." The acknowledged "reason" for college, articulated by students from all the socioeconomic classes, is that college is the prerequisite for being a successful adult.

There are other reasons too. College is "getting away. I want to go to college because I want to get out and see everything." How far away the seniors expect to go seems to lessen as the year goes on: from the other coast to the neighboring state, from the farther college to the nearer one. Still, there is a clear notion that one will benefit from a different kind of school day, a change of scene, a new group of friends. After high school, with its bondage to a tight schedule, in college their time will be their own. "Everybody glorifies college as the big party time, where there are fewer classes and more freedom," one admitted. Another senior asserted with complete conviction that "college students can pick their times when they want to go to class. It won't be like high school, when you have to be here, there, and with everybody else. You don't have the same classes every day. You don't see the same people every day. You won't even have to go to school if you don't have a class." No more chemistry at ten, day in, day out. A new schedule, seniors are convinced, will rid their life of monotony.

Most seniors expect and want change in themselves. They have faith that college will facilitate this process because they will have chosen where to go and will spend considerable time there. They differ only in what they believe will bring about that change in the most beneficial way.

Some need psychic as well as geographical distance. "I want to go to a good college, but not the one that everyone else is going to," said a confident young woman. "I want weird people and conservative people, black people, white people, Asians. I want to strike out—*not* have any comfort zones—and study new subjects." Great big introductory courses in psychology and philosophy sounded exotic. She felt she needed the fresh air, even if it turned out to be a little too bracing at times.

Other students like discovering that they "feel at home" in the colleges they visit. "I went to see a college last weekend," said one senior, giving me the impression that it was a new experience for her and for her family, "and I liked it a lot. I liked the food. I liked the rooms. I felt very comfortable there. I bet I could live there eight years, not four!" It was as if she had been sent an invitation to live inside her favorite sitcom. Or maybe a resort.

Another reason for applying to college is to gain status in high school. Even if college does not guarantee a satisfying career, even if one does not change much there, it is still considered important to go. It is the most respectable successor to high school, and many agree with the inner-city student who, fearing that he might not get into college, said, "I'll feel pretty bad if I go through these four years in high school and then have nothing to show for it."

Seniors have a confusing picture of their chances of college admission. On the one hand, they are told that it is hard to get into college. Many college-educated parents say they could not have gone where they went if the competition had been as great then as it is now. This piece of conventional wisdom makes seniors feel they are real pioneers. On the other hand, newspaper articles and TV shows tell seniors that the colleges built for baby boomers are now desperate for students: there will be a college for a senior no matter how bad his or her record is. If that's so, the seniors know they ought to feel less stress. However, the big issue now becomes: which college? This is what drives the status wars: the perception, justified or unjustified, that some colleges are "selective" and others are not. The terms *top-flight, higher-ranked,* and *Ivy* dominate seniors' conversations all over the country, although the phenomenon is more intense in the Northeast. Gambling metaphors take over seniors' language. No matter what the colleges are really like, some are *long shots* and others *safeties.* It is not just a new vocabulary to master; it is a new approach to life.

Status wars begin early. In some parts of the country, it is crucial, or so people think, which nursery school you get into. John Holt shocked people like me decades ago when he described a fourth grader he was teaching who cried because she had done poorly on a test, convinced that she would never get into Bryn Mawr. That story doesn't shock many today. More people are taking SATs and ACTs. Even if one does poorly, there is the cachet of taking them. When one becomes a senior, there is a short-term advantage in constructing a long and fancy college list. You don't need to have a prayer of getting in, or even the desire to go. The payback is: here, in this high school, in this senior class, you are known as someone who is "hearing from Harvard." There is also the "backyard syndrome," especially in relation to well-known colleges. For one senior, the local university had dominated the newspapers and TV stations, the economy, the athletic events, and family conversations for as long as she could remember. Though she knew very little about what it might offer in the areas she wanted to study, it was "familiar." Applying there was considered the thing to do: the impossible dream that might come true.

A group of students I interviewed argued for and against the importance of choosing a college for its status. "The process of applying to big-name schools is a lot of pressure," one said, "not only to get in, but to get in somewhere that is right at your peak, the best place you could possibly get into." He not only felt that pressure, he thought it was a good thing. "Accepting anything lower is looked at as slumming." College is a status symbol, but it is also a challenge, the bigger the better. "It's good to apply to places you don't have a chance to get into," another student agreed. "That would really be luck, and if you get in, great! Try it!" He derided the practice of lining up "safeties" as "selling yourself to some school that you could probably get into, but you wouldn't like it there."

Others were not so sure they should stretch themselves beyond all recognition. A young woman countered, "I think the biggest pressure is what you put on yourself. You should go for something that you know you'll like, even if it isn't up to everyone else's standards. Even if you could get into a better place, if you don't want to, why bother?" Another young man agreed. "If the higher-ranked colleges can't help me, then I don't want to go there. I need to do well," he said, indicating that he saw college as part of a continuum. It was important to get in, but where did you want to go after college was over? "I have a lot of friends who are looking at nothing but Ivies," he continued, a combination of pride and caution in his voice, "but they don't look down on me because I'd rather attend somewhere else." His brave statement revealed how socially vulnerable seniors feel as they assemble their college lists.

I asked one of the more forceful advocates for status whether going to college might be like setting up a tennis game: you usually want to compete against someone who is slightly better than you are. I expected him to agree, since he had, minutes earlier, spoken of needing to be at the top of his form. But this subject was a raw one, and he had sensed the insecurities being unleashed by it. He looked for a compromise. "I don't know about that," he said hesitantly. "I feel like you might as well play tennis with someone that's really bad, just to make yourself feel good." It was a lame joke. He was trying for the light answer, the I-understand-where-they're-coming-from response. But there was a kind of false modesty in his words and tone, and no one really believed that playing against "someone that's really bad" was a suitable metaphor for choosing a college.

Competition. Selection. Status. One reason for going to college is to look like an impressive person. Seniors do not like to acknowledge that reason, but it creeps into their language constantly. Wittingly or unwittingly, parents, teachers, and journalists contribute to this clash of values. Prestige is something the students must address; most do, and in the long run, it may be a valuable experience. But it is not a bit easy, not for any of them.

Getting Started

Going to college is more complicated than it used to be, and students start thinking about it ever earlier. College has been on seniors' minds for months—even years. But now it is time to streamline their thoughts. The buyer/seller market shifts during senior year, definitely confusing the young and inexperienced consumer. In the beginning, shortly after the student has taken the SATs and ACTs, somewhat more intensely if he or she has done well in them, the colleges seem interested in initiating the relationship. The mail arrives: letters, brochures, books, videos, invitations, more brochures, even the same brochures. What is a student to think? Why does everyone say it's hard to get into college? He feels positively courted! So do his parents. "I didn't really listen while the admissions people told us all the advantages," admitted a senior whose parents had not gone to college. "I kind of resented missing an evening with my friends. But my mom heard everything. And it is certainly a beautiful place." Most students try to keep all the brochures at first, but "after the stack grows more than five feet tall," they get a little frantic. But it is the kind of problem they boast about to their friends.

Assembling their lists is a hard job, and it has grown much harder since the adults who advise them were young. Especially in the East, where the percentage of students in private colleges is greater, an individual senior may have a large number of good options. Even in the Midwest and Far West, the greater number of community colleges gives the impression of an embarrassment of riches. One student described how her heart sank when she went into her school's library and saw all the material she would have to read if she wanted to make a thorough search. "It's unbelievable how much there is to figure out." There were books, pamphlets, and videos, she claimed, "as far as the eye could see." Not to mention websites! To give each postsecondary option the consideration it deserves is a tremendous challenge.

Many feel a rush when they visit colleges. "We looked into an amazing college with great opportunities," enthused a newcomer to the American college scene. "It was private, small—just a dream. I went for a visit and I just loved it. I said, 'Oooh! I'm staying here! I'm going to buy a sweatshirt and walk around and pretend I'm a student here!'" But others are distrustful. How do they know what is real, what is not what it seems? And what if some of their reasons for liking or not liking a place are pretty arbitrary? "I've read articles that say that fifty percent of your impression of a school is based on whether it's raining," said a determined and thorough applicant who was planning to apply to a long list of colleges. "That's sad," he concluded, but he didn't deny that it had influenced him.

The confusion is debilitating after a while, the seniors more tired than they expected to be; some order has to be imposed on all this chaos. "I haven't really looked too deeply into it," one senior admitted, "and everyone says, 'How can you be so casual when you'll spend the next four years of your life there?' And I say, 'I didn't choose to come to this high school and I like it here.' Everybody is wanting you to do first this and then that. I just couldn't have done all that research. I had to let my dad do it for me." Another senior said that he was too busy being the president of his class to bother with a complicated college search. "I easily have the grades" for the state university, he told me, so settling on that for his only application would give him less to worry about.

Seniors find interesting ways to shorten their list. One decided that since the brimming, beautiful lake pictured on the college brochure was in reality a somewhat dried-up pond, she would eliminate that college. Not for her a place that tries to fool the public. Another decided that his interests were so similar to those of a friend a year older that he'd just apply to the same colleges his friend did. And he wouldn't pursue colleges that didn't reply to his letters immediately. Anything to simplify the search.

Categories begin to be more important. How big is it? How expensive? How cold are the winters? How far from home? Even the concepts of "stretch schools" and "safeties," so intimidating at first, come to have a sort of comfort. Some of these considerations seem a little arbitrary in the middle of the night. Sometimes the seniors sense that they are not doing this job as well as they expected to. But what can they do? "At least it's a way to get some kind of handle on things."

"I've finally got my colleges now," said one young woman, revealing in that sentence a tremendous amount of emotional insecurity. "My" colleges, because she could imagine herself in each of them. Otherwise there would be no point in putting them on her list. But "colleges" rather than "college" because she would finally, for a variety of reasons—which were as yet unknown, even unimaginable to her—choose only one. She would fill out applications and send the checks. She needed to make some kind of commitment to get the process started, but it couldn't be too binding.

The Application

Applications have been removed from some of the catalogues and shifted to a more central position on the desk. Some have been lost and replaced. Others have simply been lost. Sorting them, counting them, making sure they're all there, is a frequent ritual. Finally it's time for the seniors to fill them in, but once they start marking up those pieces of paper, the momentum shifts. Now the candidates are the supplicants. Now they have to measure their own lives and accomplishments against national—or even international—standards.

The process—gather, decide, apply, wait, hear, decide—is similar for all seniors. Some students, however, are on a faster track.

They apply earlier in the fall; by early winter they are already awaiting the first round of admissions. They are usually the more successful students, but that doesn't keep them from being worriers.

With the trend to earlier and earlier admission, more and more students are afraid *not* to apply early. The "odds," as they see it, returning to their gambling metaphor, will lengthen the longer they wait. Any intellectual or emotional growth during their senior year, they believe, won't help their chances as much as getting in line first. Outspokenly allergic to stress, nervous about the prospect of selection, they opt for "a happier Christmas. I knew it wouldn't be the end of the world if I didn't get accepted," said one student, "but I thought it would make the next six months a lot more strain free."

As more students are convinced they must apply early, new problems arise. Faced with the need to choose quickly, they apply to places they have never seen or in some cases have not even investigated. Some choose colleges to which the rest of their classmates are not applying, on the assumption that they will have a better chance of admission. They do not take enough care to learn about the financial implications in early action. Since financial packages are not offered as early as admission, only the wealthier students can make final decisions early in the year.

Those who feel they have not been thorough enough worry that they won't get in; in the case of binding acceptance, they sometimes also worry that they will. And in December, those students who are rejected, deferred, or have changed their minds are plunged back into the process. They scramble to get new recommendations, to document their continuing growth. They regret the haste with which they prepared their earlier applications. The rhythm of the year has been disrupted; they are wiser but somewhat scared. And scarred.

In a few areas of the country, admission is largely or even solely by test scores, so a senior can predict where he will be accepted and avoid the colleges where he will not be. But the process is generally more sophisticated and flexible. The options are greater, the reasons for being offered or denied admission more ambiguous. This makes much more sense, but in taking the chance that a college will appreciate qualities beyond his test scores, a senior is also more likely to be rejected, which adds considerable and somber weight to the process. And even if he doesn't apply to the more selective colleges, they stand there as an opportunity somehow lost.

Everything is so final, yet so minimal. Many of the items on the application are meaningful, but there isn't time or space for honest responses. "My whole life is reduced to a piece of paper," one senior observed. "They don't want to hear your reasons: just what you did. The more I thought about it, the more I got stressed out. Not so much working on it, but thinking about it." Being a "beggar" is disheartening, and the notion that so much is riding on so little invites manipulation—and procrastination. But those applications have to be filled out.

Where do students tackle the job? One student I spoke with took over her family's dining room for several months. It was near the mail slot in the front door, there was room for everything, things were easier to find. Given the importance she and they attached to the process, her parents were willing to give up having meals there—no big deal. Other seniors carve out special places in their rooms or arrange things in bags and boxes for short-term sojourns at the kitchen table. A few set up neutral spaces in the public library or their parents' offices; a few more, the most disorganized ones, in their guidance counselors' offices.

In every school, in every year, a few "college-bound" seniors somehow never get around to filling out their applications at all. "I'm a procrastinator," confessed one student, who had "always been able to get away with it before." She had rather enjoyed the rush of adrenaline when she wrote papers for her English class the night before they were due. She even felt that she might write better under those circumstances. But her working style failed her when it came to applying for college. "College is too important to handle that way. Procrastination just caused me even more stress and anguish. The last week of Christmas break was a nightmare. And I'm not that sure I did that great a job."

The process is often traumatic. Much of it occurs late at night. Much coffee gets spilled on the pages. "Of course, sitting there typing things in little spaces is not my thing," confessed a bouncy girl who considered high school "fun" and imagined that college would be "a blast" but thought the transition between them was "absolutely dreadful. And the most difficult part of all of that was getting a typewriter that would work." Her electric one broke; the ribbon on her brother's old one "jammed itself up in some unseeable place." Her family wasn't much help, because "they were always asleep when the worst things happened. Besides, they felt that I was so disorganized that I practically deserved to have problems." Many students consider the applications needlessly repetitive, arbitrary and demanding, but they don't dare to look as if they are willing to cut corners. All kinds of people have told them that seeing through mindless projects is one aspect of "the real world": their fortitude is being tested as thoroughly as their aptitude.

Filling out applications is more than just boring, however; it's frightening. The seniors come face-to-face with the factors that make them admissible—or inadmissible. They agonize over names that are too common or too different, home addresses and elementary and high schools that are known too well or not at all. All these very personal things will now be regarded from a different angle. They have become words on a sheet. What will strangers think of these words? Will they know anything about this high school? Will they know the right things? The things that matter to me? Will they be impressed?

Seniors think harder about their high schools than they ever have before, just as they think harder about themselves: they feel they are being forced to compare their schools to others. Seniors in less well regarded schools have doubts. Some feel they have not been asked to do as much in their high school as others did in theirs. One girl I spoke with whose family had moved a few years earlier was suddenly full of regrets. "I'm doing well here but I couldn't even pass the test to get into college," she lamented. "Sometimes I wonder if they have prepared me enough to go out there. What good does my grade point average do me if I haven't learned anything? If I can't get into college or if I'm going to go off not knowing anything?"

"Sometimes I wonder if they have prepared me enough to go out there. What good does my grade point average do me if I haven't learned anything? If I can't get into college or if I'm going to go off not knowing anything?"

Some seniors wish they had been surrounded by the kinds of students who would have challenged them to do better work. One young woman complained that she had never met students who had high test scores until she participated in academic competitions against other schools. She did well in those competitions and she knew that her own test scores were low because she had not spoken English until she was fourteen. But the talk at the competitions was full of what people got on their SATs, and she was sure that "even the native speakers in our high school get only in the 400s." She also found out that some high schools offer calculus! "Everyone was so smart from those schools," she claimed. "They'd applied to colleges I never heard of. I felt out of place." She was intimidated—and bitter. She had come so far. Why couldn't she have gone to a high school that would have brought her further?

Even students who have gone to well-regarded schools worry. One presented me with quite a list: "What if too many students from this high school want to go to my first choice? What about all the work I had to do in chemistry and history, compared to the kids in the high school across town? What about the smart kids in this school, and how stingy the teachers are with their A's? Are the admissions officers going to understand about trade-offs? Will they forgive the grades I got while I was still trying to adjust? Will they understand why I quit my piano lessons, why I didn't get the chance to do out-of-school things?"

Students who have already experienced special treatment—being admitted to an exam school or placing in the top track in a public school or attending a parochial or private school—may give a lot of thought to whether they have used the chance well or blown it. "I'm not very happy here," said a student in a prep school. "But I expect this place to get me into a good college—and I'll be happy there." He felt the prestige of the institution around him like a cushion. Colleges would admire the work he had been exposed to, even if he had not always done well at it. On the whole, his assumption was correct. Colleges admit they are more likely to trust the graduates of some high schools than others. In some respects this is unfair: those who have already been able to attend "good" schools are first in line for "good" colleges. But colleges insist they need to be able to predict how well a student will do in a competitive academic atmosphere. Too drastic a change in expectations often does a college student no good. They are probably right. But as a high school senior starts to fill out his application, he is not thinking about the student he will be in a year's time but about the candidate he is now.

Lining Up

Besides the "right" school, the "right" kind of program, and the "right" grades, seniors need to enter a favorable class ranking into the blank reserved for it on most applications. Many high schools don't rank, but others do, and much angst and controversy is attached to it. I was in one high school on "ranking day" in October and it was bedlam. In the halls between classes, students were urging one another to go get their ranks. When they returned from the dean's office, their most common commment was, "Well, I guess I'm not going to college." They didn't mean it, they admitted nearly as quickly as they said it. But nearly everybody was riled up.

The only people who support ranking seem to be the parents of the top students. The students themselves decry what they call "stacking the seniors up against each other," on both theoretical and personal grounds. On the theoretical: there has to be a formula for assigning rank; in it, an A in science is given more weight than an A in art. Or it is not. Furthermore, "everybody but the formula" seems to know who the tough graders are. "The teachers you were assigned at the beginning of the year," one earnest young woman told me, "could lead to a difference of thirty or forty points!"

The more successful students attack the system as much as the less successful—at least in public. "Even your friends dispute your rank," said one ambitious young man. "The ranking makes a competitive class even worse." For weeks, he predicted, the students would compare grades, schedules, and numbers of honors courses. With so many smart students all stuffed into one big building, he asked, "Does comparing number fifty-six and number one-seventy-one really mean that much?" Seniors whose ranks are lower insist that ranking says little about how diligent a student may be. Instead it may indicate "how smart he is, what classes he took, what family problems he might have had last year." And one school leader was pretty miffed by the students "who are so quiet you hardly know they exist. And then they are ranked higher than you are! I mean, what can you say? You put so much effort into school activities" and they went home and studied. "That doesn't feel right!"

Theoretical reservations, in other words, quickly become personal worries. "Colleges only want the best," said one young woman, "so the question after my first ranking was: shall I compare and get depressed or optimistic—or shall I keep it to myself? I'm a basically optimistic person. So I didn't cry and I told myself I'd try harder, and I have." But she hadn't been told her new ranking yet, and she knew that everyone else was trying harder too. It wasn't really a matter of whether she was improving but of how she looked compared to everyone else.

Scores

A young man I interviewed had always expected to go to college, but he had taken the SATs quite a few times, and he was growing more and more discouraged and humiliated. "The question is: how do I really stack up? Sometimes I envy the people who aren't going to college. They don't have to worry about their scores. What's the point of all the work I'm doing to fill out this long application, when all they'll do is check out the tiny section where I have to put those numbers?" It was time to rethink what he wanted to do.

The disputes over externally administered machine-graded tests are never so great as during the senior year in high school, because at no other time do they matter so much to so many people. Familiarity with a mass of academic material is required not to live in the adult world but to compete for access to it. SAT/ACT scores are rarely used for any purpose other than college admission, and few seniors will take that kind of test again. Class bias is inevitable, since breadth of knowledge is clearly valued over depth, and the middle-class child is likely to have picked up more wide-ranging information. "It seems," a working-class athlete told me, "like a new game of gotcha." His efforts to master the main ideas in each of his courses were seemingly insignificant, "except to the teachers. And what do teachers matter, compared to SATs?"

Like most shortcuts, standardized tests ratchet up the sense of dishonesty, contributing to seniors' impression that they are "playing the game." Even the Educational Testing Service spokesmen agree that the tests say very little about a student's potential, even long-term academic potential, compared with such other factors as social class, energy, and persistence. Familiarity with standard English and with a Eurocentric cultural canon and the ability to follow directions may turn out to be far more important than what a student knows about mathematics or history. Also important are a strong bladder and a cool head. Students also recognize the importance of self-confidence, "but not that manufactured kind. I just saw myself as a good tester," one student remembered, "so I was." On the other hand, a lack of assurance as one approaches this kind of testing can be a serious handicap.

Although many colleges realize the potential for unfairness in externally administered tests and in spite of a flurry of announcements a few years ago that the SATs would be abandoned, very few colleges have given them up. Many colleges claim that they do not rely on test scores; "a guidepost, not a hitching post" is their explanation for requiring them. In others, however, they are publicly acknowledged as rigid gatekeepers, and reliance on machine-graded testing is spreading. After all, much work has gone into producing an easily transferred number, and—most helpful for colleges—the tests are paid for by the college candidate. The colleges also save time by using this kind of test. The number on the college application is crisp and clean. Those using the number are not expected to analyze it, and that is fortunate, because many admissions officers are untrained, rushed, and overworked.

The more selective a college is, the more it has to look for reasons to exclude people. Test scores are a "neutral" excuse for some colleges to preserve good public relations and yet deny certain kids. The alumna's son who has respectable grades and an amazing curriculum vitae but who seems a little too perfectly packaged can be set aside, perhaps even without hard feelings. The local athlete who lives in the same town as the university, who may even work for it some day, can handle this kind of rejection better than one based on other factors. In these cases, "scores" can make life seem more rational. And it will take far less time than reading a portfolio.

And what about all the valedictorians who must be turned down? I talked with one very likable young man whose spoken English was full of grammar mistakes but who had earned a high average in his high school through sheer persistence—possibly courtesy of teachers who were grateful for how hard he was willing to work. He told me he had been by to see the admissions officers of the highly selective local college. "They told me that admitting me wouldn't be a problem with my record, but I had to take my SATs." He didn't seem worried, but I secretly predicted hard times ahead.

The admissions officers were being good neighbors, I suspected, and letting the SATs be the bad guys.

SAT scores pack an emotional wallop. Some people can recite them years later. Others are like the young woman who told me, "If I were out in public somewhere, I'd take off all my clothes sooner than I'd tell my scores!" Sometimes it's a matter of privacy; sometimes of shame. Sometimes people actually do forget them, but they usually remember whether they were bad or good—how they made them feel. Teachers who know the memories and the writing skills and the work habits of their students are sometimes surprised by their scores. Sometimes not. The students, however, have now acquired a whole new method of determining their self-worth. By the middle of senior year, there are clues in the seniors' conversation and body language to how high their scores are, especially in relation to those of their siblings and their friends.

"If I were out in public somewhere, I'd take off all my clothes sooner than I'd tell my scores!"

However they perform as standardized-test takers, most of the students who take these tests consider them a meaningless nightmare. "I'm pretty nervous about college, but mostly about taking the SAT again," one diligent student said. "They're not like the rest of school. They're not something you have thought about. They're not something you can study for." This kind of test is the monster in the senior's closet, the one not acknowledged except at night. Like the monster, the tests are on the margins of the student's real life. They are not given during school hours but on weekends, often in a school far away from one's own. The students' descriptions of such test rooms usually include the word "drafty." This may not accurately describe the room itself, but it says much about their state of mind. It is a challenge just getting there on time, rested but alert, carrying one's concerns calmly but also carrying sharpened number-two pencils. The adults in charge of these test centers are nearly always strangers: serious, even stern, woodenly reading the printed instructions, bound by the clock, suspicious if a student needs to go to the bathroom. I became one of those people when I proctored those tests, and I watched as others did too. These kinds of exams are longer than those in most schools, and their format, usually the multiple-choice question, is often relatively unfamiliar because so many teachers do not believe in it and do not use it.

With those who know them best seemingly helpless, the students feel alone, even "abandoned, facing a hostile mob of fiendish little imps," each in the form of a test question. Each item is separate and has to be tackled, waded through, efficiently, joylessly, with the chief aim simply to get to the end. Reading-comprehension sections are especially deadly. Each one is unconnected to the one before. One only reads them under extreme duress. "If you took a set of these readings to the beach," one senior assured me, "you would be asleep in no time!" Though terror keeps them at their task, they cannot bring much interest or enthusiasm to it. Even students who really like school and really like to solve problems rarely describe the SATs with anything but loathing and contempt. Instead, they develop various strategies to stay calm, most of them centering around denial and bravado. Some students take expensive preparation courses, but even after taking practice tests several times, they are not confident they will do well. The designers of the tests are too distant from their world.

High school seniors are an unusually moody lot. Since their plans are uncertain, their relationships in flux, this is not surprising. Also not surprisingly, it affects the test-taking experience. "Maybe something really bad happened to you the day before, but you still have to take the test," said a young woman whose nerves seemed as steel-like as any I saw. Even she had to fight off the urge to get up, scream her loudest, and flee. All over the country, students echo her observation. One calm but angry young woman pointed out that the test was "always on their time, not mine. I am not a morning person, but do they care about that?"

Time matters in another way as well. Teachers know, but test designers seemingly do not, that the time students need to perform various tasks well varies tremendously. One of my best students was a direct and effective writer. I always looked forward to reading her essays because, although they were not long, they included the details she needed to make her point. More than most students, more than required by multiple-choice tests, she had, and kept, focus. She also made wry, astute observations in class, comments directly connected to the homework and showing an uncanny sense of where we might be going. How could a teacher not admire such a kid? And since these are the very qualities that colleges say they value, I thought she was a natural.

But an outstanding college candidate is not always an outstanding test taker. My student did not work as quickly as standardized tests require. She considered each option on a multiple-choice test carefully. This is just what we are trying to teach our students to do, but it hurt her score, which hurt her college admission prospects. It was as simple as that, and she accepted it. She didn't even blame me, as far as I could tell, for encouraging her to be a careful thinker. But even though I knew I should not show it, I was terribly upset for her. I couldn't help but blame myself—and, I confess, "the system."

In recent years, more students have come to realize that doing poorly on standardized tests doesn't mean that one is fated to do badly in school or college. "I don't do well in standardized testing," said a scholar-athlete in front of other seniors, some of whom she did not seem to know very well, "so I'd rather write an essay. It's easier for me to express myself so they can see more of what I'm like from my writing than through a test score. How can you take those little boxes so seriously? My ACT score is simply not me. In fact," she went on, growing bolder as she watched the others nodding, "I don't think that test scores are representative of a student's ability to do work."

Many adults agree and have gathered considerable evidence to buttress their position. But disagreements among scholars and educators about what the SATs measure just made it harder for seniors to know what to make of them. "One college says your scores are low but we know from your record that you can do the work," said a senior in slightly accented English. "But another doesn't seem to have the same perception about me. They seem to think that because my SAT scores are bad, if I were to go there, I couldn't keep up."

The seniors also feel ripped off. Although only a few have thought through the reasons for standardized tests, they all know how costly they are, and many have heard about the lake and green grass at the Educational Testing Service "campus." "I don't think we'll ever get rid of the SATs," complained one high scorer, "because it's a huge money-making business. They say they aren't important, but I think they are. It's a corrupt system, I think. A lot of the time,

> "I don't think we'll ever get rid of the SATs because it's a huge money-making business. They say they aren't important, but I think they are. It's a corrupt system, I think. A lot of the time, it's who can afford to take the review courses."

it's who can afford to take the review courses." Any system that can be manipulated, she believed, could not really be objective. But none of the adults in the seniors' world—not parents, not teachers—dare to counsel them to bypass these exams, let alone organize a revolt against them. On this issue, therefore, seniors grow increasingly cynical and sullen. One told me, "We are just objects to be played with, and in a matter that will really affect our lives."

What are the seniors to think? That these tests are objective, unless you don't read standard English with speed and facility. That they are fair, unless you value other forms of expression and talent as much as you value memory and the making of minute distinctions. That it's "part of the system," and that most people, even themselves, see no alternative except reluctantly to go along with it. However they experience the process of standardized testing, it adds to the seniors' sense of vulnerability, even of shabbiness, as they go through their last year in high school.

The Rap Sheet

An increasing number of colleges have begun to ask students to explain their disciplinary record on the application form. This may be sensible on the colleges' part; they will, after all, be living with these young people for a number of years, so the seniors' past behavior is of relevance and concern to them. However, the requirement is a painful one on a number of levels, even for those who have no disciplinary incidents to report.

What is the role of schools as shapers of their students' morals and the behavior that follows from these morals? Infractions of the rules are frequent in high school, even by those who are never caught. In most cases, the physical exuberance of the early high school years gives way to a more considerate form of behavior. Wrongdoers respond to the school's scolding/counseling/punishment regimen and evolve into better citizens. For the school to ignore these lapses in judgment would undermine its responsibility as a moral arbiter; inattention in these matters would teach the wrong lesson. Once having engaged the problem, or problems, however, both teachers and students want to learn from them and then move beyond them. As one senior put it, "I'm so different now," and with most students, this is indeed the truth. Thus the college's request for a list of disciplinary incidents keeps old and often outdated concerns alive.

Some colleges ask for this kind of information and others do not, which is another source of confusion for the seniors and their advisers. Stories abound about colleges that have withdrawn admission to those who reported honestly—or dishonestly. Boarding schools, which monitor their students' behavior for twenty-four hours a day and on weekends, will inevitably have more infractions to report and may feel their students are at an unfair disadvantage. Strict schools and large schools, which require more rules, may feel the same way.

One young man expressed his dilemma forthrightly. The year before, he had shoved another student who was taunting him. He regretted the fact that he had "lost it," but he thought premeditated verbal bullying was as harmful to the atmosphere of the school as what he had done. The teachers saw it differently, so he was officially punished, and he never had that kind of trouble again. But now he—not the other kid—had an incident on his record that threatened his place in college. Since he believed the school had treated him unfairly, he proposed that he—and the school's record keeper—leave that question blank.

Teachers tend to believe that colleges need more information, not less. The function of high school is to provide an education, not identify criminals. We celebrate our students' improvements as profoundly as their successes. Many of us count ex-wrongdoers among our secret favorites. We want colleges to take an interest in matters of morality and behavior but in a way that elicits the whole story. The mechanistic nature of this question on a college application makes us wonder. A list is too simplistic, too easy to lie about or misunderstand or manipulate. Asking the student what she thinks about a past disciplinary incident would give the college a better notion of how the student processes such things and put the student's behavior into context.

What Did *You* Do in High School?

So far in crafting the application, the seniors' urge has been toward conformity: the best schools, the "most demanding program," the highest grades, and the best scores on standardized tests. Finally it is time to distinguish oneself, to pull apart from the rest of the pack. "Well, of course, you have to have a whole lot of interests," one senior told me. Also a whole lot of contacts. Membership in certain organizations also helps. This emphasis on their differences is summarized as the "angles." The word has a manipulative connotation. Having tried to look "all-round," they are now turning angular.

Nearly every student I talked with was aware that American colleges like to "put together a class." At least in theory, our nation is rich enough that college can be open to a wider variety of academic abilities, can wait for the "late bloomers." Offering a social as well as an academic experience, colleges need "greens and reds and blues," the tortoises and the hares, the children of alumni and the underprivileged, the musicians and the athletes, to create that "complete picture." Since students also teach one another, they can do so more effectively if they have different qualifications. All this makes good sense in the long run; moreover, seniors appreciate being able to present themselves more fully than they would be able to do in a single exam.

But seniors are still troubled and intimidated, especially as they look for ways in which, "without looking *too* wacky," they can stress their uniqueness in a way admissions officers can recognize and assess. How much of a "hook" are they supposed to have? On the one hand, this "hook" is their capsule identity, the characteristic that will make them stand out, seem different and accomplished and passionate and interesting. At the same time, the "hook" is the quality that will make them an especially good match for a specific college. It is ironic: at a time of life when wearing slightly more flared blue jeans than other kids can lead to social disaster, these teenagers are looking for a quality, a talent, an experience, that will set them apart.

In a group interview in September, a few suburban seniors discussed their dilemma. On the one hand, they agreed, this was meant to be the year when one would become the best soccer player, flutist, class leader, whatever, one might ever be. The "amateurs last year will become the professionals"; the followers would turn into the leaders. So the best idea, some of these seniors claimed, was to decide how to present oneself, which single aspect of oneself to emphasize. "Polish it into a rich deep glow / send it in a portfolio." We all laughed at our rueful little poem.

But some enjoyed the joke less than others. They could not even crack a smile when I mentioned "left-handed tuba players" or "albinos from Idaho." The very word *hook,* one of them noted, had a menacing sound to it. They insisted that senior year was the very time to branch out, to take up new interests. Eighteen was a great age for looking around the world, in every sense. But they felt that would be a risky undertaking, especially during the first half of the year. If you took a physics course, for example, you might risk getting terrible grades. "It might not be the way you think," said one, "even if you did well in biology." If you gave up a leadership position in the environment club to be in a play or learn how to play chess, you might be penalized. These decisions led them to panic, to the fruitless urge to control the unknown. How good is my "hook" ("am I the best quarterback applying this year?") and how valued is my category ("will they accept one or two—or three—quarterbacks?")? And what if I choose to play up my musical side instead of my interest in becoming a scientist and this is the year their string section is already full?

There is a certain amount of confidence in most seniors at the beginning of the year. If someone will just tell them what they need to do, what they need to be, to get into college, they are willing to do it. Each college, however, needs to paint its own picture, and the colors it needs depends largely on the colors it already has. When the seniors ask, "What's the key?" and no one can answer their unanswerable question, they collapse in an emotional heap, even when they try to keep it well below the surface. They are overwhelmed with confusion but also with the pervasive feeling that the world has no right to be so confusing. I tried saying, "What if there *were* one thing? It's grades, or sports, or race, or connections, or your score on the SAT. Now you know what your choices are. Go after it." This was even more painful for them. When they thought about where they stood in relation to each of these narrow dimensions, they decided that confusion might not be so bad after all.

In the effort to look accomplished, most seniors hedge their bets: they pad their curriculum vitae, their contacts, their racial diversity—anything they can think of. "I need extracurricular activities to dress up my college applications," one student admitted. "One way or another, I have to pump the stats." It's dishonest: the students and their parents know it deep down, the teachers and college counselors admit it openly. But adults encourage this inflation. Teachers announce in all-school meetings that community service—or entering a contest, or going to Europe—"will look good on your CV." Any wider purpose seems secondary, and anyone who protests this order of priorities is "being naive." Dressing up college applications is one more form of manipulation that we as a culture have permitted, even encouraged, and that seniors feel obliged to perpetuate.

Students all over the country try to get "something—anything—to put in the activities section." Very often, a flurry of civic-minded activity follows the first trip to the college counselor's office. Suddenly, students who have never participated in extracurricular activities decide they need to be class president. Some insist that the big jobs should be passed around, so more kids "can get the benefit of their titles." Students often refuse to vote for these suddenly enthusiastic candidates. They are on to their scam, and say so openly. But the leaders of smaller clubs are appointed, not elected, so deals can be arranged.

Phantom clubs, often centered around acceptable activities like protecting the environment, peer tutoring, or Students Against Drunk Driving, rise up during the fall like mushrooms after a rain, seemingly out of nowhere. They have a full roster of officers but not much of a program, and then fade in the winter and spring. "I stayed in the same clubs, but I made sure I got a title," one senior said. The club of which he was vice president was "not able to do much," because they weren't very strong to begin with, "so it was a building year." But he never answered my questions about what they were trying to do, and I got a little suspicious when all his verbs were in the past tense. It was only January.

The seniors know it's a game, but most of them feel they have to play it. One senior, who had complained of being so behind in her work that she might not finish her senior project, said she had just agreed to be on a committee at a local community college. When I asked her why, I expected her to tell me she was just too interested to resist, or that extracurricular activities were a lot more fun than schoolwork. But interest and fun were not among her reasons. "It will look good on my résumé," she said, "and especially on my college applications. You're so busy during your high school years, but when you write it down on a piece of paper, you think, It seems like there was more than this." It's a demoralizing moment. "You look through your life and you think, I wish I'd done that and I wish I'd done this, because if you had, it might have made you look a bit better on this piece of paper. And you start to hate yourself for that." Did she hate herself for what she did not do, or for enhancing her record on a piece of paper? "Both, really. I guess both."

"You look through your life and you think, I wish I'd done that and I wish I'd done this, because if you had, it might have made you look a bit better on this piece of paper. And you start to hate yourself for that."

Many senior activities are interesting and worthwhile, but seniors are not asked on the application to choose the most important or to write about them. Many are serious, longstanding interests, and even when they are new, some lead to lasting involvement. But they are all cheapened by being seen as something that is vital for college admission. Elizabeth's dilemma—do I dare present myself as I really am?—applies here too.

Contacts

"A lot of the time it's who will write for you." Advisers give out more than advice. They are "connections," another factor in the application, another word with a dishonest aura. *Legacy* is an ironic word in these meritocratic times. A legacy in terms of college admission is a "legup," a payback to the candidate for services someone else rendered to a college in the past. Who from the senior's family has already attended this institution? If so, have they been active alumni, well known to the college or to a wider circle, generous in both time and money? Suddenly Uncle Jack, whom one has avoided at family occasions ever since he said something obnoxious a few years back, is a fascinating member of one's very own gene pool. One senior was grateful to his father for his longstanding work interviewing for his college—"even though I would actually rather go to Mom's college."

Legacies are the center of an enormous amount of speculation and emotional energy all through senior year. Contacts matter all one's life, but for this year, and this selection process, they are especially mysterious, because although one may throw a particular name out there, one has no idea how "they" will react to it. It is obvious that you got into a certain nursery school because your older brother went there, or that some day you may be hired in your dad's company because he wants you there. These contacts are straightforward. You know what they did for you, and what they did not. Connections to colleges are different. For every story about a kid who got into college because of his contacts, there is another about a kid who did not. And these are stories; who knows what the truth is?

Legacies are also divisive. Some seniors are embarrassed that they have one. A few refuse to apply to a college where they may have an advantage, feeling they need to take the chance, to grow outside their parents' shadow, afraid of never knowing whether they would have been able to get in on their own. Like most brave people, these seniors are sometimes called foolish, and not only by their parents. "I would use every advantage I could get," said a student whose parents had not gone to college. Though he resented all the students with legacies for their extra advantages, he also thought that failing to "apply where you had a legacy, for example, the Ivies, is just another way of showing off." On the other hand, he felt that if he wanted to go to that college, he would be glad they were not applying. He was already preparing to use his lack of legacies as an excuse if he did not get in. And if he gained admission, he would be "prouder than anyone else," because he would be able to say that he did it on his own.

Colleges admit that they accept people because of their legacies, but they rarely explain why. It is not a good subject to debate: its arguments are particular and emotional. The most worthwhile explanation is practical: colleges are small businesses, and they need to attend to all aspects of their community or these businesses will fail. Their community is built on an idea—the idea that learning is valuable in a person's life—but it is also built on relationships and on personal values like loyalty. It is more than just the money that may have been donated or will be donated in the future; it is the bond between a family and a college that has grown up over the years.

This explanation, with its emphasis on longstanding connections, is hard for seniors to understand. At eighteen, longstanding connections are exactly what they as individuals do not have. They are just beginning to learn to think of themselves as being on their own. They are trying to think about the personal attributes and individual attitudes they need in order to operate as adults.

And so they become cynical: the decision doesn't rest on individual characteristics, on person B bringing more qualities to the college than person A. "If the two candidates had swapped names, the admissions picture might have been quite different. Plus they said that the movie star got into college because of his test scores," one senior said. "But that is not true! I know a lot of people with test scores better than his, and they didn't get in. It's just the way things are." They can't give an explanation. They only know it bothers them.

A related issue is racial and ethnic identity and how it helps or harms one's chances. Affirmative action is as controversial with seniors as it is elsewhere in American life. Like legacies, the process can be seen as mysterious and divisive. But in the case of race, colleges can claim sound abstract reasons for accepting one person rather than another. Person B is accepted for one or two of her own particular qualities. She will also bring a diversity the college needs "to paint its picture" and to provide a rich social life. And in the longer run, she will—or at least she might—use her college education to create a different and more just America.

This is hard for many seniors to accept, especially those who feel their own candidacies are a bit shaky. Diversity and justice, the abstract reasons cited most often, are notoriously difficult to apply to an individual life. I may be diverse in a hundred ways, and you may act justly in a thousand, but when people are choosing between you and me, which aspect of diversity will they honor? Which aspect of justice? By one definition, they will choose you; by the other, me. The abstraction grows crucially—and cruelly—personal.

In some contexts, there is no mystery; it helps to be a certain race, and the fact is openly admitted. I listened to two students discuss, with admirable civility, the fact that the one with lower test scores had been admitted to a local college because he was black. The second student was Asian and had been denied admission because her scores were not quite high enough, though they were higher than his. She liked her classmate and did not want him to lose out on any chances he might be offered. That was not her point at all. She did not claim that she was being denied a seat at the college because he had taken it. But she needed to make the point, and to make it forcefully, that "it's just not fair." Strict equity was her definition of justice. She did not consider the challenges her classmate might have had to overcome.

College, she declared, ought to be offered first to people who have shown that they really want to learn. Accepting the argument that test scores reveal whether one wants to learn—though she fiercely resented that assumption in her own case—she was willing to go further than most defenders of machine-graded tests will go. She seemed to believe that such instruments can measure not just knowledge or intelligence but even one's capacity for hard work. Rejecting the argument that colleges ought to reflect a diverse community, she insisted, "The point of school is to get an education. I think the ones that are going to go there and work hard, to be successful in the end, should be the ones first given the opportunity to go. We need the others, but it's not like they are guaranteed to stay there, and get the best that they can out of the school. So it just makes me mad."

It was a civil discussion because the young black man did not seem to take umbrage at what she said. He kept the subject off social policy and on himself as an individual, and since she knew him and liked him, she could accept his arguments. He did not claim that he had earned a seat in the local college as definitively as she had. But he was clearly growing more serious as a potential college student, and he made the case that people who needed a second chance would also work hard in college, maybe even harder, because they would owe the college so much. His implication was that the opportunity to go to college should be about the future as well as the past, and she agreed with him there. Like most good conversations, it was ultimately inconclusive, but it shed a lot of light on the subject.

The Essay

Filling out a college application is surprisingly difficult—far more complicated than "typing in a lot of little spaces"—but the hardest work is yet to come. "The essay takes *days* for me to think about," one senior remarked. "A few hours wouldn't be enough. These questions are so *big*."

Seniors see the purpose of the essay much more clearly than that of any other part of the application process. The grades in the transcripts have been earned years ago. Test scores can be explained. Recommendations often depend more on the teacher's writing ability and energy than on the student's worth. The essay is the seniors' chance to show themselves exactly as they want to be seen. They can take as much time as they like. It's an opportunity to put their own spin on the facts presented on the application form and to show the flair, the imagination, or the understanding behind the numbers, letters, or titles. And that's exactly what scares them about it. They are being given a chance—and they can't throw it away.

Most seniors feel the time the essay takes is well spent. "Anything that makes you look at your life is good," said one, who found writing college essays intensely uncomfortable, "even if you don't like it. This is a chance to look at my time in high school and see what it really was about." Still, it was even more important to connect her past accomplishments to her future plans: to the world's life, to its business, to the need it might have of her talents and energy. "You're supposed to condense your entire life—and what you have to offer for the rest of it—into a three-hundred-and-fifty-word essay."

"Anything that makes you look at your life is good, even if you don't like it. This is a chance to look at my time in high school and see what it really was about."

What do you have to offer? is the ultimate grown-up question, one with which many seniors have little experience. Getting started is the biggest problem. "In my college essays, if I didn't have a perfect first sentence, I couldn't get anywhere with it." In the "perfect first sentence," the connection between the "way too general" topic and the fascinating particular—themselves—has to be established. Essay topics and questions can be as straightforward as "Describe your best qualities" or as oblique as "What would you do if you had William Shakespeare as your roommate?" One student complained about "questions like How has your high school academic career changed you as a person? or What are your political beliefs? I mean, how do I know who I really am, anyway? These were things I hadn't spent much time thinking about." Despite what seemed like hours devoted to self-scrutiny all during her teenage years, much of her energy had been focused on what she *didn't* like about herself, what she was going to try to change. "I didn't want to brag—it didn't feel right. Because you cannot judge yourself—at least that's what I think." In her family's culture, it was appropriate for parents to boast about their children, but *not* for the children to boast about themselves. Now, invited to present herself at her best, she did not know what to say.

In the case of college-bound seniors with an essay to write, this ambivalence is not only frustrating, it is costly. Many seniors feel their school has not given them enough practice at writing about themselves. Some are right: in many high schools they have not written much about anything, or their writing has been the objective third-person variety used in literary criticism and history term papers. Even if they have kept journals, this may be the first time they have attempted high-stakes personal writing. "You're writing to a person who indirectly will determine the course of your life." Who is that person? There are rumors about seniors in last year's class who were told their records and personal impression—in the essay or interview—struck the admissions officer as "too perfect." And what about that dip in your grades during the last half of junior year, when you and your mother were getting along so badly you had to leave home for a while? "Should I explain it exactly as I explain it to myself—that it's all her fault—or would that seem too self-serving?" What if the admissions officer who reads it is a parent with a troubled teenaged kid? Tone is the hardest aspect of the essay to establish, because the readers are unknowns. Furthermore, as one young man put it, "They don't know who *you* are." Everyone else he had ever had to impress with his writing had been known to him and vice versa. "When the teacher knows who you are, you can really shine," he said. But when the readers are faceless, the writers are clueless.

Others believe it is easier to impress strangers than it is to impress their own teachers. In college essays, one young woman said, "You're trying to present the best of you. When you're writing an essay you try to come up with the biggest words and more elaborate things to say." When I asked her whether she felt honest doing that, she said that it was expected. "I don't think they get a clear picture," she admitted. But, she continued, "You are supposed to dress things up."

It's fakery, they know, but in their minds a necessary fakery. The vocabulary is full of what they call "SAT words," and the phrasing is polished. It often sounds unnatural and stilted, but the students are too panicked to write more directly. Other forms of dishonesty also creep in. Teachers are often asked to "proofread" college essays. Depending on the atmosphere of the school and the teachers' own feelings about it, which are inevitably conflicted, some seniors ask their teachers or other advisers to see the essay through several drafts. "Sometimes you'll have to rewrite it three or four times," one student explained. But he felt he was acting responsibly. "It's up to the student to get the teacher's help." Parents and other adults regularly "type" these essays, which usually reduces errors. Besides making the essay different from what it claims to be—the student's own work—this puts having more well educated parents at a premium, widening the opportunity gap once again. Most seniors, however, can't take the time to worry about justice; they just assume they can't do it alone. One student feared that the new college counselor in his school was not going to "ride" him enough to finish his essays. "The old one was real fussy," he said, and superintended most of the process, but the new one expected the kids to be self-motivated. And for him, he believed, this might not work out. "I need help," he said, "but I'm not one who normally asks for it."

It isn't just concerned adults who pitch in when a senior is struggling with the essay. One senior admitted to me, in a roundabout way, that he had helped one of his friends with his college essays so much that he felt "bad about it." Why did he do it? They had grown up together, and had always "helped each other out" with writing and math. It just seemed that his friend had turned to him more this year, and everything was so late, and anyway, they were headed in different directions. He didn't want to get stuffy right at the end. He finally confessed that he had essentially written his friend's essay. "This won't become a habit, since we'll be so far apart next year," he said, but he also took some pride in the fact that his friend was "applying to some pretty big-name schools." If his friend got in, he could privately take some of the credit.

Dishonesty also determines what some seniors choose to write about. One student told me that she felt that school should never interfere with her "real education," which was "having fun." When I asked her what she wrote about in her essay, she said she focused it on her plans to become a doctor. Another student said that his essay described all the hardships he had overcome. In his school, however, his reputation was that of a person who had brought on most of his own hardships. To be a victim was fashionable, though one had to be a "recovering" victim rather than a whiner. Many of the essays I heard about concerned learning difficulties, family problems, social and racial isolation, or what-I-learned-when-I-broke-my-leg.

Students like to write their essays in (or about) strange places. Foxholes, hospitals, even jails, may well be an advantage as a dateline. One student wrote his whole essay looking down from the top of a Ferris wheel. "More than anything," he told me, "it is important to be memorable." Yet it is hard to decide how many risks to take, how much to reveal about oneself. Will an off-beat answer or a wacky essay seem impulsive? Not serious enough? Years ago one of my students showed me an essay she had already sent. She was much more self-mocking and imaginative than I would ever have dared to be when I was seventeen. I concluded that if the college took her in spite of the risk she was taking, it would be a good enough place for her.

There are still other worries. If the application says the essay should be two hundred and fifty words, and you usually write shorter or longer ones, should you shape yourself to these expectations? If your essay is shorter, will the college think you are too casual? Will they wonder what else you might have said? If it is longer, will they think you do not know how to follow directions? Will they think you do not know how to discipline your verbose impulses? How tolerant do you have to seem? Can you admit how much those kids in the settlement house seemed like total brats at times? Should you reveal that no matter how many environmentalists scream in your ear, you will never ever give up your car? Do you have to say you liked the museums and hated the bullfights in your trip to Spain last summer when it was really the reverse? Do you dare to be average? Fun-loving? Selfish? "I'm not sure that I'm very different from all the kids who want to go there," one senior admitted, "and I'm not sure that I want to be. But I want to be accepted to college." So for the sake of his future, he described his present in a way quite different than he knew it to be.

These exertions also prompt seniors to cull their lists and refine their objectives, to center on the ideal: the ideal college, the ideal candidate. "You have to make everything perfect," said a young woman who was the first in her family to apply to college. No matter how many people checked the application, there might be a simple spelling mistake, and that, she was convinced, would instantly disqualify her. "I don't want anything to be wrong with it, or it will ruin my chances of going to college." With so many issues at stake, and with the tremendous fear of sending off something less than outstanding, it's no wonder seniors procrastinate. Quite a few report losing a serious amount of sleep.

"Writing the essay is your last chance," one young woman declared. "Before, you could always do it again. And coupled with all the other things I'm thinking about, that got me very stressed out. I don't handle stress very well. When I have a lot of work to do, I get excited. Little things that wouldn't normally bother me seem very big because I don't think they should take my time." Observations like these, admirable for their honesty and their self-perception, indicate an emotional resiliency that will be helpful in the first year of college. Yet they could never be admitted in a college essay.

The Interview

A college interview is an intimidating experience no matter how it is conducted. At a self-conscious age, one's appearance genuinely matters. Clothes can make or break the boy—or girl. A bad haircut is hard to camouflage. Weight, braces, hair, all carry messages. Adults and older friends pass on lots of advice; everyone seems to "know" the "right" thing to say, but so much of it is contradictory! Should you behave yourself or be yourself? This classic conundrum is discussed with family and friends for weeks. Seniors have had few extended, serious conversations with adult strangers. They are desperate for coaching, resent it, are indifferent to it, all at once, in different phases and with different people.

The college interview is generally stilted. First of all, it is less and less important in the admissions process, at least to the more selective colleges whose applications have soared in recent years. Many colleges no longer grant them. Others arrange group interviews that nearly everybody finds unsatisfactory. Some ask their alumni to interview, but without any real faith in their judgment, which frustrates both the candidates and the alumni. In spite of these trends and of their own trepidation, most seniors seek out individual interviews, convinced that their own uniqueness will emerge only in that setting. When individual interviews are conducted, their settings are often unfortunate. Crammed into summer days, they are often held in the small, hot offices of the most junior staff people, those with the least experience at reading body language. There are inevitably too many interviews on a given day, so for the interviewer, they become a blur. As questions and answers grow more wooden, the seniors fear the smallest and least important flaw may stand out.

The two people talking in a college interview are not only strangers to each other; they will never work together, perhaps never see each other. But seniors know they still have to act as if they are embarking on a lifelong friendship. There is the mysterious process of "hitting it off." Most seniors can tell whether they liked their interviewer, but they are far less certain whether their interviewer liked them. Even when their words are, "He seemed to really like me," their voices reveal uncertainty. "I need to learn to present myself well, because all of that makes a huge difference," said one senior wistfully. He could not explain why he thought so. Like many other aspects of senior year, it seems like something one "knows" only because one has heard it so often.

There is a clear sense on the seniors' part that they are at a disadvantage, that the "elite" is being defined by the people who already belong to it. "His attitude," one senior complained, "seemed to be, Are you college material? How do I know what college material is? All I could do was hope that he'd think I was. I couldn't think of any way to be sure." Another senior, the favorite of her high school teachers, said, "A lot of my interviews didn't go well. The strengths in my personality don't come out in questions like, What are you going to do with the rest of your life? Because I don't yet know, and I would feel dishonest pretending that I do." Even a budding mathematician had complaints. "I knew he'd just been dragged over from his office to talk to me. He didn't really seem interested in much that I'm actually working on. It turned me off the college for quite a while."

The seniors are marketing themselves, and they know it. "It makes me feel a little cheap," admitted a smooth young man. "Maybe I'm being cynical about the whole thing, but that's the way it goes." When she went to her interview in her mother's suit and high heels, a young woman asked herself, "Is that the person I want to sell? Or is it the person I think they want to see?" Or perhaps the person her mother thinks they want to see? She did not know. But what she remembered best was that "I looked nice that day."

Elizabeth's dilemma—do I dare present myself as I really am?—permeates much about the application process. The emphasis on quantity of achievements rather than on carefully expressed quality is what drives so many seniors to "play the game." The student who works hard, pays his bills, stays healthy, and is nice to his dog and his grandmother does not get into college. Or at least not the "right" college. At least according to the conventional wisdom of the high school seniors and the many, many advisers who counsel him not only to "look nice," not only to "get his act together," but also to doctor up his image.

Seniors feel as if they have been asked to present their own eulogies: to describe themselves as impressive products rather than as works in process. And so they add metaphorical lifts to their shoes: the enhanced curriculum vitae here, the expensive test preparation course there, the short-term community service, the essay about that community service that has seen the benefit of a variety of editors. Each "lift" is added without much worry about being dishonest; each is tolerated by the culture that surrounds the seniors. Added together, the seniors hope, these things will make them stand out. But the growing disconnection between the person presented in the application and the person who still has to live with herself, her family, and her teachers can't help but undermine what is left of the senior year.

5 Grandstanding

Bill, co-captain of his soccer team and its most enthusiastic and skilled player, had helped his team play well enough to reach the tournament. "You get a lot of publicity when you win tournaments," he confided, "and it's real good for college," so he was even more eager than usual to win. "I'm the only senior who wants to play after high school." He was playing a new game now, using athletics as a way to somewhere else, lining himself up for the best life possible. He was counting on soccer to help him get into college, and his teammates were prepared to pass to him, let him make goals, see his name in the newspapers. It was an unspoken agreement.

In one of the tournament's first matches, however, he came up against a frustrating situation. The other team had only one good player, but it took all Bill's energies to keep him from scoring, so there was little chance to score himself. His team was still ahead by one goal, but when he was taken out, three quarters of the way through the game, the other player scored a minute later. "After that goal, my whole mental structure just went down the tubes," Bill confessed. "I wasn't focused or anything. I got put back in, right after the goal." But the other team then played defensively, to hold the tie, and that just made Bill more frustrated. "I then decided to play breakaways, which was probably one of the worst decisions I've ever made. But that's the way I am; I figure all or nothing. So I played offensive and decided the two fullbacks could cover this guy."

Bill was wrong; the other team's star player scored again. "It all went by so fast." In less than seven minutes, they went from being ahead to losing the game, the tournament and, for this captain, the season. "No one knew what happened, and then after that goal we played the best soccer of the whole season," but never made another goal. "I went home as discouraged as I've ever been," Bill admitted. "I felt inadequate as a leader and foolish as a player. Everybody must have discussed my unwise decision." As he saw it, the whole town was punished for his "glory moves." As Bill saw it, he had precluded triumphant memories for his team, his class, and his school.

Bill realized he was grandstanding when he abandoned his defensive posture to try to get the goal that would break the tie. But he needed to think about more than the present situation; he needed to think about future games and future teams, games in college, games he would never play unless he managed to impress others now. There was something ignominious about a tie. Ties might keep the team in the tournament, but they would not contribute much to his or his fellow seniors' memories. He was "not running out the clock" but searching for memories that would last a lifetime. He wanted to be the one who scored the winning goal, even if this meant taking risks with his team's reputation as well as his own. Attempting to keep all these needs straight—his own and his teammates', the needs of today and of next year and of all his life—caused an emotional overload and led to a reckless decision.

When Bill told me about the incident a couple of months later, the sorrow and shame in his voice made it clear how wrenching the experience had been. "I try to ignore it most of the time," he said. "It's hard when people try to talk about it," although it was he who brought up what he called his "grim scenario." He would not have been able to describe it, he said, for the first few weeks after it happened. At this point, he could. He was on the rebound, he claimed, and the way he "got better" was to work very hard in his courses. He had pulled up every one of his grades except math, and math, he insisted, "wasn't my fault. The teacher is new, and she definitely doesn't understand seniors."

Earlier, he had presented himself to me almost exclusively as a soccer player, but using athletics as a point of leverage had taken its toll. By January, he was grateful that the season was over; the constant need to think of soccer as a way to promote himself had destroyed his pleasure in competition, at least for high school. His picture of himself was altered. He was grateful that he was able to move from one arena to the next; his resilience augured well for his ability to face other disappointments, which were sure to come.

* * *

Bill's story poignantly reinforces the corrupting effect that pressure can have on extracurricular activities during the senior year. So many aspects of it are tied up with the time dimension in which seniors are trying to live. Athletic and other extracurricular activities emphasize the present tense. Every outcome is in the balance. Each match varies, depending on the competitors, the weather, the amount of sleep gotten the night before, teammates' reliability. Nothing matters in the heat of competition but seizing the moment. Nothing can undo a terrible two minutes. Nothing can outdo a brilliant, spontaneous masterstroke, a caught pass, a wrestling pin, a last-lap spurt. The decisions, the emotions, the reactions, are particular. If a game—or a concert, or a speech—could be predicted, it would lose its fascination. It is a supremely human exercise, subject to all of a person's foibles, an occasion to rise to for those who can.

Most seniors still look at their out-of-class activities the way they always have: as excitement, as camaraderie, as something to do, as fun. "You devote so much time to it," said one senior, trying to assess the importance of the newspaper to her life. "And that's how I met my first friends in this school." Her school year was built around the newspaper's deadlines just as surely as Bill's was around the soccer season. However, during this year of transition, the natural orientation toward "now" comes to be shaded more and more toward "then." The school play is videotaped by the senior's parents. The game becomes an investment, the season a way to contribute to school history. Win-loss numbers establish not only a school but also a class record. The homecoming victory, the award-winning yearbook, the state drama festival production, are part of the seniors' sense of entitlement, of the spotlight, of having come through for their school. Even senior-class spectators feel they "deserve" to witness an outstanding performance. Anything else is unthinkable, because it won't be fun to remember.

The best trained and most talented—or those who fantasize that "this is the year when it will all come together"—approach their extracurricular pursuits differently in their final year. The need to honor and enjoy the present butts up against the need to develop a future. The team becomes less meaningful, the game less playful. A talent or skill becomes a route out of the ghetto, a ticket into a certain college, a way to pay back Mom and Dad for all the lessons and all the driving. Seniors who have loved sports—or music, or school politics—all their lives continue to respond to the thrill of the game, but they look at the game differently now.

To Play or Not to Play

Athletics in particular plays a central role in high school. Sports teams are especially important, in part because they become a measure by which their members gauge their personal progress. These growing teenagers, adding inches and weight and skills and finesse, are able to do more every year. They go from junior varsity to varsity to starting player to co-captain. What they can do physically is more discernible than reading and writing; it is more celebrated than research. They couldn't outrun the others at the beginning of high school. Now they can, or nearly can. In all senses of that term, it's a rush.

I taught a highly academic Korean teenager once who made me promise not to tell his father what a good soccer player he was. In the United States, however, the concept of the "scholar-athlete" is alive and well; nearly everybody approves of sports as a way to spend one's time, and at the beginning of high school, there is a lot of time to spend. Being out on a field for the afternoon seems a healthy and pleasurable way to live. As a pastime, it is one of the few likely to gain approval from both parents and peers. Even teachers profit from the sense of agency students often gain from sports: I-am-a-separate-individual-who-can-do-this-if-I-work-hard applies to schoolwork too. Sharing goals, sharing strategies, sharing the limelight, working effectively with people who are not close friends, figuring out how to pick themselves up after losing a crucial match and trying again: all these lessons are noticed, and, like other lessons, mostly learned.

All eyes are on varsity athletes, even more so than on seniors in general. Hometown newspapers describe their "long workouts" and their "grueling schedules" as if they are local warriors in a crucial regional contest. Their talent is publicly displayed, their feats have a mysterious hold on adults who are no longer prime athletic specimens themselves. Most varsity seniors expect the adulation to be short-term and learn to take it in stride. Less-noticed aspects of athletic competition—and those most germane to the culture of senior year—are the conflicts between now and then, the team and the individual, that plagued Bill.

At the beginning of senior year, most team athletes are at a crossroads. If their position on the varsity is at all vulnerable—if the previous season was not what it could have been, if they have let themselves get out of shape, or if new, better players have shown up—they face disaster. If they do not play well enough to make the varsity in their final year, they will probably not be able to play at all, since many high schools exclude seniors from junior varsity teams.

Most of the seniors who mentioned this policy to me seemed to agree with it. Such a senior, they explained, just takes up space that ought to go to a younger player. Coaches would rather "invest in a person with more talent," someone who can help the team win in future years. One has to think of the payoff for the team, the rights of the school. In a sense, nonvarsity seniors have already forfeited theirs. The fact that the school is already assuming, even planning for, their departure is an early intimation of these seniors' replaceability as individuals in their community. The school celebrities are learning that the spotlight, though bright, is also narrow, fragile, and short-lived.

And seniors who *are* bumped down to the junior varsity roster may quit. "It's like staying back, in a way. The same onus." Then, too, sports purely as a pastime has less appeal, since seniors have less time to "pass." They tell themselves they will "use all that time in better ways." Some even do.

Quitting the team seems counterintuitive, however: they have emphasized their success as athletes in their applications; there is more time toward the end of the year and lots of nervous energy to wear off. During the long period of waiting for college decisions and job hires, sports can be an effective diversion. But all over the country seniors who have played competitively for eleven seasons are not signing up for the twelfth. Some of the most talented and enthusiastic players seem to lose interest. Senioritis has started to settle in, even in sports. In the beginning of the year, most agree with the girl who said, "Though it adds a lot to the stress, I can't imagine a senior year without athletics." But as Bill's story indicates, somehow, after a season or two, many of them can imagine exactly that.

Why? "I'm awfully mentally drained," one senior insisted, though he had always considered sports to be the only important thing about high school. "I haven't had any time off from the beginning of the year to now." Adults may well consider *sports* as "time off," as a chance to leave work, have fun, and be admired at the same time. But for this senior, "At a certain point, enough is enough. They take it out of you every day. I feel as if I paid my dues so I'm taking a break." Being on the team had come to feel like work. The focus of athletics had been on his performance rather than his attitudes and preferences. He knew now that he would "not be recruited," although he still hoped his "athletic record may somehow have helped" his college chances. During senior year, so many of his motivations had become external—for the team record, for his own college admissions—that he had forgotten what he really wanted. He felt low on energy, nearly depleted of good will, but by having played, he felt, he had earned respect. "Now I'm going to spend some of that equity. You get annoyed with the hassle after a while, and I ought to be having fun."

Another athlete suddenly realized how much sports depends not only on the actions but also on the decisions of others. His individualism inflated by his college applications, he was angry at the vulnerability he was made to feel over others' mistakes. "The win-loss record during my senior year was affected by some sophomore. My memories of my senior year," he complained, "are at their mercy." The whole thing made him so disgusted that he did not want to go through it again in the spring, though he realized his teammates on the baseball team considered him the selfish one.

Like so many decisions seniors need to make, this is a difficult one. Taking off the uniform turns out to be surprisingly painful. "I cared about the uniform when I realized I was wearing it for the last time," an eleven-season athlete said about his last basketball game. The uniform had been his official attachment to the institution, his way of representing and defending it, and in setting it aside, he was setting aside a role he had savored. "The name of the high school on my chest and everything. It's like your last game ever. It's the last time you're going to play—the last time you're going to wear the name. Officially, I mean. With your number." It was not so much the people who were causing him trouble but the abstraction. He and that uniform had been through so many momentous times together. It still had meaning for him, no matter how much he was trying to move on. And even though he would never have been able to wear it anywhere, "It would be nice to be able to hold on to it." He felt the pain of everybody who has ever moved off the center of the stage, who has ever been replaced. "I wonder," he mused, "who will get my number."

Seeing the Big Picture

The high school seniors who do manage to join and stay in the varsity teams usually dominate them. Raw talent, of course, is spread across the high school, and there are many underclassmen on varsities, but the seniors determine the team's morale and act as its leaders. The team's hopefulness—and its willingness to work hard to achieve its dreams—is often fueled by the seniors' achievements. Besides models, the seniors are teachers: their knowledge of recent team history is firsthand, vibrant, and full of cautionary tales. One senior did a fabulous job as a goalie on a JV team. She had been on the varsity as an eleventh grader, but faced with an amazing new player, she gracefully picked herself up and played with the younger athletes. They idolized her, especially as her work in the goal led them to a season in which not only were they unbeaten but no other team even scored. And they learned from her about the game: specific techniques, but also what the chance to play on a team can mean to a person who really loves it.

Another senior described a different kind of leadership. "A lot of people think of me as a dumb jock," he admitted. "But I'm really number ten in my class. I want people to look up to me. Even if they don't have the same talent, they can see me work hard." He wanted to be even more than a role model, however. He had some advice: "Take your time." Taking one's time, keeping one's head, seeing things in perspective, are the result, the seniors think, of their hard-won maturity. They value their increased stability as the season progresses. "I did manage to settle down," one young man boasted, after what he admitted was a rocky start. The seniors often grow closer to their coaches and are frequently asked to act as a go-between. They sense when a clique is beginning to form; often, they can break it up. "We'll stick up for the younger players," one explained, because "seniors realize that new members of the team need to be brought along rather than constantly criticized." He claimed that he could remember what it was like to be a clumsy sophomore better than the juniors did.

> "A lot of people think of me as a dumb jock. But I'm really number ten in my class. I want people to look up to me. Even if they don't have the same talent, they can see me work hard."

Though seniors believe they have helped the team in the matches, they admit to being casual about practices. They want to stay on the coach's good side, if only to get to play more, but the co-captain who is gamely trying to lead the practice isn't going to be making those decisions, and everybody knows it. Circumstances are changing. Loyalty as a virtue doesn't seem as important now that they are in their last year. How can it? Flexibility is supposed to be more important at this point. In school after school, the refrain I heard from dancers to football players grew louder and louder: performance is still important, but preparation is "more and more meaningless, and it takes time—time that I simply don't have right now." In a year loaded with irony, here is another: despite their mixed feelings about practice, all seniors want their teams' records to be perfect. "I have real high expectations in basketball," one young man said. "Probably too high, but I tend to do that. This certainly seems as good a year as any to win the tournament."

Many of the most ardent athletes don't expect to play again, which only adds to their motivation to do well during senior year. One girl I talked with was resigned to the end of competitive sports in her life. "I want to make the best of each season," she insisted, "and even more, I want to go out with a good season to end on. The fact that I'm a senior has made me more focused on athletics than I have ever been. In soccer, when I was playing my last game, I thought, Well, I'm never going to be here again. It won't happen next year." Just as high school coaches are beginning to imagine life without the seniors, she was beginning to erase the high school and its playing fields from her own future. Not from her self-image, however; she was determined to end on a proud personal note. "I better play my heart out or I won't have much to remember this by. I want to look back and remember how well I played in my last game."

"I Was Counting on a Miracle"

The culture of senior year is long on fantasy, and fantasies involving sports are probably the most fantastic of all. Perfection is the only option. "I have to play smart and not make any mistakes." Very few scholars expect to earn 800 on their SATs, and very few adolescent musicians think about playing in Carnegie Hall, but all kinds of athletes are dreaming of the big breakthrough. One young man admitted that he fully "expected to make a winning shot from eighty-eight feet," even though he had never even come close before.

Some even achieve their dreams—or part of them. "I had a fantasy of scoring the winning touchdown in a state championship game," said one young man. "And we never got that far. But I accomplished some great things through football. I'm looking forward to receiving a scholarship. I've had that big dream, and some of it did happen." He was waiting for the news that his SATs had improved in his most recent try. Until they did, he reported with an air of disbelief, his scholarship was still not certain. Still, "We got a chance to play in the pros' stadium, and I scored two touchdowns there, and man, I was excited. Oh, that thrilled me! That was one of the great moments of my life."

Seniors who have demonstrated their talent expect to be admired—and rewarded. "Before the season started," one admitted, "I was expecting more, to receive offers from all these colleges. I had dreams of sitting in a room with coaches, and having the scouts come talk to me." He had not heard from a single one, while rumors abounded about the attention other young athletes got. Phone calls, letters, dinners, visits: they were out there—everybody knows it—but why weren't they happening to him?

Anticipating the big breakthrough adds tremendously to stress during the senior year. Every game is an opportunity not only to play well but to be seen as playing well. The sports section of the local paper becomes some kind of Bible if it talks up one's talent—talent matters more than effort—or a dirty, biased rag if it does not. "Seniors need to get good press for colleges and stuff," said many seniors, and one of them admitted to "becoming a little obsessed for a while." Coaches, too, have to watch what they say about their seniors to reporters; quoted or misquoted, it causes them tremendous problems if it isn't wildly positive. Some seniors, discouraged with the lukewarm advocacy their coaches and the local press are giving them, send their own videotapes directly to the colleges. They never really know, however, whether the college coaches look at them, and the controversy poisons the atmosphere of the high school.

Adding to the stress is the constant fear of injuries. One student still winced when he described his. They were doubly poignant because, like so many young players, he was improving very quickly, but he was mentally a little unsure of his returning skills, and he was trying too hard. After a few weeks of healing, "I had to work my way back on the team," and he never really recovered his stride. After two games, he was damaged again; it was all snatched away from him in a moment. Moreover, the culture of the senior year made him believe that he needed to carry the hurt and look brave—even blasé—about it. He was also convinced that more colleges would have accepted him if he had not been injured—and he may have been right.

These young athletes also have money on their mind. One student's parents had paid for her to go to a bigger public high school in a nearby town "with better coaches and a more competitive schedule." It also had a better academic reputation, but she did not mention that as being among her parents' motivations. Now, she said, she had a limited range of places where she could apply compared with her classmates. It would have to be the kind of college that recruited and paid middle-income athletes. Ever since she was thirteen, however, she had "known what the deal was," and it seemed entirely reasonable to her. Her parents had done their part, for four years. Now it was her turn—but only if she succeeded as an athlete.

To do that, she felt she should join a regional league. "If you only play high school soccer, there's no way you'll be recruited." It was flattering to be "asked to perform at a whole new level"; she enjoyed the faster pace; and she admired her league coach, whose "recruiting connections are wonderful" and who knew the game much better than her high school coach did. She also appreciated the "chance to meet a new bunch of kids, even though it's more like being on an all-star team, so you don't feel as close to the others." She felt she also needed to stay on her high school team: for the camaraderie, the chance to be its star, and her loyalty to its coach. "He may not know the game as well, but he knows me." Still, the time demands were extensive. "My family's weekends are pretty much dominated by my soccer schedule, but I know it's going to pay off."

Another athlete had a less-satisfactory league experience. Having decided during her sophomore year that her high school was "not very competitive," she felt she needed to join a state team. "I hoped to show the coaches what I could do," but she learned that she was not as good as she had previously thought. "It was a reality check. The realization was gradual, because I had been trying out for the state team for years, but finally I saw how good the players were. This year I finally made the team, but I was really frustrated when I started." She felt like a latecomer, like a person who could never catch up. Her family and her high school coach were excited she was on the team, but she played so little and was so intimidated that she wondered if it was worth it. What was athletics about, anyway? Establishing a certain reputation or actually taking part? Being there or doing something?

Even those who enjoy the league games admit that a lot of grandstanding takes place. Loyalty to their friends and to their hometown is replaced by loyalty to the game and to themselves as individual players. Appearance matters more than anything else. Exploits like Bill's are relatively cost-free in league games. The recruiters invite it, the coach expects that kind of playing, and the players don't have to face one another in math or English during the coming week. "In the league games, you get a lot of people running around doing things with the ball that are stupid. Of course, they are all the glory moves, but they look good." It becomes important to the seniors to outdo their teammates, one athlete admitted, "especially when they are aware that coaches are watching them." Or when they are trying to get into the same college.

Leadership

"I never wanted the spotlight," one sparkly young woman said a bit disingenuously, "but we do the announcements now, which gives us notoriety. I think your whole senior year is leadership. It's just one big leadership experience." Seniors are expected to represent other students to the public at school events and to the faculty in school matters. They lead as parts of committees and as individuals, each with its very different challenges. They preside over senior class projects, edit and produce the newspaper, and assist the drama, dance, and music directors. In some schools, they direct performances themselves.

Depending on the size of the school, the percentage of the seniors who are considered leaders varies tremendously. In small schools, there is some kind of job for almost everyone. Even in big schools, the prevailing opinion in the fall is that all seniors are leaders. Seniors who take part in extracurricular activities—the sports teams, the band, the literary magazine, the prom committee—say they are important to their school, are giving something to it. This is a new feeling for them; it feels burdensome at times but welcome at others; they expect to work hard but also to be appreciated. Their activities are prime reasons for spending many hours together, comparing and refining their vision and getting things done. Once they had friends; now they are learning to work with colleagues.

Though nervous about their new responsibilities, seniors tend to want to put their own stamp on things. They don't seek much advice from last year's seniors. In September nearly every leader enjoys the firm conviction that he or she will do better than any predecessors in the role. Despite the suspicious relationship between their newfound visibility and their college applications, as the year progresses many seniors get past their titles and concentrate on accomplishing something. By springtime most of them can cite a product or two; some of them have done a lot.

Leading one's peers, however, is hard work, especially in school. Caught between the faculty and its expectations and the students who may have elected them, the leaders loudly lament the power they do not have, quake more quietly before the power they do have. In some arenas, it seems important for student leaders to have talent and skill that are clearly greater than that of their peers. "It's tough to lead someone who feels he is better than you are," a team co-captain confessed to me during the fall. "You need to be good enough so that you can tell people what to do without its being, Well, you can't do it either!" The pattern in sports is to consider skill first when choosing leaders. This is tricky in activities like tennis, where skill is determined by ongoing matches. The captain, perhaps not at the top of the ladder to begin with, may descend it during the season, which usually affects her credibility as a leader. Skill is also cited as crucial to leadership of music groups, drama groups, newspapers, yearbooks. "You have to be a good writer to be the head of the newspaper" is a universal conviction.

The qualities that bring student leaders to the top, however, are often not the same ones they need once they get there. "I hadn't really been much of a leader and suddenly I'm the editor with a staff of forty people," one senior acknowledged. The school's best photographer has to weather the emotional stresses and strains of the yearbook. The star chess player has to risk his personal win in order to play for the whole team. An outstanding musician has to be willing to work in groups with struggling members of the band. "Junior year is for developing yourself," a senior told me somewhat ruefully. "In senior year, you need to be a teacher."

"Junior year is for developing yourself. In senior year, you need to be a teacher."

Under the onerous shadow of the CV and of "the definite need to look good," seniors are constantly recalculating their priorities. A passionate dancer has not been elected to be a leader; does that mean she should quit dancing and do something else? The student who spends all his free time writing a novel has never been published in his school's literary magazine; does that mean his talent, his drive, his purpose, are less genuine? "I was *always* in a play," one girl lamented, "but I didn't like the one they were offering this fall, so I decided to skip it. That was probably a mistake." The seniors' feelings about their interests have much to do with their perceptions of how "successful" they are—or are seen to be. Getting a position, getting published, getting the lead, will help their chances more than the careful, persistent development of their interests and abilities.

For leaders, it is easier to discern success when the product is clear: games won or lost; newspapers gotten out on time or not; crisp or blurry photographs; articles proofread or riddled with typos; editorials admired or criticized. Like so much else about American culture, one is perceived as doing either very well or very badly and in that atmosphere, numbers are useful. Even though sincerity or compassion or the uplifting time everyone had on the hunger walk may be more important, it is less measurable. One needs to cite the number of participants and the money earned, so leaders do, early and often. By the middle of the fall, accomplishments are already being tabulated. This is scary, even for the seniors who are only looking on. "They have such a burden on them," one commiserated. "Everyone's going to blame them if something goes wrong."

Maintaining Authority

Even in the most successful enterprises, seniors are discovering how hard it is to gain authority over one's peers. "People respect the person, not the title, which is the way it has to be," declared a young woman who was a leader in one club and a follower in another. "I think leaders should be prepared to accept others' ideas rather than feel that theirs are the correct ones all the time." The student head of the school band recalled her early struggles at finding the right tone. "There's a lot of proving that you have to do," she said earnestly. "I had to show that I could conduct, that I knew what we had to get done. I knew that I had to have some respect from the band or I was not going to be effective at all." She realized that it was going to be tricky: could she "be herself" or would she "have to put up a front"? "You can feel a little manipulative," she admitted, "or a little manipulated." As she saw it, there were a number of ways in which she might fail, but "I shouldn't have been there if I wasn't going to get the job done."

A band member offered a critique in the gentlest of tones. "Watching how people reacted to her in the first few weeks when she was trying to establish that respect and power from the people, I felt that a lot of people resisted just because they had known her from before when she was just equal to them. And now that she was one step higher they couldn't quite accept it yet. Because they weren't sure if she was just going to be a dictator, or whether she was going to interact with us, yet keep some authority over us."

That was the bandleader's problem in a nutshell, and she took the criticism well. "I've learned from this. You have to cater to people's needs and communicate on their level and not on yours. You have to figure out what their needs are and help them solve their problems. It's awkward. But you get used to it. You have to." Later she said, "I am very sad to be leaving my high school band. I've been so involved in it and loved it so much. Band has drastically shaped my personality." Drastically? Well, substantially, and she seemed to believe it was for the better.

Seniors have so little experience to guide them that personal development is mentioned whenever leadership is discussed. "I never really thought about leadership qualities, and at first I was reluctant to use them," one senior admitted. What are leadership qualities in high school? How much should one stand out? How much should one work by consensus? One's answers often depend on one's school culture but also on one's instincts. For one senior, leadership felt natural, since he enjoyed the image of himself on a white horse, ahead of the others in his class. "I'm comfortable saying I'm a good leader," he said. "That's what I like doing. I like to take charge. I like to make sure things are going well. I don't like chaos." The isolation so many student leaders feel didn't seem to bother him. "This year was my test. I've made an effort to do everything I could, and I've discovered that I'm a very good leader. I consider myself as very different from my classmates, even people on the same level as me, because I have it together. I know what I'm going to do, and I'm organized."

"They need to look up to you a little bit," another leader agreed, but she insisted that being liked and working hard were as important as talent. "Sometimes you kind of emerge as a leader, but you don't stand up and give orders," another young woman believed. "Still, you can't show your leadership if you just sit back and be quiet." She was making herself be "out front" more than she had before. She was also discovering how complex leadership can be: how many personal traits it seems to require, often too many for one individual. She was grateful for the virtues of her co-president. "We complement each other. She's quiet and talks to people individually. I'm enthusiastic and think of the club as a whole." Because they were able to draw together two quite different approaches by respecting the need for each, and because their adviser was making it clear that he depended on them, they were exercising leadership.

More seniors, however, experience the frustrations in their jobs. I heard about problems with faculty advisers—too bossy, or, more often, not helpful enough—and between the student leaders themselves: co-leaders who gave lousy advice, griped a lot, acted arrogant or—most common—"were never there." One co-captain, fresh from a study of the U.S. Constitution in his government class, spoke of the possibility of "impeaching" the other co-captain. "We lasted out the season, finally," he said, but their problems clearly absorbed much energy that might otherwise have gone to the team.

> "When you're in a leadership position, it's like they want you to be perfect. [The demands are] practically inhuman. Inevitably, you will miss with somebody. You can't please all of the people all of the time. Nobody wants to help but everybody wants to criticize. There's a lot of animosity toward some seniors who are not getting the job done."

Senior class officers are very dissatisfied leaders. "When you're in a leadership position, it's like they want you to be perfect," said one senior president, echoing others. They need to be on their best behavior, every minute of every day. The demands are "practically inhuman. Inevitably, you will miss with somebody. You can't please all of the people all of the time. Nobody wants to help but everybody wants to criticize. There's a lot of animosity toward some seniors who are not getting the job done."

But what job? Running good meetings? Raising money? Organizing trips? Choosing a class gift? Since their jobs are ill defined, so are the talents and skills that may help them perform well. It's hard to measure respectability, organization, effectiveness, teamwork, making the whole thing fun. Yet a class leader's reputation and sense of self-worth can rise or fall on such gossamer wisps. Moreover, adults tend to intervene when the student leaders are in trouble. It was the coach, for example, who convinced the two co-captains who were not getting along to last out the season, and in most high schools, newspapers are essentially censored and managed by the faculty adviser. When the students' own activities are the only real product, however, their teachers tend to back off. When the school's reputation is not as clearly at stake, the kids may as well be given the opportunity to sink or swim. So sink they mostly do, at least in terms of client satisfaction.

Three senior class leaders in a tough urban school helped me analyze the problem. Comparing their jobs with those of team leaders, they said that the members of an athletic or debate team "know they want to work together because they know they all want to win against the other team." They have a common "enemy" and defined goals. "If you make the senior class win, that should make you feel good too." But it's hard to tell what a "winning class" looks like. These seniors felt their experience leading the class in earlier years—"before it became so popular"—should be honored. "When you're a senior," one declared, "you feel like you want to win, but it's *you* who wants to win—the election. You may say, 'I want to win. I want to be the leader.' But you do it for personal recognition. You don't do it to help the class. We've been through all the negatives and pitfalls before. We know what will work and what will not." Nearly every class officer I spoke with felt unappreciated. Strangers may be impressed by their titles, but those around them, especially their fellow seniors, seem to concentrate on their mistakes. "We're on top but they're trying to knock us down, because they didn't do what they had to do to get on top."

School politicians also have to juggle the special demands of senior year. "There are a lot of special traditions—a lot of stuff already made for you," one explained. In other words, his tone implied, not much room for creativity, and a lot of potential for messing up. The calendar matters. When seniors have the motivation—in the fall—they don't have the time, and when they get the time, they don't have the motivation, even for important final activities. "At the beginning, it was all right, but it's hard to get the class to work together in senior year. You try to do things for the class and they just throw it back at you. It's definitely harder to get them to think about things. They're doing other stuff, or they have already gotten into college so they're all set. I don't think they want to deal with issues like what gift the class will make to the school."

One class president was particularly beleaguered. A group of her male classmates had been blatantly heedless both of school property and of their female classmates' feelings. As a result, a special room set aside for seniors had been taken away from them, and it was up to her to get it back. Right away! She agreed with her class that the room was a necessity, amounting almost to a right—an indispensable component of the "class unity" seniors believe is so crucial to a successful last year—but she also agreed that the behavior of some of the seniors had been offensive and that some of the proposals they were making for dealing with the situation were ill advised.

"Sit-ins and hell-no-we-won't-go posters won't work," she insisted. "That's not going to set an example and prove to the faculty that yes, we deserve this room. It's going to backlash." But most of her fellow students weren't even using the words "example" or "deserve." They wanted action! Leadership! And she felt they blamed her for trying to steer a course between the opposing sides. She had the ever-increasing feeling that "in their lives at home, whining and complaining might actually be a solution. But here it isn't working at all, and it certainly isn't working fast, so they make me out to be the monster. The fact that we don't have the room back yet? Well, I must be doing something wrong!"

The situation, she reluctantly concluded, was made worse because she was a girl. "I don't think students are used to having a female leader and I think particularly the male portion of my grade has a hard time with that. They really do. I never thought it would be the case, but I think it is." Her voice was troubled. "They're more willing to listen when a man says please be quiet than to me. Even the girls! They doubt me more. They doubt my ability. It takes getting used to." There was a long silence.

"You have to be tough," she continued, with a new resolve in her voice. "You can't be nice all the time. You have to be very direct. And when you are, there's the classic title. You know, it rhymes with *witch*." She smiled then, a wonderful smile, part shy, part sardonic. And she wasn't giving up. "As president, I had to learn that you can't please everyone," she concluded. "I just have to take the stand that I think is fitting." The well-worn phrase *alone at the top* applied to her and for the first time, which made it extra painful. Still, she meant to demonstrate that seniors could set good examples, both in making their case and in deserving their privileges. "I have a couple of ideas for the room. I'm not guaranteeing that they are going to work, but I think we should be given a chance to try them."

Leading acquaintances is one thing; leading friends, another. If the essence of leadership is inspiring others to do what they do not think they want to do, where better to start than with those who know and like you already? One leader, in particular, was grateful for a classmate who "shared my vision. We were good friends before but now we're better friends." But it did not always turn out that way. "I've noticed that people who I thought were my friends really aren't," one class president said. "Either that, or I've lost a lot of friends in this job." Nagging was an inevitable part of student activities; so were disagreements. "I had a lot of friends on the staff," an editor said, "and I found myself sometimes being torn between them." As each side of a controversy hones its arguments, it finds it hard to appreciate the leader's desire—even duty—to be above the fray.

By spring, a very few seniors still see themselves as leaders. "This job is going to be over," one senior I spoke with supposed, "but it hasn't hit me yet." They are "training" their successors. "I feel like I have to help the underclassmen learn how to manage, so that when I'm gone, these things will still get done." Some seniors even use their senior projects to create videos and write handbooks so that "younger students can benefit from our mistakes." They seem to have forgotten how unwilling they had been a few months earlier to take advice from their own predecessors. All the time, all the energy, all the homework not done seem worth it to this tiny percentage of genuine senior leaders. Even those who are eager to stop leading for the moment admit they will remember their senior year largely in terms of the leadership experience. In their nostalgia-management phase in late spring, they know they will remember themselves as captains, as editors, as class presidents for many years to come. With rest and perspective, their memories may even become fond ones.

For most others, however, the widespread impression as the year progresses is of people who are letting one another down. "At the beginning they were excited about our plans," one leader claimed, "but at the end they said everything we tried to do was lousy. People wondered why we didn't do everything they had in mind, when sometimes they never even told us!" They are tired of responsibility. "When I get overwhelmed, I try to put someone else in charge but they don't know what they are doing. What they do, they only half do, and then I have to do it all over again. When I set up a committee and they don't do the work, it's on me. I sometimes feel as if I'm on that committee all by myself."

By the end of the year, the senior year as "a big leadership experience" for all is a hollow, often bitter, memory. It is tainted, even for the leaders themselves, by the general impression that it is only another form of grandstanding. Preparing to hand over their jobs to underclassmen, all but a handful are ready to give them up, happy to join the ranks of followers again. "People see you in a certain way when you're the president of your class," one observed. "You're automatically labeled. I'd like to blend in for a while. I don't really care about the prom that much, but I was in charge of it, so I had to put in all this time and energy. Maybe I'll be able to pick and choose more next year. I want to personalize what I'll put my energy into—like maybe a women's activist group." Participation in such a group might not impress a college admissions officer as much as the presidency of the senior class, but, next year, that wouldn't be her problem.

Like so many other aspects of senior year, the time and stress which leadership requires—in athletics, clubs, class offices—now seem inappropriate. It has all been too much. Even when seniors have reason to be proud of their accomplishments, they feel that school leadership is cheapened by the obvious manipulation involved. It is also harder and more thankless than it has any right to be. Once again the situation is riddled with irony. "Seniors have gotten to the point where they don't want to be led around," one of them observed, "but they don't want to lead either."

* * *

Extracurricular activities in high school have for decades been essential vehicles for the development of a clearer sense of one's own potential in a variety of areas. They have enabled seniors to think about their future—not just where they will go after high school, but what they will do with their education, what kind of career they might envision for themselves. Tying these activities to the colleges' ongoing programs and to their admissions policies means that seniors are in danger of being subsumed by the immediate challenge of selectivity and manipulation. This is troubling, warping, and it borders on the dishonest: it is also a lost opportunity.

6 Senioritis

Lisa didn't seem like a candidate for "senioritis." The stereotype of a lazy and entitled student couldn't be applied to her. But she too felt more and more restless in her last months of high school; she too felt demoralized by her acquiescence in "the system"; she too faced the challenge of being chosen and rejected and then having to make choices herself. Her emotions overwhelmed her. The result was an unexpected disorientation during the second half of her senior year that affected her mood, her self-esteem, and her academic achievement.

Lisa's case of the disease set in shortly after her college applications had been completed. All through the fall, she had felt superior because she was handling the challenge in a sensible and measured way. She had known what she wanted for years. Her search had been relatively focused; she had applied to only four colleges, and "I probably spent five hours tops on the applications over the course of three weeks, so for me it wasn't very time consuming. Applying to college is not painful, but I was glad when all the interviews were over and everything was sent in the mail. It's out of my hands now. Let *them* do some work for a change! I was just so happy to get back to my real life. Whether I ever get into college doesn't matter to me at this point. Forget it."

She intended to isolate herself from the whole process. "I feel like my brain is fried. I'm trying to push every thought of essays and college out of my head until it is absolutely necessary." But those thoughts kept sneaking back. "I kept thinking about the fact that the colleges would be getting my applications and looking at them. Just thinking about it made me very stressful. When I sent in my applications, I was feeling really confident. I'll get in, sure; they really want me. But two days later I felt, No! Why would they want me? It's that kind of torment—self-torment, up and down." She thought for a while, recovering her balance. "I'm sure I'll be accepted into at least one of them," she said, but the tone in her voice relayed another message entirely. First, she was not as sure as she wished she were. And second, would one acceptance really be enough?

Yes, it would. "You can finally only go to one college. I just realized that the V in CV—as in, padding the old CV—that stands for *vita*. Life. *My* life! I want to work on being in the play. I want to work on doing my assignments. I want to see people that I haven't been able to see or talk to for I don't know how long because of these stupid things." She was even able to weather what would have been a disaster earlier. "I felt pretty good about the job I'd done," she remarked. "Two days after I sent out one of them, I realized I hadn't filled in one whole section. But I just thought, Oh well."

Adjusting to life after applications turned out to be more problematic than Lisa had expected. Convinced that there was little left that she could do to improve her chances, she was nevertheless not as elated as she had expected to be. She had not anticipated this period of limbo. After months of hyperactivity, she seemed almost passive as she awaited her verdict. But intense self-scrutiny lay underneath the surface. She needed to decide how much others' impressions of her corresponded to—or would influence—what she thought of herself.

For a few days in April she "got into the frenzy" after she was turned down—"not even on the waiting list"—by one college and put on the waiting list by another. Neither had been her favorite, but now she wanted to feel validated by acceptances to the other two colleges, even if she could only go to one of them. The rumor circulating in school was that acceptances were being sent out later than rejections, so waiting for the mail was agony. She wanted to hear, but she did not want to hear what she did not want to know.

She finally got in to the other two schools, but the experience was unnerving. "I really didn't work very hard on my applications," she now believed. "I wish I'd done a better job. The other ones, it doesn't—I mean, I got in, so. . . ." She couldn't know either why she was rejected or why she was accepted, which gave her a strange hollow feeling she couldn't shake. She had thought she knew exactly what she wanted, but now she wished she had more options. The fact that her best friend was awash in possibilities made it harder. "When she started hearing from schools, I almost wished that I'd applied to more places, maybe one a little closer by, so I could choose whether or not I really wanted to go real far away or stay closer to home.

"For a few weeks, all my friends wanted to talk about was, 'Should I do this or that?' And 'I got in here and I got in there.'" I reminded her that she, too, had good choices: admitted to two fine colleges, and with relatively little strain on her part. "I know," she replied, her guard down now, "I do have a choice, but. . . ." Her voice trailed off, then returned at a lower volume. "It seemed right, the way I did it. But for a few fleeting moments I thought, I could have done it differently, I guess."

What would her senior year have been like if she had applied to more colleges? Is suffering over one's applications an inevitable, even a desirable, ritual for seniors? She wasn't sure. "I wanted to get out of it as a rite of passage," she remembered. "Even with four, I was always complaining about how impossible it was to finish the applications." There didn't seem to be any "right way" to do these things.

Lisa finally cheered up. By May, she had enrolled in the college that had been her favorite in the fall. Her friends had made their choices too, and things seemed much more equal between them. "It's not like everyone has all these choices now," she consoled herself. She was back where she had been months before. "In the end, you can only go to one college."

All those months of worry, the choices, the regrets, had taken their toll, however. The voice that was bold and purposeful earlier in the year had grown whiny. Lisa may not have felt a strong pull to any college, but she knew she had to get out of high school. Though she had "been on the honor roll since kindergarten," she dropped off it. "A lot of things I'm letting go," she admitted. "I never thought that would happen." A person who normally had strong, individualistic ideas, she cited the effects of peer pressure. She was reverting to immaturity, losing the good habits that had taken years to build. She sensed her teachers' disappointment in her, but she didn't know how to explain herself—so she didn't. "It would make me feel even more awful." She would be leaving the high school soon, anyway. "I can't explain it. Every year, people have just gone right down hill. It's not bad. I mean I can think of a lot of things I would rather be doing than homework. So," she hesitated, "but I guess—I don't know. It's pretty bad sometimes, especially since getting into college isn't just a ticket to do horribly. Everyone says, 'Oh, it's just senioritis.' But sometimes I wish I were working a little harder." She planned a demanding career and had always been good at facing external challenges: dozens of athletic opponents, calculus, unexpected setbacks in her health. But now she no longer felt she could stand up to things. Moreover, instead of external forces, these "things" were interior: her own motivation, her own will power. Was she really the person she had planned to be by the end of high school? Lisa wasn't sure.

She blamed herself. "It's the end of my senior year and I want to have fun, so I should make the most of it and improve my attitude," she lamented. "But I can't stand this school one more minute. I'm looking for a way out every way I can, and counting the days, and there's nothing the school could do to make it better. It's really how I take it, positive or negative. I can sit back and not do anything, not get involved—but then it's a drag. The last two months have been terrible—terrible! But that's nobody's fault but my own." She had added self-loathing to her list of feelings.

"They Can't Really Get Us"

Lisa defined senioritis in strictly behaviorist terms. "Oh, you know what senioritis is," she chided me. "It's simple. You don't get your work in on time, or you don't do it at all." It isn't at all simple, however. It is first of all an emotional state: a complex combination of vulnerability, nostalgia, restlessness, weariness, disappointment—and laziness and entitlement. The behavior generated by these feelings receives more attention—and it too is highly problematic—but it will not be understood until the emotions are.

The medical suffix *itis* is instructive in describing both the emotions and the behavior: it means *inflammation.* Inflammation of the senior. Seniors are larger, more tender. They irritate the context they have been part of as surely as if they were an inflamed appendix trying to survive in a formerly adequate space. They can no longer function; they have lost their purpose, their sense of a working order. It is time for them to be removed.

In the middle of their sense of accomplishment, seniors feel pain. In the middle of their future planning, they are drifting. Many lose the ability to perform even so fundamental a task as getting their work done, staying healthy, or telling the truth. They conclude that they have simply "had enough." There is no energy left for any new challenges—"at least not now." And therefore not here. They try to explain themselves to themselves—and to others—but they don't find an easy explanation. Why do they feel this way, behave this way, when they are supposed to be at the most impressive time in their lives?

It's a hard question to answer. The reasons for senioritis are legion, and most seniors exhibit a number of them, even when they too are contradictory. Perhaps their reaction has to do with the difficulties of transition, perhaps to the stress they feel each time they negotiate the next step. Often they claim that slack ought to be given them because they have achieved so much; just as often, they are disappointed in themselves, and they expect to be treated with sympathy and concern. Some are just plain worn out, unable to process all the aspects of a senior year that has been momentous or difficult or troubling or not what they expected. Some are confused about how they ought to view themselves: as manipulators of "the system" or as victims of it? As cynical or as vulnerable?

Senioritis is considered a rite of passage in nearly every high school—at least by the students. In most cases, it enters the seniors' lives as a strong and precise expectation well before it is felt directly. The overall tone is one of entitlement. "I personally think we deserve a mental break," said one about-to-be-second-semester-senior. "First semester, school was fiendish." They have worked enough; a long hard trek is over. They have been duped into thinking that senior year will be confident and carefree—and then it isn't. The second half of the year has to make up for the disappointments

"After tomorrow we'll be second-semester seniors and it won't really matter. There's still the waiting period to see what school you're going to get into, but there's no more to do. It's over. I mean you have to just sort of sit back and watch."

of the first half. "After tomorrow," another student said, "we'll be second-semester seniors and it won't really matter. There's still the waiting period to see what school you're going to get into, but there's no more to do. It's over. I mean you have to just sort of sit back and watch."

How will they be able to adopt such a passive attitude when they are still in school? The most common plan is to ease their workload. "I'm dropping courses. I'm taking two arts, two independents, and I'm dropping math." Can they? They will lose the credits, and they may not approve of themselves for doing it, but they are going to drop them all the same. "We don't want to sign up for hard courses," one student explained, "because the majority of us realize that there's going to be a lot of other things at the end of the year that we're going to care about besides school." So they go through their list, dropping the courses that were there primarily to impress the colleges, substituting them with others that would have been harder to explain in their applications. A student who wanted to become an engineer had postponed a difficult course until the second semester. Doing it that way would make it too late for him to be penalized for the bad grade he expected to get in it.

"The senior slump," one student candidly admitted, "is the first chance to break your routine. It is a chance to change focus and look for something new. I signed up for two half-courses in the fall purposely, so I could switch to easy ones in the spring." Some of the new courses reflected real interests on their part, but mostly, the students admitted with a kind of bravado, they were "outright hacks." Most of all, homework and tests were to be strenuously avoided.

Even when they are not changing their courses, they plan to change their work habits. "I'm sure the workload will be pretty much the same," said one young woman, "but I'm just not going to let things bother me as much. I'm just not going to worry about as much stuff as I normally do. Little things, like doing the extra reading assignment that the teacher said you could do? *I'm not going to do it!*" she fairly shouted, her face reddening. "But," she continued more calmly, "people don't turn their minds off. All of us will do the major assignments. We're not going to fail the class. We're going to get pretty good grades, I would assume. I'll do stuff in school, but as soon as that bell rings, I'm through. We're just going to be more lax. And we'll go out on Friday night when normally we'd stay at home and study." "People will still do at least some work and they'll get a C and they'll pass," a young man agreed. "They're not going to get thrown out of a school they got into. Big deal. They can't really get us."

Teachers don't usually hear this language as baldly expressed, though most of us suspect that these are the students' thoughts. My status as an outside researcher was helpful in getting at the truth, however painful. The most startling part of these revelations is that these students are not describing the present so much as they are outlining the future. They know ahead of time what they are going to feel, what they are going to do—and *not* do. The culture is that strong, that pervasive; most of them, it seems, have bought into it. The seniors they have watched the year before, the little stories inside their heads, the sense that "everybody's doing it," exonerate the dramatic change from intensely active, self-directed people to new versions of themselves who are going to "sit back and watch." They are exhibiting the salient aspects of senioritis: a phobia about work, a phobia about accountability, a sense of getting away with something, a distancing from their context, an impatience with authority, and a strong, troubling feeling that they are somehow "on hold." Some call it "the limbo period." Important changes will soon be occurring in their lives, but not quite yet.

Crunch Time

For most seniors, the where-next problem is solved during the spring. "It's crunch time," one told me, and her adjective seemed very apt. Despite all the preparation, all the steeling of themselves, all the increased knowledge of their options and new awareness of their disadvantages, in these last weeks before crunch time most seniors carry within them a small persistent voice. "You deserve everything you want," the voice says, "and so do your parents and so do your friends. You have worked hard. Besides, change is hard enough. The last thing you could do is to adjust to a place that is not even your first choice. So: expect a miracle!"

A miracle? "It's not going to happen, or it could happen," one senior told me, demonstrating the vacillation he had been experiencing for weeks. The gap between prospects and dreams seems so thin, and some miracles do occur. Some students are admitted to their "stretch schools." Others really do get in because they are good in chess. Still others, sometimes even shy ones, hear that their interviews carried their candidacy. Every year, enough obstacles are overcome, enough surprises produced and remarked on, to create a whole new generation of miracle seekers.

The emotional highs and lows of this period are the most intense of the year. A conversation in the lunchroom of a public high school I visited in early April centered on when Harvard's letters were going to come versus when Amherst's were. I looked around at the students at the table. They seemed divided into three groups: the intensely involved candidates for these colleges, who were leading the talk; a few students who had already heard from other colleges but who seemed glad enough to be caught up in the excitement; and a few shy—or perhaps insecure or resentful—students who were quite visibly doing homework. I could understand the quite distinctive reactions of all three groups: to life and to each other. The ultimate tracking—for some, the purpose of high school—had begun. After years together, they would soon be peeling off to quite different places.

All the other issues of life are seemingly put on hold. One student called home from school several times a day "just to check up on the mail situation." He wanted his mother to stay home so she could get the mail and be there to answer his call. In an age of instant feedback, it was especially difficult for this generation to accept the fact that somebody knew an all-important fact about their lives but they did not. There were no emails, no faxes: just the postman. "I'm scared to call," he said, "and every time, my heart is beating all over the place. But I'd be more scared not to."

When the letters come, the seniors feel cornered, pelted by little pieces of paper that feel like bombs. In every high school, there are the horror stories, the shared folklore of the seniors' predecessors in this great migration, this trail of tears. Everybody knows about someone who "had everything—I mean *everything!*—going for him, but still got left out. How can that happen?" There are dramatic tales about the student who decorated his bedroom door with his seven rejection letters. And the one who closed down emotionally and had not been the same since. And the one who hanged himself. These stories are told, but even more often they are alluded to. And even more often than that, I suspect, they are harbored deep inside the seniors and those who love them.

For some, the relief is palpable. "I liked getting accepted," one young athlete stated gleefully. "It's nice to know they wanted me. The only regret I have out of the whole college thing is that I wish I'd applied to some harder schools." He did not feel that he could take credit for his unexpected success as a college candidate, but he looked at himself differently now. "I'm just so grateful that there will be *someplace* I can go. After the acceptances had arrived, it seemed like I was so free. There was nothing to worry about. I couldn't get used to it."

"I'm just so grateful that there will be *someplace* I can go. After the acceptances had arrived, it seemed like I was so free. There was nothing to worry about. I couldn't get used to it."

Others, of course, have a different experience. Some are turned down even by their "safeties." The disappointment is wrenching, especially for those who have studied the process carefully and lined their ducks up well. "To keep yourself from wishful thinking is the hardest thing there is," one told me. She had been accepted by a college but one "way, way down in my list," well below those to which less successful students in her high school were going. Another student had compiled an outstanding record and was proud of the job she had done in high school, but she had also set her heart on a certain college. "Much to my dismay, I was not accepted," she told me. "I *really* wanted to go there—more than you will ever know—and it *really* hurt when I didn't get in. When I called them, the admissions office basically said I was completely qualified, but that there were others who were slightly more competitive. Duh!"

Faith in themselves is hard to sustain for all those who receive the infamous "thin letters," especially those who are turned down at places they expected to get in. But nearly everyone has to accept the paring down of his or her hopes in one form or another. Most have at least one rejection letter, and the patterns of where one is accepted and where one is rejected often go against conventional wisdom. Perhaps she has been accepted for her first choice but rejected for her second, which leads to a new round of soul-searching right in the middle of what should have been self-congratulation. Perhaps he has been told that his scores are too low, but he learns that someone else who got in has lower scores than his. Perhaps she has been admitted but told she will have to do remedial work in order to earn college credit. Perhaps the job he counted on has been given to someone else, or the program that seems perfect has been discontinued. Perhaps she got into a college she would be happy to go to, but the scholarship package is lower than she needs. "This is not only hard," one such senior told me, "it's insulting!" Even those who are admitted to several colleges dwell on the "one that got away." Months later they still refer to it. "I can't tell you about the college I'm going to," one young man said, "until I tell you about the college I wanted to go to."

"Once you get into college," predicted one student during the winter, "you'll be like a little kid in a candy store." But it doesn't turn out like that. What surprises even the seniors who are offered the jobs or get into the colleges they wanted—even, in a few cases, ones they "didn't deserve"—is that they are still restless and unhappy. Partly it's that not all their friends are as contented with their choices as they are. In that environment, one has to be cautious. Freedom of speech is definitely curtailed; many seniors feel guilty. It's hard to feel serene and settled when their friends are still uncertain and upset. It's hard to feel happy when those around them have not been as lucky as they are. "If you feel you deserve it," one senior asked me, "does that mean you think your friends do not?"

Compromise has up to now been considered a dirty word. Now all that has to change—a seismic shift. "My senior year taught me a lot about compromising," one young woman told me. "Wanting things to happen doesn't guarantee that they will come true as you have planned. Something similar may come true, which may be better than what you really wanted to happen. But you are constantly compromising between the college of your dreams and the college that gives you the most financial assistance." A school leader summed up his year as "fantasy-to-reality time." His college plans, announced so proudly in the fall, had changed. Reality sounded like a great word, an adult concept—until he had to live through it.

"The competition that you face when you're a senior! It really hits you. You have to work twice as hard if you want something. And sometimes even then, not everything you want you're going to get. It was a smack with reality." Another senior was more philosophical. "There's graduating from high school, and then there's acceptance into college. At least I'm doing one of them." By May, most seniors are making acceptable plans. But they are not exactly the plans they had planned to be making.

Acceptance. Admittance. Rejection. The very words carry a tremendous weight. Americans are not comfortable introducing those concepts to their young, at home or in school. We like our children to be able to have a childhood, and part of an optimal childhood is to be in an atmosphere of welcome and admiration. Earlier generations—those who reared children during depression or war, or who had more children than they could provide for—may have done a better job of introducing their children to reality. "Fantasy-to-reality time" may not have waited until senior year. In those families, there may have been more forthright conversations about what one could not have as well as what one could. Modern middle-class parents, however, expect to be able to shield their children better than that, which makes this first experience with significant rejection an extra hard one.

The Buck Stops Here

Why have they been rejected? "Partially it was my fault," one student admitted. "I was in a lot of denial at the beginning of my senior year." She had had so many family problems during her junior year that she had missed a lot of school. She started off the year "farther behind than anyone else" with considerable academic work to make up, plus the applications. The applications suffered; she never got most of them in; those she did were rushed. "I just kind of messed around my first three years," another senior admitted, "and I didn't listen to anybody. I thought, Yeah, whatever, I can get it done; I can work under stress. And I never got the portfolio together and I just plain don't have one." He applied to a local college he had disdained earlier. What changed his mind? "I don't want to preordain myself to no life at all. I want to have the college experience, and I think

I could handle it. Then I'll try to go to the college I really want to go to." But his observations were permeated with uncertainty and regret.

Some seniors are nervous about their bad habits. "It's great to be self-directed," one young woman told me, "unless you want to go in the wrong directions. Seniors are not that clever; we just brag a lot. I sometimes think that we're just a bunch of know-it-alls." Another wished he knew more. "Am I a hard worker? I'm not sure. I want to prove to myself and others that I'm not just a person with potential, that I actually *can* get my rear in gear. But trying only gets you so far." Others were growing up at a faster pace than he was, but it was about more than just will power, despite what everyone said. He lamented his own childishness: "As soon as I get constructive criticism about almost anything, I kind of give up. It's a pretty bad problem of mine, I guess, and it doesn't make for teachers liking me that much."

An even larger proportion regret their poor grades, especially the ones they earned in their first years in high school. Why did it take them so long to get the message? "I didn't really do anything grades-wise until my junior year," one commented. "Some people realize that they need the grades to get into college. I had Bs and Cs and I was here every day and I tried, but I could have applied myself a lot more. Some people realize that right away, but I had a hard time doing that." The result is terribly painful. "You look back and you look at your grades and you say, 'I'm not so sure a bigger college is going to look at me.'" Sure enough, they do not. "My high school transcripts," another senior said, "are like big old dumbbells stretched out behind me." Illegal drugs—one form of wishful thinking—had played a part in that record. Now in the spring he was reaping a bitter crop.

Even more poignant are the confessions of those who fear they do not know enough, especially in math and writing. They think they can probably improve in writing but with math it could be too late. "In math, I feel I'm going to mess up, no matter where I am." They may just have to avoid it for the rest of their lives. Besides disappointment at their lack of aptitude, there is a sense of lost time. They are just plain unqualified to achieve their dreams, a fact surprising to them. One student in a vocational school described the tribulations in his internship as an electrician. "I would ask my boss something, because I didn't understand it. But he didn't explain it to me. He just screamed at me. So I decided to get out of the trade." Electricians were "money-hungry" anyway, or so his friends had convinced him. He definitely did not enjoy the work, and he knew it was more dangerous than he could handle. But the most disappointing part was his conviction that he could not do the work, even after several years of studying the subject.

As the seniors describe the process—not only what is happening to them but how they are handling it—their thoughts come back to central concepts in their identity with a poignant combination of bravado and sheer panic. "For me it's hard to promote myself," admitted a plumber in a technical school who had not been able to line up an internship. "I don't know why: I probably need to learn more about myself. What exactly do I want out of my life? What's my purpose in being alive?" What could he do until he knew the answers to those questions?

It can be heartbreaking. "One day not long ago I woke up and realized I was unhappy with my life," an articulate young woman told me. "There was just nothing going on. I had no goals whatsoever! I didn't know what to do with myself. People would ask me, 'What are you going to do when you finish high school?' and I realized I have no ideals. What kind of a young person am I? That is so bad!"

"One day not long ago I woke up and realized I was unhappy with my life. There was just nothing going on. I had no goals whatsoever! I didn't know what to do with myself. People would ask me, 'What are you going to do when you finish high school?' and I realized I have no ideals. What kind of a young person am I? That is so bad!"

She held herself to a different standard than some of her classmates. Trying to stay "cool" and strategic, they felt they needed only to pull all the proper levers in order to survive the year. Paralyzed by competition and status, they were not sure they had the time or energy for deep thought. Thinking about themselves as candidates was useful, but thinking about the meaning of life itself might be more than they could manage. But she believed that students all through history had been engaged in a quest to find the deeper truths behind what they could see. Now she wanted to join the search, even if it made her noticeable or embarrassed. "Sometimes I sound so mushy and idealistic," she apologized, "but I guess it's just something that young people do." Or at least the young people—wherever they were—with whom she wanted to ally herself.

Or Does It?

Seniors may blame themselves, but they are also blaming others. The "system," of course, is full of corruption and injustice—they have been saying that for months—but they now feel especially burned by falsely high hopes. "For the last four years they've been telling you that you can do it," one senior complained, referring to her teachers as well as to her parents. "And now you find out that you can't. I don't blame them, I guess. But if I'd had warning it would have been better."

The question of whether they are in this alone or with others is one of the most confusing aspects of senior year. "The teachers now say, 'You were a teenager; now you're an adult. You're on your own now. It's up to you to make your own way. Do what you want.'" This young man's voice held a mixture of amazement, pride, and a sense of abandonment. "It's different. You go from being dependent to being almost totally independent. You have to take care of yourself. No one else is going to be able to apply for college. And they can't do your homework. It's just a total change in everything you have to do." He stopped and seemed to reconsider. "What you ask people to do for you is totally different." He held to the word "totally," but he was admitting he was still asking for—and getting—help.

Another student echoed this confusion as to how autonomous seniors really are. In our interview, she said, somewhat bitterly, "You have to make things happen and go after it. You can't depend on others." And where were her parents in all of this? "They used to tell me what to do all the time and now they don't even ask any more. They're just kind of like there." Clearly their attempts to give her some space were not being understood or appreciated—at least not today. "I'm glad I'm getting out of here and growing up. But you have to learn how to adjust: your parents aren't going to be there any more to help you out. All the action your senior year is on you," she insisted, forgetting for the moment the dozens of adult hours that had been expended on her behalf. "And even though it should be that way, the fact is that I didn't know that was how it was going to be."

Seniors feel lonely. One self-described "laid-back procrastinator" said that the only way he could survive the senior spring was to "shut out all those frantic voices." No one could help him. "Everything's so definite now. All of a sudden it's your own success or failure," his voice slow and deliberate as he pronounced those powerful words. "And you have to make it happen."

Ready or Not

This is the moment. "So much is going to happen this year. I graduate; I get to register to vote. Oh, I'm just ready. I'm *ready*! I'm ready to be an adult." One of the adjectives high school seniors like to use to describe themselves is *ready.* It is part of the status of being a senior. If you ask seniors how they are, they reply in a single word, "Ready." If you ask their parents how the senior is, even they say, "Ready." But ready for what? The same word can be used to describe both the qualities that will enable them to survive in another place and the impatience that the seniors are increasingly feeling where they are. Many seniors are not making the distinction between these very different conditions. Still, "ready" or not, they need to make their plans to move along.

At first it's fun. Once admission letters are received and job offers collected, the "baton" passes back to the seniors. They have won—or received second or fifth prizes in—the contest. They are being courted again; "visiting days" are offered; once again they are the ones who need to be impressed.

Making general plans for the future earlier in the year has the aspect of a chase. There is so much emphasis on the competition, they haven't internalized the fact that they will be living their lives in a different time and place. Once they get in, college is seen less as a prize, more as an environment, an important part of life just as high school has been. The more they leave the contest behind and realize they are committing themselves to one course or another, the more anxious they become. And since anxiety rarely enhances the human personality, most seniors are as difficult to live with as they have been all year.

What to do? "It's the only thing I could have done," a senior told me years ago, "because that's what I did." It is a wonderful example of teenage hubris, and ever since, I have envied his certainty.

Indeed, many American children have had considerable experience making decisions. People in other cultures find the latitude we give our young quite disconcerting. I remember an older Australian friend warning me that I would turn my two-year-old into a neurotic if I continued to ask him to choose which cereal he wanted to eat in the morning. Although high school seniors may be experienced in making low-level decisions like that one, they truly quake before ones this large. At stake is not just next year, "It's having to figure out what you want to do with your life." It's where they will live; it's what they will study; it's whom they will meet; it's how they will play—and in the case of college, it's how much they and their families will have to pay to make it all possible. Adjusting to and then picking among their options is harder work than they have anticipated. They shudder under its emotional weight. The conventional wisdom is that this is the first major decision that is theirs alone to make. "You need to go on your own," said one student. "If you have any responsibility, it's to yourself only. Not to other people." Yet their choices clearly have an impact on others—an impact that although often unmentioned, adds to their gravity as they stand at the crossroads.

Since this is much more complicated than just getting a placement for the fall, a new round of soul-searching begins. How can they make their decisions unless they know what they need to prosper elsewhere? Not only *from* the new environment, but as participants *in* it? Ever since the public version of their collection of virtues has been exhibited and sent off, many seniors have begun to compile a private version. Now they stack up their particular characteristics against what they believe there is to do in this world. In their applications, they have portrayed themselves as serious yet lively, serene yet focused. "Not too much of a nerd," as one put it, "but worth backing." They recognize themselves, but just barely, in such portraits.

For years they have worried about whether they are smart, good-looking, funny, friendly—not to mention tall or thin. Now their personal inventory, influenced by the colleges that have chosen them—or not chosen them—centers around their own maturity and especially around qualities such as ambition, autonomy, confidence, and growth. Maturity implies a certain knowledge of themselves, a self-definition that they can count on and carry with them.

Many seniors speak with pleasure about the greater maturity they have discovered in themselves, sometimes unexpectedly. "It's amazing how much you can change in four years," one declared. "I used to worry about a lot of things—some pretty stupid. Now I just laugh about how hard I had to work to pass that one class. Back in freshman or sophomore year it seemed so hard and miserable. I used to be so emotional that I got upset when people even looked at me. It got in the way of my friendships, but now it's over with. I consider myself ten times more mature than I was freshman year."

Ambition determines the heights some seniors intend to scale, but also the depths they need to avoid. "I've been brought up to believe that no matter where I am, I can succeed," one senior said. But at what? And how will his credentials and income, his jobs and houses, compare with those of his parents? His siblings? His friends? After several months of performing at a breakneck pace, at being better than they really are, writing papers every Sunday, producing essays that have no spelling errors, seniors have to decide whether the fast pace suits them or whether they need a good long breather. "You have to either pretend to be," one of them told me, "or really be."

"There's a lot of pressure," one African American in an inner city said, "but it sure beats having people say I'll never amount to anything. Now everything is up to me, and my destiny lies in my hands." His first-choice college had not accepted him, and the scholarship package was crucial in his decision about whether to go to the other. Yet he didn't feel these two limits on his freedom so much as the freedom itself: it demanded his best efforts. A number of immigrants I talked with also had fixed self-portraits as "people on our way up the ladder" that also made them feel they could not afford to take any time off. But ambition is evident in all the socioeconomic classes. "I have felt a lot of responsibility all through high school," one upper-middle-class senior said. "It's not been just carefree for me; it's been a lot of work. I guess it's just the way I am. I always push harder and I imagine I'll be that way in college. I can persuade myself into a better result as long as I work harder than I would like to." Although these days she occasionally

"There's a lot of pressure, but it sure beats having people say I'll never amount to anything. Now everything is up to me, and my destiny lies in my hands."

felt like going home in the middle of the day to take a nap, the important thing was that she never did.

All these character traits have to be reviewed in order to move forward wisely. "One thing I can't stand to do is to make decisions," one senior told me. But they have to—and they do. The first step for some is to return to the issue of whether to go right on to college at all. One senior admitted during the spring that he'd just heard about the City Year program the day before at a school assembly, but he thought he would try it. Unaware that it too had entry requirements, he believed, "Experience sure beats another year in school." In the fall, he had intended to go to college, but after all that competition, he needed relief. Another senior was also taking a year "off the treadmill," but in a completely different way. "I had known for a really long time that I wanted to do something else before college," she explained. She had made careful arrangements, both for college and for the community service she would do. A number of seniors, however, fear any break in their studies. "Most of my friends aren't planning to go to college," said a senior in a troubled urban high school. "They want to take a year, and figure out a way to get to college after that. But I think it's a waste of time. I'd be afraid to put it off, afraid I'd drop out, afraid I'd be too tired to come back to school." His winter of thinking about himself had made him more certain of his goals, more aware of his frailties. "I have to get ahead with my life."

Since most seniors have never left home for a substantial time before, how do they know how far away to go? Even when the head is working effectively, the heart keeps butting in. "Part of it just has to be subjective," explained one senior. "You can research and you can analyze and you might determine that there's a place far away that's equal to a place here. But then it comes down to your comfort." Some seniors, for one reason or another, separate themselves with longer distances, but one girl I spoke to knew she could not go very far. "I need to let go of my mom and dad at some point, but I wouldn't last one semester if I went away to college. I would be a *mess*." She would have to go to a local college as a day student, at least for a year. Another came up with a different distance. "One and a half hours is perfect," he believed. "I want to be on my own, but I want to come home every couple of weekends so I can hang out with my brother and some friends. It's bad enough that I'm going there not knowing anybody."

In the heady, tense days of spring, status is still on many students' minds. One senior could not imagine going to any but a Division One school, now that he had been accepted to it. Another explained her decision to go to a college that was less prestigious than another to which she'd also been accepted. She had attended a very competitive high school, and in that atmosphere, she said, "It gets sort of frustrating which acceptances are considered these big victories and which are squat." The small college was going to suit her better than the university, she believed. She liked the way the kids looked, the clothes they wore, the fact that "people could explain what it was about the college that made it better. I just felt that this was the right place."

Her parents agreed with her, so she did not need to think of a lot of arguments to convince them. The problem was with her friends, who did not understand why she had not chosen the higher-status option. They pretended not to be able to pronounce the college's name, reinforcing the idea that it was "out in the boonies," that no one had ever heard of it before. This made her a little frantic. "I still feel like I have to explain that I got accepted at the more prestigious university even though I'm going to the college," she said. She did not know what to be mad at: the situation, her friends' attitude, or her own insecurity. Maybe all three. "It's like I have to explain that I really am smart enough to get into a really good school," she lamented, clearly conflicted about what "really good" was for her. When she was offered a small merit scholarship at the college, she snapped it up: now she would be able to justify her decision to go where she preferred.

Even in these high-stakes personal decisions it's hard to avoid being swayed by the opinions of others. In the case above, the parents' opinions were good; the friends' were bad. More often, it's the reverse. "They say, 'It's your decision,' and then they criticize you for it," said one senior angrily. "It seems like every decision you make, there's always someone there to criticize it. I didn't like that feeling at all." An excellent athlete, he expected to go to college, but he was the first person in his family to be offered the opportunity. So everyone was interested, and their nerves were beginning to get on his. Not all relatives get in trouble with the seniors, however. One brother was quoted often by his older sister. He had ideas about everything: what would be important to study, how far away to go, what price was the right one. At first, this scenario startled me: she was such an assured young woman, I couldn't imagine why she wanted to defer to anybody, let alone a freshman brother. Slowly I began to see that her instincts were pretty similar to his. By asserting his opinions, and watching others' reactions to them, she was coming closer to her decision. He was acting as her mouthpiece. Soon she would be able to speak for herself.

Many hours are spent by seniors and by their various counselors discussing where exactly a decision could go wrong. "My nightmare scenario," one senior confessed, "is that no one does any work and they're always partying and they want me to party. Or else," he continued glumly, "the total reverse of that." The social scene is the hardest possible aspect to determine from far away. Very little is written about it in the official literature, and even a visit can be misleading because it is so short and dependent on a small number of impressions. "I just don't want to spend a lot of next year," another senior said, "wishing I were somewhere else." One year like that had definitely been enough.

"Sometimes you have to make awful choices," a senior told me, when she realized that no matter which of several colleges she chose, one or another important aspect of her life would be lost—or at least jeopardized. "Everybody is always asking, 'Which one are you going to go to?' and I'll say, 'I don't know.'" A large part of the challenge of the last year in high school is this place at a crossroad. Two paths diverge, and the seniors believe that the one they choose will be crucial, will make "all the difference." They have picked up Robert Frost's image, but not his fundamental equanimity. "I have to admit I am surprised at myself—and not particularly pleased," this young woman concluded. Admired by others, at the top of her form, she felt the need to shrink back into childhood again.

And while she struggled to regain her bearings enough to make the decision, she managed to offend a number of important people. She grew too distracted and dispirited to attend to her schoolwork. She exhibited the classic symptoms described by Lisa: she stopped getting her work in on time, or even at all. Her teachers, believing that she was confident as well as competent, could not understand the turmoil she was feeling or her dissatisfaction with the way she was trying to tackle what she saw as one of the central tasks of adulthood. They only knew that she had stopped being engaged in their courses. The reasons for senioritis may be complex, but the resulting behavior is predictable.

Most seniors are able to steer their way to a decision with more equanimity, but mostly, they just want the whole thing to be over. "You make your final decisions and you're off. You can't go back. You can't change anything," was the way another senior put it. He knew that transfers are more common than they used to be, but he could not imagine going through the admission hassles again, at least not next year. And he wondered whether the whole process had been worthwhile. "I feel that no matter how much you plan during your senior year, everything will change once you walk out of those double doors for the last time. Nothing can prepare you for what lies ahead, and you cannot plan for what you cannot foresee." For him, it was time to stop getting ready for life and to start living it. Seniors have had their chance to decide; now they are going to have to adjust, and let their decisions influence their lives. That's the way things have to be.

Seniors on Strike

For most seniors, schoolwork loses meaning gradually, as more and more attention is paid to pressures outside school. The restlessness and introspection that is so often a part of impending transition grows slowly too. Now that most of them know where they are going next, they certainly have the time and they may be able to summon the energy to return to their schoolwork. But it's particularly difficult to refocus. Most seniors claim they can still work very hard, but only if they are interested and have a talent for it. Nearly everyone, like Lisa, identifies one subject, art, sport, or cause to "return to" once the applications are done. "I am what I do," they say, so maybe that's what they should concentrate on. Developing their passion will pass the time that has been dragging, and it will keep their energy flowing—or so they hope. But the intense feelings of crunch time and making decisions have robbed them of the desire to prepare for the future in constructive ways. They long for it and fear it at the same time.

Are they ready? They can describe their restlessness articulately enough, and they do, constantly, somewhat to the distress of those around them who will be left behind. Most of it centers around the aspects of home or high school that feel like constraints. These constraints may have been necessary once, as one senior admitted, "like last year, when I needed to keep my focus. I felt like everything was very important then." But during the senior year rules and mores seem more and more bothersome, especially around the issue of time. They have more time, but they are very possessive about it; it is still at a premium, especially as a topic of conversation, and they resent the demands others make on it. Whose time is it? Theirs? Their family's? The school's? Living in two time dimensions all year has put an emphasis on how time is to be used. Now they are watching the clock, watching the calendar, as never before, yet these are supposed to be the times they will treasure. "The days are so long," one told me, "but the weeks are so short." Their time in high school is nearly over: it can't go either quickly or slowly enough.

The school day and the school calendar, they believe, are susceptible to evasion but not to negotiation. Thus their absentee rates are legendary, but not for serious purposes; instead, they do a lot of hanging around, with little work or play to show for it. Seniors feel they deserve the relative relaxation of the summer, but it hasn't come yet; and anyway, they'll have to have jobs then. "I'm tired of doing what someone else wants, when someone else wants it, and at someone else's pace," one told me. He blamed not his own late hours but the high school's early ones for the fact that he needed sleep but was not getting it. Increasing autonomy after school hours allowed him to devise what he considered to be a more appropriate schedule. He and his friends were going to bed a lot later, waking up a little later, skipping breakfast, getting to school on their own. They regularly boasted of cutting the time between waking up and getting to school. Homeroom procedures, since they came at the beginning of the day, a time when seniors function particularly poorly and in haste, were seen as particularly "arbitrary" and "mickey mouse," designed for younger people. "I only have four more months of high school," he declared angrily, in describing new regulations for lateness to homeroom, "so what's the point?"

Seniors are obsessed with time. Many have new problems sitting still, "stuck in the same seat for forty-five minutes," as if they have never had to do it before and will never have to do it later in their lives. One school leader said she "could have skipped senior year entirely and still survived college. I only stayed so I'd have a place to apply from." Certain classes are particularly bothersome because they seem like "time fillers." "I've had the same current events class since fifth grade," this same young woman continued, blithely ignoring the fact that the events and issues being discussed—not to mention the depth with which they might be discussed—had altered considerably in nearly a decade. (The history teacher inside this researcher was perhaps reacting a bit too sensitively here.) Besides that, she knew her classmates and their politics so well by now that she considered their reactions "too predictable. I really have better things to do with my time."

Although time is cited often to explain behavior, some admit that they aren't using it well. One student told me in great detail about how much time he had wasted the day before, "a day which I badly needed to use to cram for a big test which I haven't studied for hardly at all." First, he said, he helped his friend's mother out at her store, which took "way longer than I thought it would." Then he and his friends "always get together to watch a couple shows on Wednesday nights." When he got home, he had some calls from friends to return. "One I haven't seen for a while, and the other's going through a hard time." Neither was a close friend. "Where did the day go? I have no idea. If only I would think ahead more I'd realize that I have time for both my work and my friends," he commented ruefully. "And it's too early in the year for this to be happening." What bothered him was not the phenomenon of wasting time, but how soon he had started to do it. But his use of the passive voice betrayed his bemusement rather than a sense that there was anything he could do. He described himself critically, but as if he were looking across the room at a stranger.

Autonomy—the development of a separate sense of self and a sense of agency over their own lives, the ability to leave their moorings and to create new moorings for themselves—accelerates during senior year. Now that seniors can choose more, what they love to do gains more and more importance in their lives. It is a natural part of growing up, but can look like confrontation. "Senior year, I've done some things that were out of character, kind of in a rebellious stage, more than I have ever done before," one said. "I've had my hair a different color, and I got a tattoo." Why would she do that? "The soul-searching thing. I needed to find out about myself."

It's a short step from restlessness and autonomy to frustration—and malingering. "People have started laying off already. I know I have," another senior admitted, sounding as if she had been released from a factory. "I'm bored because I'm looking ahead. I'm not thinking about school or its work. I'm bored because that's not what I'm excited about. I'm excited about college and so I'm offended because they're asking me to do this work that I'm not thinking about. I don't think there's any importance to it." The grade was important, of course—at least if it got bad enough—but not much else.

Even those who consider themselves hard workers begin to see a limit to their energies during their senior year. "I was trying to take too much on," one admitted. "I probably knew I couldn't handle all of it, but I wanted to and I had to." Will power is not enough; by winter, she was looking for a way to reduce her workload. She did not respect the seniors who "got their mothers in to complain to the guidance counselors about how much work their babies were being asked to do," however, so she figured she would just try to stick it out. She noticed she was growing lazy about some things, especially those concerning school. "Maybe we need to set our own goals. Or maybe we're just getting too selfish," she admitted with a big smile.

Procrastination is such a problem for spring-term seniors that many of their teachers give up assigning long-term projects, afraid their students' graduation will be put at risk. The seniors simply don't get to the work. "You have so much to do, but you aren't doing it," one admitted. "For a while I tried hard—for a couple of weeks. I mean, I'm an ambitious person, but procrastination defeats everything. Other years you'd start the night before, and this year you're starting the morning of." So little time is put into it that the quality declines sharply. "My standards have gone down at this point." He wasn't sure how long they would stay that way. "I have no desire to become a bum the last month, but blowing off homework would sure relieve the stress." He had lost his sense of being responsible for his own actions. He was watching himself with distaste, preparing for others' distaste, even giving others permission to feel distaste.

In that atmosphere, work itself is anathema. "I just can't do the things I don't like any more," one said, blaming her disinterest directly on her status as a spring-term senior. "A lot of the time, my learning priorities don't correspond with getting schoolwork done. Since it's our last year, we don't want to be bogged down with all that work to do, and anyway, I feel like I've put my time in. I think since it's my senior year I shouldn't be bothered with having to take trigonometry. I used to love math; my father is a mathematician. My mother always says there's no excuse for my not doing well in math, because I come from a long line of mathematicians on my father's side of the family. But I was just doing my homework and thinking, It's my senior year. I'm going to take the math anyway in college. I don't want to be bothered with it now. But," she continued, candidly, "maybe that's because I don't understand it."

She had advertised her plans to become a scientist in every one of her college applications. Math would be necessary for that, and it was a clear hurdle for her, one that she would find to be challenging whenever and wherever she tackled it. Math classes were likely to be smaller and more flexible in high school, she admitted; if she were ever to "understand it," now would be the best time to get started. But she seemed bent on giving herself a break. Within two minutes, she used the words "since I'm a senior" three times. The culture of apathy that surrounded her seemed more important than the personal integrity that would lead her to be who she said she was.

Another said about his senior year when he was only half way through it, "I just took it as it came. Didn't plan much," minimal even in the way he spoke, and already describing the year in the past tense. In a firm, don't-try-to-talk-me-out-of-this tone, he said, "I do what I need to do, and that's it. At this point I don't do extra credit." It was a revealing statement. He may have seemed diligent and dutiful once, but that was in a different time—at least a few weeks ago. Extra credit was for people who, for whatever reason, cared about getting good grades.

Besides a phobia about work, most spring-term seniors have a phobia about accountability, which in most schools is expressed through grades. Grades have been the seniors' big—for some, their primary—motivator for as long as they can remember. Since the colleges are no longer looking over their teachers' shoulders, they think their grades don't "count." But the change is too sudden for them to believe it—at first. The recent high dosage of adrenaline makes it hard to let go. Some students feel guilty for slacking off; at the same time, they feel a little sheepish about still expecting to do good work. Many people, even their parents, are telling them to take it easy, that the judgment—and, thus, sorting—part of high school is essentially over. Still, one senior I spoke with sensed the hypocrisy in writing himself up in glowing terms, "and then just goofing off when the ink is barely dry."

Others adjust quickly to the new norms. "People generally do things for two reasons: either out of fear or out of desire," one senior said. "But at this point in your senior year, there's not a lot left to fear." (He didn't explain what had happened to desire.) It is among the seniors' most steadfast convictions that they have been in high school primarily to get somewhere else. Since grades have been a crucial component of that process, and since that process is mostly achieved, the importance of the academic side of the high school—with which sorting by grades is inextricably entwined—is essentially over. And that is how the seniors seem to like it. As far as assessment goes, they like pats on the back, but not much more.

"People generally do things for two reasons: either out of fear or out of desire. But at this point in your senior year, there's not a lot left to fear."

Facing such widespread and determined opposition from their seniors, some schools stop giving grades. Graduation averages are important in these schools—all kinds of honors depend on them—but they are computed without the seniors' last semester. Grades are downgraded: they become less important as motivators but also as careful feedback. Tests and written responses to student work are far less frequent during the senior spring. The locus of academic accountability and authority is no longer in the high school. It is not in the considered judgment of a teacher who knows her students well. It has been transferred to the college admissions offices, and once they have made their decisions, it evaporates.

What replaces the lost grades? Not much. "A lot of kids learn just for the grades," one senior said candidly. "As much as teachers would like you to learn for the sake of learning, it's tough when the teachers aren't motivating you either. Some of them can motivate you naturally, in their personality and in the way they run their class, and others try. But it's obvious that going without grades is not what they would like to do. They need those grades, or they can't function. My math teacher says he has plenty of motivators—bad grades—to keep us working. But by spring, we aren't as intimidated, so we aren't as organized. I think it's remarkable the work we *are* doing."

Slipping Away

Seniors are caught in a cultural moratorium: neither children nor adults, neither in this time nor the next. One student in a group interview said he liked being a senior in the middle of the year. "You don't need to be worried about anything but yourself." At this, the others nodded vigorously. Their demeanor was confident, even cocky. They clearly saw themselves as self-reliant individuals, moving along smartly into the prime of life. But when he added, "You're not married or anything. You don't have kids," the alarm in their faces was obvious. Maturity is a great concept, but it can only be taken so far. Seniors are still struggling to free themselves from their high school, from their parents. This is no time to mention having kids!

They expect to be exultant at their new status. "For so long I thought all I wanted was to get into college!" one senior told me. "I thought I'd be really relieved, and I was relieved—at first. But it's sort of depressing knowing that now you're definitely going. I'm getting really tired of high school. But it's hard: leaving my friends and my parents is more a depressing feeling than a feeling of relief." And she had seen it before. "I watched my sister. During the beginning of her senior year she was keeping on top of everything and toward the end I could see her slipping away. I'd sort of kid her about it. Senioritis! Look at you now! She tried—just like I'm trying now. She tried to keep her balance, but in the end, she slipped down. And now I have a friend who's gotten A's and B's her whole life. And ever since spring she's not there any more. She just doesn't—it's just not easy for her to do what she has to do any more." Seniors all over the country are struggling with "slipping down," with whether they are "there any more," whether they still belong in high school.

They fear they are coming out on the losing end. Extra energy even for their favorite pursuits is flagging, stifled by their new realism and their weariness. They are what they do, but they're not doing much. The trouble with "interests" at the end of high school, as opposed to interests earlier in their lives, is not only that they have been cheapened by their use and even outright manipulation in the application process but also that they come with new emotional and intellectual price tags. The seniors know themselves better now. The star in the brass section realizes he can't go to music school or handle a life with a lot of travel in it. The young woman who loves animals finds out that veterinarians have to take a lot of advanced biology courses. The passion for the local ball team that has characterized one young man for years looks distinctly unmarketable—then somewhat quaint. Even to him.

Since most seniors do not see a connection between schoolwork in high school and work in the future, they reason that hanging back in one environment will give them more momentum in the next one. Searching to explain their loss of incentive, they decide they need to take a break now, regroup, the better to return to a questing and competitive spirit when they start up in another place. One senior told me that he had no academic goals for the spring, because when he went to college, "that will be the time to move to the next level. I haven't done as much work as in previous years, but I found myself doing more than I wanted to do. The biggest thing that I have learned during senior year is balance. You need to balance time with your friends, time to study, time with your family, time in English, math, and music. You need to keep things in proportion." His tone went from earnest to sheepish. "I got this out of high school—even though it was not what my teachers wanted me to get."

"The biggest thing that I have learned during senior year is balance. You need to balance time with your friends, time to study, time with your family, time in English, math, and music. You need to keep things in proportion. I got this out of high school—even though it was not what my teachers wanted me to get."

Long after the ostensible reason for their anxiety—where to go after high school—has been taken care of, their anxiety persists, interrupting their sense of purpose. "It's strange to be in the middle of what's called a slacker year," one serious young woman said. "I think you need to learn to work hard and have fun at the same time. But a lot of people say, 'I'm going to be working for the rest of my life so I'm going to have fun now.'" This reasoning was not yet being presented as her own, but it clearly appealed to her. Whether or not they are diagnosed as such, seniors are dealing with attention deficit disorder. They can't study like they used to. They blame it on their "crazy schedules," but they also describe themselves as "too jumpy to read" or "too jittery to think." "The kids aren't necessarily rude," one senior believed, in describing his classmates, "but they're more antsy, fidget in their chairs more." They are like eighth-graders finding "seat time" harder to deal with. But since they are not eighth-graders, others might reasonably interpret their behavior as rude.

And entitled. A few outright refuse to take on assignments, as a matter of principle. "I am a spring-term senior" is their terse explanation, often accompanied by a bold stare. Most, like Lisa, avoid explanations because of the arguments they might engender. The obligations seniors are shirking are not just homework in a class where the teacher doesn't collect it and does all the talking but also contributions to group work. Even outside the academic arena, many don't do what they promise they will do. "The seniors are just so immature," said a sophomore who was trying to organize a debate conference. "They don't think they have to work to be the best team." The tone in his voice indicated he'd been burned often: there was no sense in relying on them. He placed the blame on them as individuals, but also on the senior culture that "allowed" them to be irresponsible.

High school requires organization: the creation of routines, but also the energy and motivation to carry them out. And for one senior, both energy and motivation seemed to have deserted her. "I do my homework, but I don't really feel like I need to. If I don't want to do it, I won't. I wouldn't have dared any other year, because I was afraid my grades would go down, but now I just feel I'm already accepted. It doesn't matter. I don't have any reason to get good grades unless I want to prove to myself that I can. And I always thought I would want to, but now I'm not so sure." She could not live up to her earlier goals, which mystified and discouraged her.

She had not expected to feel so weak. "I thought senior spring was going to be a big deal. I was very excited by it. But really it's turned out to be something where I come to school and then I leave. Right now, I'm just so tired. I don't want to do any homework. I don't want to do anything, really. For a while now I have felt like I shouldn't be here. Like there's no point. I'm already accepted into college and there's this mentality that occurs: things just seem to glide off you. You ought to be doing something else—I personally ought to be earning money for college—and you're just here because you have to be here and it seems like—I mean, look at me: I'm just sitting here in the school cafeteria."

Their performance is slipping away and slipping down at the same time. "It's like a job," one explained. "You get to work right on time the first day and you pay a lot of attention so you'll do it right, but gradually you get to work later, things don't seem as important, you can cover up your mistakes, and you think, Nobody's going to notice. You start cutting corners to make your life easier." He paused to think for a while. What was happening to him and his friends? "Right now, what we're doing is getting stuff over, finishing up things, waiting for the prom. We just want to breathe awhile. We'll have more energy later."

In fact, a number of seniors show clear, classic signs of depression. Frantic to give up stress, they find it returning in unexpected places. They can't get up in the morning and they constantly feel tired, listless, unable to show much sparkle or to stand out from the crowd. Spring-term seniors get sick a lot. They aren't enjoying the activities—in school or outside it—that they have always enjoyed. They have lost the sense of agency that, a few months earlier, was steering them through complicated and dangerous shoals. "I feel faded, somehow," one admitted. "Sometimes I feel as if I'm already gone and it's kind of depressing."

The culture of deception that has come to surround the college admission process has dispirited them. Even those who have been admitted to their first-choice colleges are not really sure why. Is it the tests they were prepped for, the essay their teachers helped them write, the presidency of the club that, in fact, rarely meets? Is it their race or the part of the country they come from or the fact that their parents went to that college or can pay the full fee? If so, how can they help but feel uneasy? Like Lisa, they wonder whether they have really accomplished anything in high school. And those with fewer acceptances are haunted by these factors even more and in reverse: they should have had more help, gotten more "breaks." The wrong people are rewarded, the wrong values upheld; the "real world" reveals itself as a shabby place. Much of the seniors' cynicism may be a form of despair.

Intensely aware of where they are in their lives, one thing they do not want to be is depressed during senior spring. But the nerves that have been necessary to survive the year are starting to get to them. "I'm at a point in my life," one explained, "where I see this big, long table of food. It's a feast, but it's out there and I can't get to it. And I'm starving right now! I know it's for me. I have all this opportunity waiting for me: I could travel, go to college. It's exciting! All these things are about to happen—all this freedom. But anticipation makes this year really difficult. To keep up the motivation and the desire to do anything about closing off this period of my life." Seniors, who have expected to feel like the kings and queens of the jungle at this time in their lives, are feeling instead like caged beasts.

Farewell to All That

As seniors begin to imagine themselves in another place, their attitudes grow harsher. They are not only disengaged from high school but also disenchanted with it. They believe their listlessness comes from their eagerness to try something new. They'd do even more than is asked of them if they could do it somewhere else, away from this place in which they have grown up. One senior, describing her weekend in another city, lamented, "It just reminded me of how much I need to get away from this town! I've outgrown this school, and it's time for me to move on." Though she had worked hard, she did not consider it "a place for thinking or even for learning. You took chemistry so you could go on to physics or chemistry AP. Requirements were there to get out of the way." Nobody cared what her real interests were, and she had little faith that what she was learning would actually "stick." "When I have to go through these things that I don't want to, it really irritates me. I feel like I'm being treated like a kid. And I hate it when I meet new people and they ask, 'Are you in college?' and I have to say, 'No, I'm in high school.'"

"High school takes up so much time just sitting in class doing nothing," another complained. "Senior year is the same stuff—only less of it. It feels like it's just something to get this time over with. I just want to get out of here to do things that I want to do." What those things might be, however, were not as clear in her mind, so she had not taken any steps to secure them. She had no plans for either college or a long-term job after graduation. All she was sure of was that the present was unacceptable. And she was angry. "School is forced on you: you know, Get up. You have to go. Come on. It's time to leave. I never have any trouble getting up to go for a walk in the woods; I'd love to get up and do things like that. But at school you have to learn things you don't care to learn. For example, some of these graduation requirements are so stupid. I'm taking blow-out classes just because I need them for graduation. I don't know what you learn from ceramics. I could be at home right now, but instead, I'm making a birdhouse." She was getting desperate. "I've been pretty set on graduating. I've got to keep up this routine a while longer. But I despise it all the same." The closer graduation got, the less she believed that she would last.

Some seniors move away from their formerly dutiful selves. "I have worked so hard and concentrated on every rule and made sure I did the right thing," one young woman told me. "I was so tense and always knew what everybody else thought and whether I was going to get into trouble. But now, I don't feel that pressure. I'm very passive. I have learned not to feel too bad when I haven't done my homework. For the first time in my life, I read one of my French books in English first. It was a shortcut. I may do something wrong and the consequences don't even scare me! I do what I need to do. If I'm going to fall down on myself I totally won't do it, but if I want to skip class because I know it's a substitute that doesn't know French so it's going to be a study hall anyway, I would rather go out and get something to eat." This was, she believed, more sensible than the mindless obedience she had adopted earlier. She would know when she had started "to fall down on herself" and she would be able to avoid it. "I think it's probably irresponsible to skip the class, because every other person can't do that," she reasoned, remembering that for years she had viewed herself as a person who helped the institution run smoothly. "But I don't see anything wrong with it." She was a person with limited time, with specific needs, with choices to make. When the institution has grown illogical—as she believed it had, hiring a non-French-speaking substitute to run a French class—she needed to think for herself, even if she looked irresponsible to others.

This environment gives rise to the ritual known as "senior pranks." Societies all over the world tolerate a short period of hooliganism that marks the transition between childhood and adulthood but is subject to the limitations of neither. In the United States, high schools both promote and harness the seniors' need to move away from a familiar context with its atmosphere and memories of imposed authority. Since pranks are about resisting authority as well as about resisting lugubriousness, adults need to be at least a little upset for a prank to "work." Many pranks flaunt the high school's obsession with crowd control: there are bunk days, pajama days, water pistol days, and mischief nights. Seniors deface property, break dress codes, and go where they're not wanted. In one school I visited, the seniors stayed out of class for a whole week—but spent their time doing chores around the school.

"Senior pranks are a lightning rod," one senior said. "Or are they the lightning?" Like everything else about this year, the line is a fine one. Do pranks fit into the "roasting" tradition that allows people to insult one another as a form of tribute? Like a lightning rod, do they absorb criticism and take it humorously and harmlessly away? One group of seniors treated me to a long discussion on the difference between good and bad pranks. A "good" prank is "the perfect blend between being smart and being a kid." An example? Taking apart a car and reassembling it around the large tree in the school's courtyard. It is good because it is very visible, it is clever, it hurts no one "except those who refuse to take a joke," and it will be remembered for years. "A good prank lightens the emotional load. Everybody's worried about the future and all that, so a prank takes your attention away. You can kind of kick back for a moment and say, 'Don't take life so seriously.' After all, you don't become outstanding by sitting in the library. Acting the clown around school is the way to stand out." Pranks need to be seen against the "heavy atmosphere of the spring. The fact that you're going becomes real, and then you grow all solemn and just wait for graduation. The mischief time gives some relief from it."

Or, like lightning, do pranks reflect an urge to strike? A "bad" prank, these seniors said, is something like filling locks with superglue: it is too predictable, it doesn't take any brains to do it, and it hurts people and property. "Really damaging pranks don't help at all. They just unsettle you even more."

Somewhere in the middle are the kinds of "jokes" seniors love to sneak into their yearbooks: the insults, the shocking photographs, the secret messages. They defy the restraints of high school not by creating their own yearbook but by undermining the official one. Underground communication is delicious and effective, although only if the right people "get" the jokes and the wrong people don't. Gentle teasing of the adults in the institution is considered fair game and even affectionate, but frequently, in end-of-the-year skits and publications, "jokes" are designed to be intensely painful. They are a chance to attack the do-gooders, a chance for the class ne'er-do-wells to become part of things. One yearbook editor tried to justify such humor. "High school can be a very cruel place at times," and bringing it out in the open, she believed, takes the edge off that kind of teasing.

Seniors don't expect to be seriously punished for these pranks, and most are not. Still, pranks are about humor and authority and cruelty and reputation, words that mean very different things to the younger and older generations. Many adults feel muzzled, afraid to look like bad sports just as the seniors are leaving high school for good. Others react strongly: they stop the presses on the yearbook or delay diplomas. The resulting turmoil dominates conversation as the spring slips by and inevitably affects the end-of-school rituals. The pranks a senior class "chooses" determine its reputation. But just as it is important to have a reputation, most seniors want to pull off pranks that will seem funny, at least to themselves, for years to come.

"Senioritis is actually logical," one insisted. "You're rebelling against a giant new step." The transition out of childhood is, in fact, never very far from the surface. When asked to define the role of senioritis in senior pranks, one young woman said it was "the temporary return to childhood when you're facing an adulthood you're not sure you're ready for." When her boyfriend was going through it, she continued, "I would ask him, 'Why are you being so immature?' and he'd say, 'Because I'll never be

"Senioritis is actually logical. You're rebelling against a giant new step." It's "the temporary return to childhood when you're facing an adulthood you're not sure you're ready for."

able to do it again. I won't have this freedom any more. Because after I get out of high school, I'll be considered an adult.'" Her brow furrowed as she tried to perfect her definition. "This is the last moment the seniors can ever be a child. And they want to use that time."

Goodbye, Mr. Chips

In the midst of so much emotional turmoil, seniors' relationships with teachers suffer even more than their grades. "No one's going to look at my grades; no one's going to look at my papers; it's not going to make a difference what I do," one senior stated belligerently. When reminded that his teachers still cared whether he did well, he insisted, "It's not going to make a difference in my life." He and his teachers were about to part—forever. He needed to insist on the mechanical nature of their relationship.

On their part, teachers are often mystified by the seniors' behavior, and they fear that many of the good habits the seniors have developed are being lost. After years of admiring their students' progress, they watch them lose ground. Last year, she wrote a fascinating research paper; this year, she spits out a couple of pages of predictable speculation. Last year, he designed his own experiment; this year, he can hardly make it to the lab. Rebuilding a car around a tree is cute, but what else does it demonstrate? Is this a normal way for human beings to develop? How permanent is this lapse likely to be? And—even more pressing, because our time together is short—will *I* ever see good work from her again?

Teachers are demanding people to get along with. As one senior commented, "It's pretty hard to stay friends with a teacher. So much is based on these little things like whether you did your homework." The daily rhythm of assignments, of classes that depend on preparation in order to function, of power and accountability on both sides, makes it a complicated relationship even when it is going well. "I can see it from the teacher's perspective," he continued. "They have only so many ways to read your feelings about them, so if you don't do your work, they might think, What does that mean about how they value me or my class? But I just wish the teachers could understand where we're coming from too.

The fact that I'm not working doesn't express how I feel when I'm in that class."

One student, camouflaging considerable anguish under his "cool," described for me the way in which he had allowed his relationship with his favorite teacher to deteriorate. His history teacher believed in him and, during junior year, had helped him "go from a C student to a B. He made me realize that I was better than I thought I was." During senior year, he took both of this teacher's electives, even though they were considered difficult. During the spring, however, the magic was over. "I just blew off his class," he confessed. "I was unmotivated. For a few weeks I was here in body but not in mind. I would just grease by. I didn't want to finish off my high school career in a real slump and I didn't want to let my grades slip that I had worked for so long to get, but I just relaxed where I could. I had other things on my mind. Every time I got a bad grade, I thought, Oh, I can bring this up. Maybe I wanted to see what it was like to get a D in his class! I didn't even realize how bad it was until the week before the quarter ended and it was too late."

He hoped, but only hoped, that he could pull himself together in the last weeks of school. "I'm trying not to have senioritis," he insisted. He wasn't blaming his history teacher. "I respect him more than ever, because he makes you work. That's the only thing I ask for in a teacher: that he's fair. I was pretty conscious of the fact that I wasn't doing the work. But I was wondering: do I really work that hard for a B in his class? And obviously I do, because when I stopped, it showed." There was no getting around it. He had disappointed a person who had advocated for him, who was important to him, and because of that, he had disappointed himself. He was willing to look at the experience straight in the face, although he still—possibly naïvely—hoped to repair things before he left high school. "I don't really like history," he admitted, "but I do like him—even in senior spring."

Most seniors explain their changed relationships with their teachers in more self-serving ways. Although they know that being an adult also means doing at least some things they don't like, they persist in their fantasy of adulthood—or at least college—as boredom-free. "I kept waiting for an exciting moment, but it didn't happen," one said, explaining his poor record in one of his classes. Only excitement can still make seniors feel connected to school, yet they watch with amusement as their teachers spice up classes to hold their interest. One skeptical senior told me that her English teacher had assigned "a novel that was, I'm not kidding, *much* juicier than usual. Really! It is not really a schoolbook! I guess he has to attract us to school, because otherwise nobody would come. It's kind of pathetic in a way. I don't want to end on a rotten note. I want to finish up pretty strong, to maintain a certain degree of—I mean, so my teachers won't think I'm harassing them."

Other seniors stop worrying about what the teachers think and begin criticizing their teachers' professionalism. "The teachers here don't know how to do anything but keep school," said one. "They don't know how to help students through transitions. Some teachers have senior slump too. They have kind of shut down—just teach to get the paycheck. They've kind of lowered their standards just not to give us too hard a time. It's dishonest, but we're not complaining." But he *was* complaining. "We get lectures every other day about how we still have to work, but they don't give us the work," which he interpreted as weakness or even laziness. "You find yourself with a lot of free time on your hands that you didn't have before, so now you get bored, and have to do *something*." With less to do, classes are tense, but at this point, teachers who still ask their students to do a lot of work may face more than disengagement; they may face punishment. "I have to admit," one senior said. "Seniors can get *ugly*."

Now that the seniors consider themselves adults, they demean the teachers who were willing to take them seriously when they were younger. "He's just so high school" was the way one student described it. "We've been going over the same thing the same way. He explains all the time. I wish he'd tell us to learn it on our own. In college, you'd have the sense to stay home if you weren't going to get anything out of it. In senior year, you build up your independence. Part of that independence is stubbornness and that means that if someone tells you to do something and you don't want to do it, you don't. You say, 'No, I have ten million things to do and that's not one of the things on my priority list.'"

Growing up, in the seniors' minds, now means growing away. "High school is just not where it's at," one girl said. College professors would be smarter, more impressive. "I love my school and everything but I've had enough. When I have to go through these things that I don't like, like math homework, it really irritates me. I feel like I'm being treated like a kid. I used to look up to the teachers so much that they didn't even seem human, and now that I see human flaws, I'm kind of disappointed in them. I see them more clearly now that I have more time to think, and they're hypocrites! I find myself not talking in class, just watching people. I don't have to raise my hand any more and answer the question, just to make sure that they know I've done the work. And I'm getting tired of people who are still showing off that way." She admitted that she sounded critical. "I've been grumpy lately. I'm noticing what's wrong here to get the energy to move out. If the people here aren't perfect, then I won't be missing as much. And they won't miss me either, if I'm obnoxious just before I leave."

"Grumpiness" is the tone of high school's last weeks: seniors tangling with but mostly overcoming nostalgia. Their discomfort comes from many sources, but they blame their teachers for at least some of it. Knowing that they need to move away from those daily relationships, seniors consciously or unconsciously create distance between themselves and the people they are leaving. The essence of the student-teacher collaboration has been in shared work and the sense of achievement and progress that can come from it. Senioritis interrupts that pattern even before graduation, and in the process threatens or destroys earlier memories. Despite the handshakes and hugs they may exchange at graduation, too many teachers and seniors end these once constructive partnerships on a sour note.

PART THREE

7 Supporting Transition

Certain inevitable things about the last year of high school had best be accepted graciously. For one, it is a year of transition, with all the academic, extracurricular, and social dislocations this entails. The ways seniors experience these changes are investigated in Part 1 of this book, and it would be a callous adult whose heart did not go out to them in a time of such turmoil on so many levels. We should not try to remove the challenges of transition entirely, of course, lest we sacrifice a vital component of growth. We can, however, remove those aspects that have become unnecessarily destructive and support the seniors as they deal with the rest.

"I just wish someone could help," one senior observed, though she was clearer about what she was not getting than about what she needed. "It seems that every week I learn about a new thing I'm supposed to do." She was not wrong, and the first thing the adults in her life can do is acknowledge how much is on her plate. But we should not shy away from our responsibility to assist and guide the seniors. We may not be able to do it the easy way: give orders or even very clear advice. The seniors' position on the edge of adulthood precludes that. Nagging, also, is often counterproductive—though, as we have seen, not in every case. But as people who have faced a multitude of demanding and even contradictory expectations ourselves, we can appreciate the dilemmas seniors face, and our interest in their situation and our belief in their ability to handle it will provide the confidence and steadiness seniors so badly need.

Sensitive School Policies

What can a high school do to ease this important but inevitably sometimes painful process? In a nutshell, it can reallocate spending and time priorities so as to offer seniors and their families the support they need. The most important changes will be to offer the senior seminar, the senior project, internships, and exhibitions (each described in detail later in this section) and to offer political, financial, and emotional support, via bold and sensitive school policies, to the teachers who oversee these activities.

Other school-sponsored activities are needed as well. Many schools offer the parents of seniors considerable help in negotiating their child's transition out of high school. They compile a list of the tasks involved in deciding "where next," concentrating on the importance of finding a good match rather than on meeting someone else's expectations. There is a lot that needs to be done, but also a lot of help available for doing it.

Seniors should of course complete all applications themselves, but school counselors can show them where they can accept help from others without painting a false picture. Some schools use role plays to address difficult questions while they are still hypothetical, such as what parents should do if they sense their son or daughter needs more help than he or she is asking for. Role playing brings out the complex nature of this familial experience—the senior's own record and expectations, the parents' ability to support their children, the imminent separation—and how all these strands need to be seen in relation to one another. After group sessions like these, each family is likely to find itself clearer and stronger as it modifies the list of possibilities to suit its own circumstances.

Once the school's philosophy is made clear in its written communications and in these group meetings, later individual meetings and phone calls will go more smoothly. Separate meetings on ways to plan for college expenses are particularly helpful, and other counseling efforts can be coordinated as part of the senior seminar. Though the majority of these efforts will seem to be made use of by a small minority of the seniors and their parents, the benefits of these activities will nevertheless be substantial for all.

The school can also reduce the chance that seniors will become alienated from one another in their last year by ending class ranking. The effect this has on college admission is often debated, and there are strong opinions on both sides of the issue. What is not debated is that getting rid of ranking has a good effect on the relationships within the class.

Some graduates of course do anything to avoid their high school. But others do a better job in a new place if they know there is a healthy, regular way to retain contact with the old one. Many high school seniors like knowing they will be able to stay in touch through an alumni bulletin. Communications technology has improved so much in recent years that even less wealthy schools can provide a forum in which people who once meant much to each other can exchange news.

Seniors also need to know they will have the chance to see acquaintances again, and not just at the five- or ten-year reunion; the school should offer frequent minireunions built around the activities the students took part in while in school. Graduates can also remain part of their school experiences by being welcomed at games and musical performances. As individuals or panels, they can be a crucial part of a school's curriculum by sharing the knowledge and insights gained in college or on the job, from academic qualities needed "out in the world" to what it feels like to move away from old friends. (If these meetings are kept small, more seniors will be able to ask the questions that are troubling them.) All graduates, not just the famous ones, have plenty to offer the students in their old schools. Visits from those who have left and survived encourage seniors to face the future more straightforwardly. And since social isolation is a large part of why so many college freshmen are unhappy and drop out (often forever), the high school can consider such invitations and the time set aside for them as part of its mission to help its graduates to be resilient.

All graduates, not just the famous ones, have plenty to offer the students in their old schools. Visits from those who have left and survived encourage seniors to face the future more straightforwardly.

School policies can address the issue of money by making a concerted and well-publicized effort to keep the costs of the senior year down. Expensive club dues and multiple memberships should be discouraged, and school officials should tell the colleges and local benefactors why they believe that "less is more" when it comes to school clubs. Scholarships for unavoidable school fees should be offered. Teachers know many of their students cannot afford the kinds of proms and school trips that have become the norm in so many schools and can speak for those who do not feel powerful enough to speak for themselves. Although the school wisely doesn't get into matters such as how much a prom dress should cost, its administrators can insist the prom be held in less expensive venues and discourage using limousines to get there. If the parents of the richest students want to send their kids off to Cancun, they will. The school, however, has the right to insist that it not be called a school trip, and it also has the responsibility to explain why such a trip does not square with the ultimate values of the school. Schools should uphold the principle that everyone be able to take part in a commonly recognized rite of passage, albeit by persuasion rather than by instituting inflexible rules.

As for before- and after-school jobs, teachers will be persuasive only if they recognize the legitimacy of the argument that how students spend their time and money outside school is none of the school's business. A certain amount of autonomy is needed to achieve greater maturity as a teenager makes mistakes and then learns how to rectify them. Each senior has different financial resources and a different curriculum and feels the effects of diversion from schoolwork differently. Any one-size-fits-all campaign is therefore inappropriate, but teachers of senior seminars should provide information and activities that will encourage each senior to get beyond the autonomy argument and consider other facets of the issue.

School policy should encourage the wisest possible use of time, which means starting and ending later in the day. This not only allows teenagers to follow the sleep patterns scientists say are most helpful for them but also tends to preclude early-afternoon jobs, which have the biggest effect on homework and on sleep. Changing school hours isn't easy—there are strong factions who oppose it—but it can be accomplished over time if the benefits are made clear.

Schools should expect seniors to be leaders for the whole year. Playing on a varsity or junior varsity sports team, working on the school newspaper, or holding a class office reinforces the idea that one can stay engaged in one community even as one prepares to move into a new one. Seniors should be considered elder statesmen, not fickle infants. Senior year may be most teenagers' first experience with transition, but it will not be their last, and the graceful leaving of a place is an important skill for them to acquire.

Steady Parental Counsel

Children need their parents at the important crossroads of their life, and the senior year is one of them. Being realistic about their children is not in the job description, but parents are the adults who know their children best, who watch over their minds and habits, their talents and challenges. Since realism is too strong a word and carries with it the strong implication of compromise, we can better express this watchfulness as aligning the seniors' talents and habits with their dreams. This allows parents to be advocates for their child while at the same time working with the school to identify the environment in which he or she is most likely to thrive. (The particulars of honest presentation, in which parents must take a crucial part, will be discussed in Chapter 8.)

Parents' most useful activity is helping their children explore their particular options, not all at once but in dozens of short and long conversations. After years of encouraging their children to become autonomous, parents now need to be nearby, available for talks around the kitchen table or for long drives in the car. Though the approach is informal, the subject can be serious. Parents need to be willing to talk about expectations, both in the abstract and in the particular, telling stories about when they or others were unable to realize other people's real or perceived expectations. Sharing such memories gives the two generations a chance to talk about perceptions, reality, and the strong emotions understandably attached to both. The tales parents tell should be full of detail and reflection but should not include black-and-white heroes or villains. This will give the seniors a rich mine of experience into which they can dig, but in their own heads and on their own time.

"Crunch time" is a phenomenon that has to be handled mostly at home, since school is so public and much of what students may be feeling is sadness for their friends or anger at "the system." The most immediate help parents can give is to sympathize. It does no good at this point to minimize the depth and variety of seniors' emotions—they just need to be helped to get through it. Parents are the ones who should stay calm, who should remember that more than anything else, their job is simply to care for the kids whose lives are at this juncture. As adults, their biggest contribution is to keep their clarity and their senses of humor. They must avoid clutching at the flimsiest straws, consulting and even pressuring strangers on their children's behalf, or mistaking the seniors' short-term passions for sustainable activities. They can and should insist on a careful and thoughtful process, but once the process is in place, they must keep their faith in the essential good judgment of their progeny. That is how the seniors will be helped to move on with surer and more appropriate steps to the next phase of their lives, to the interesting and crucial challenges still to come.

Another crossroad is actual departure, both from the school and the home. A metaphor may provide the needed perspective. The students I talked with portrayed this as a tense, exciting, glorious, unnerving, and confusing time for both generations. They quoted their parents as saying they were little birdies about to leave the nest, an analogy they accepted grudgingly but without much thought. In fact, as a frequent observer of each phenomenon—young birds and young people leaving their childhood berth—and a participant in one of them, I see a number of similarities.

During the stressful period just before the little human birdies leave, they sense there is something they ought to be able to do, but they have not quite done it. They need to convince themselves there is a reason to undertake such a dangerous voyage. And since they do not really know the benefits of the wider world, they concentrate on what they do know: the inadequacies of staying where they are. "I can hardly wait to live somewhere else," some say. The nest is getting tight. They blame this not on their own maturation but on a fundamental problem in the nest. This cold climate. These restrictive parents. This boring school. This straitlaced town. So they get grumpy and critical, and they tell their parents, in so many words, "How can you have offered me such a soiled nest?"

Some parents try to reply. They say, "The nest is fine; it has been what you needed, and we did our best. It is simply time for you to leave." But there are hard times between the two generations while they argue about whether or not the nest is soiled. Finally, the endless arguments themselves pollute the nest, and it becomes a desperately uncomfortable place. Only then do the birds find the courage to fly, and once they have flown, they find the ability to survive the flight. Or—here's the parents' greatest fear—they do not.

Still, no one expects these birdies to stay permanently in their nest. Seniors have the sense that everything is about to change for them, but many do not seem to be able to move from one place to another in their lives without leaving behind a pretty dirty nest. And here's where the analogy breaks down, because two thirds of American parents now bring "worms" to their children as never before!

The Senior Seminar

Clearly, the high school curriculum needs to be restructured in order to address the problems identified in Chapter 1, to make the senior year seem more coherent and engaging, to extend the intellectual work of the school, and to reinforce the value of consistent learning. But how can an institution built around the premise—even the promise—of uniformity and efficiency handle the wide variety of support the seniors need? After years of learning to read, learning geometry, learning United States history, all more or less in lockstep, the seniors now have only one thing in common: they are leaving the school and are uncertain about where they are going next. Or, if they are certain, they are worried that they may have decided too early. Seniors need to be treated in a new way, by all their teachers. As much as possible, the students should decide what papers to write, what characters to analyze, what historical figures to research, what chemical to isolate. They need to practice setting goals and seeing them through.

The seniors' needs divide them. Some need to build up basic skills so lacking that unless they improve they will not be able to get a decent job in the local factory or be admitted to entry-level courses at the community college. One needs to find a strong graphic design department not too far from home so that he can commute. Those with stellar academic records or lots of money or both may feel the sky's the limit—and opportunity can be burdensome. Some need to resist the pressure to decide quickly, others need to get busy.

A senior seminar is a way for students and teachers to navigate the academic and personal dilemmas that plague this year. It is a serious, intellectual undertaking. If successful, its chief outcome is the steady, effective use of the mind and the ability to channel the work necessary to address both short- and long-term challenges. Since the teachers of the seminar need to coordinate the assignments they give and the guidance they provide (including college counseling, perhaps even advocacy), the classes should be small. The seminar should not be a tack-on; it should be heterogeneously grouped and required of all. It should replace one or two of the seniors' courses, depending on how much it asks them to do. The sessions must be a regular and important guide for student work, though they may well be less frequent than those for a normal course. (The seminar is also the logical base for the senior projects and internships described in Chapter 9.)

A senior seminar is a way for students and teachers to navigate the academic and personal dilemmas that plague this year. It is a serious, intellectual undertaking. If successful, its chief outcome is the steady, effective use of the mind and the ability to channel the work necessary to address both short- and long-term challenges.

The small class size and interdisciplinary nature of the seminar allows teachers to structure a course both intellectually demanding and relevant, one that enables the seniors to process the experience of crossing the stage for all its worth and meaning. This is a venue for reading novels, memoirs, biographies, and plays about leaving home, about formative experiences, about autonomy and community. This is a venue for learning about how people all over the world, in our age and earlier ones, have handled the tremendous challenge of becoming adults. Whether the seniors realize it or not, their agenda goes well beyond the concrete tasks lying immediately before them. They must think of themselves as part of a worldwide, ageless process. They should investigate not just the rituals of transition in Zimbabwe and in Borneo but also what each aspect of these rituals means to those who engage in it. Reading about how Helen Keller or Martin Luther handled similar "rites of passage" can help seniors see some aspects of their own situation more clearly.

What tasks is an eighteen-year-old expected to face in India, in South Africa, in France? What similarities and differences are there between these young people and American seniors? Which challenges are universal for those on the cusp of adulthood? Which are particular to the Western tradition? To the American tradition? Do they vary by race or class? Are they avoidable or unavoidable? What did society think about high school seniors in 1920? 1950? 1980? How might that have influenced the expectations their relatives have of them or they have of themselves?

An early topic for the seminar should be the expectations summarized in the introduction. To expect much of someone is to pay him a tremendous compliment, but just now, seniors feel overwhelmed. They need to feel that the adults in their lives realize how much they are being asked to do, that time and guidance will be made available to sort it all out. Since expectations will not go away, no matter how hard one tries to squash them, it is wise to understand where each expectation came from so that the seniors can gauge its importance in a crowded field. One senior described expectations as "the baggage that is on the senior train." Most students manage to carry this baggage, though each one spends a lot of time repacking these expectations into his or her own mental and emotional backpack. But if their challenge is acknowledged, and if they are helped to address it more squarely, methodically, and in a wider context, their load may be easier to bear.

The senior seminar is also the time and place for varied writing assignments. Everyone should be writing a lot, but some should be composing scholarship essays, others preparing reports on local job options, still others ruminating about the experience of being a senior. Writing down the thoughts floating around in one's head has a way of taming these thoughts, putting them to work. Journals are a particularly useful way to prompt seniors to face and demystify the plethora of sometimes contradictory challenges. This helps seniors handle a welcome but unfamiliar load, winnow out what is unnecessary or could be postponed and set up avenues of reliable help.

A yearlong seminar inevitably takes on an important counseling function. Deciding what's next requires knowing oneself well, never a quick or easy project, especially in a person who is changing a lot, but talking helps. The rhythms of the year affect each student differently, but the changes in mood are substantial, and the job of the counselor changes accordingly. In the senior seminar students and teachers can stay in touch throughout the year, offer one another support, inform and cajole one another, and combat the fear and doldrums so often associated with waiting.

But there are often more than two people in the teacher-senior relationship. The ghosts of seniors' freshman selves are looking over many of their shoulders. However childish, those ninth graders had had their high school careers ahead of them, and their goals may have been very high. They are the seniors' sternest critics. Has high school really been all it should and could have been? Have all their expectations been met? It is an uncomfortable question to have to answer, especially when it is forced on them by being scrutinized and then judged by strangers. If the seniors still have not figured themselves out, it's not for lack of being interested. The topics taken up by the seminar and the ongoing relationships with the teachers and one's fellow seniors are likely to help.

Another purpose of the seminar early in the year is to get seniors to set priorities. One assignment can be to gather their tasks into categories: what is more important, what less; what is important to others, to themselves, to both themselves and others, and why; what must be done this week, what can be done next month. This is such hard work that the seniors are sure to grumble, but most will be grateful for the perspective they gain.

Short-term projects should be combined with a distinct effort to reinforce wider skills that ought to be mastered by the end of the year. For example, a teacher who wants to instruct her students in doing serious research should see to it that the research they do is original, significant, and shared and leads to the idea of research as a way to lead one's life, not just as a way to please a teacher or produce a paper that has little personal meaning. She should make assignments that involve using the Internet and the library and interviewing authorities and the general public. She should teach her students the weight to give the resulting information and how to assess and record it in expository or analytical essays.

A teacher who wants to give his students experience in writing comparative essays can ask them to compare two, three, or five college courses on the same subject, or how the study of business is different from the study of economics, or how this college's approach to teaching communications differs from that one's, or how considering two options compares with considering five. What aspects of intelligent decision making are brought to bear in each process?

The senior seminar can also take up what higher education costs. More than two thirds of a senior class enrolls in college these days; others embark on training programs paid for by the government, their employer, their family, or themselves. Seniors should therefore learn about the history of funding postsecondary education in the United States and in other countries. They should think about the nation's priorities in this respect and be familiar with which politicians have proposed what and why. Funding issues are related to the purposes of higher education, so seniors can fruitfully discuss why it may or may not be in the public interest to help pay for an individual's education. Discussing the arguments behind needs-based versus merit scholarships helps the seniors who are going on to college understand the process of which they are a part.

The seminar can also teach students how to look for scholarships, how to understand the guidelines, and how to determine where they stand within them. Information on local options and scholarships is of special help to those who may not otherwise be aware of them. When this material is not available, the seniors should produce it—in English and Spanish, in both oral and written form (possibly in a video and on a website).

Seniors will appreciate doing well what they might otherwise have done badly. By writing and rewriting essays and sharing them with others in the seminar as well as with the teacher, the writers will attain not only more clarity but more depth. Communication forces one to summarize data, make a case, see what is most important. Just choosing what to compare will help seniors understand their own limitations and priorities, and reading and discussing the essays of their peers will help them understand how different someone else's path is likely to be. Yet they share the struggle to find and to shape that path. These problem-solving skills are emphasized by employer after employer when they hire both high school and college graduates.

A student's progress through the seminar should be constantly and thoroughly assessed, with written reports presented to the seniors, their parents, college admissions officers, and prospective employers. Two portfolios can be developed: one for each student individually, and one for the class as a whole. Though teachers, fellow students, and parents who work in the fields being investigated should provide careful feedback, grades should be downplayed. Answering one's own questions, and in a way designing one's own future, requires comments, not a grade. Pass/fail for each activity may make sense, if only to give closure, but each student needs to concentrate on the complicated job at hand rather than how he or she stacks up against others. Besides, each student's work in the seminar will be different. Some will come from families who have been researching colleges for years; others will have a hard time persuading themselves that college is a necessity or even a possibility. Some will think abstractly with ease and grace and will enjoy common discussions; others will need much more practice and help and time. The students who are ahead can help those who are behind, reducing competitiveness and at the same time deepening their own understanding.

Breaking the seminar into small groups to tackle jobs that seem too large to handle individually is especially instructive. Working successfully in groups is an important quality in nearly every corner of today's economy. We all say this, and those of us who work have experienced it, but we do not teach it adequately in schools. Indeed, we stress individual accomplishment so much that we may undermine any natural aptitude for working with others that our students possess.

A few years ago, I tried to set up an exercise in which my seniors would read some primary sources in groups of four, discuss them, and then write a paper comparing them. It sounded like an interesting way to collaborate; the students realized from class discussions that they gained different insights when they read the same material; and they could divide the work. So far, so good. It was only when I told them that the grade earned by the group would be each person's grade that the fur began to fly. In class they still seemed amenable, but several of the more ambitious students came to me as individuals to express their outrage at such an assignment during the fall term of their senior year. They could never rely on the writing ability of even a good friend for something they considered that crucial. They would have to rewrite it, and the assignment would turn out to be more, not less, work. I stuck to my guns for that assignment, but I didn't try it again. What a shame. Our nation needs to produce people who can trust one another more than my students did if we are to do the vast amount of work that lies before us.

Richard J. Murnane and Frank Levy, in the provocative book *Teaching the New Basic Skills*, describe the way workers are hired at an automobile factory in Michigan as an example of a progressive company in the modern workplace (1996, 22–23). Many of the requirements are predictable: potential employees fill out applications, take paper-and-pencil tests on their verbal and numerical skills, and physical tests of their manual dexterity. To assess the candidate's potential as a team member, however, the company puts applicants into small but diverse groups and asks them to undertake a complicated job together. Directions and the final product are described, but the way the job is done is up to the team members. Members of the hiring team watch the process carefully, noting which applicants do what. They are interested in how clearly each one sees what has to be done but also in how effectively he or she works with others.

Reading that book, I thought back on the students who had trouble working together in my senior course. Could my students have performed well in such an exercise? Probably not. Yet there are examples of the need for that kind of teamwork all over the country and all over the economy. And too many of today's high school seniors are like my students were. The individualistic, competitive short-term challenge of getting in to college or work has overwhelmed them, but it is important to keep them aware of long-term challenges that will dominate their adult lives. A prudent collection of both individual and group performances will help keep that balance in their minds.

In my more recent teaching, I supplemented group work with a small amount of direct instruction about working with others. I asked how students normally reacted when a job was to be tackled. Did they like to be well informed before they spoke about a subject? Did they enjoy speculation for its own sake? Did they feel an urge to get something done, even when they knew there might be more to learn? What inspired them to rethink their opinions or to dig up more facts? Once they had done the thinking necessary to answer these questions, they were more aware of what their contributions to groups were likely to be and more tolerant of the contributions of others. Some feared they might not be allowed to develop as members of a group, but on the whole their greater sensitivity to the process fostered growth.

In addition to this kind of practical help, the senior seminar can offer a number of wider angles on the subject of transition. These may not seem as "useful" at first, but they help seniors think through the two separable but necessary aspects of their journey, that of the body and that of the heart. We can help them see themselves as important, as unique, but also as part of a lifelong process of making changes and of making decisions. My students in the early nineties were shocked when I told them they might change jobs several times over their working lifetimes. Most were appalled at the prospect. They wanted to "get it right" in the choice department so they wouldn't have to do it more than once. Many of them said outright they would never face such changes, and some could point to their parents as "proof" that this kind of uncertainty would not be their fate. However, this point has been driven home by a variety of people and factors in the last ten years, and more seniors are beginning to believe it. Some are even excited by a life in which there will be different phases, different training, different responsibilities.

In addition to this kind of practical help, the senior seminar can offer a number of wider angles on the subject of transition. These may not seem as "useful" at first, but they help seniors think through the two separable but necessary aspects of their journey, that of the body and that of the heart.

Still other seminar work should revolve around the thrilling and frightening fact that in crossing a stage, a diaspora is about to begin. Many seniors are trying as hard as they can not to think about the friendships that are about to be severely tested. Breaking up is hard to do in any context; not breaking up when the context is radically changing may be equally difficult. The vicissitudes of friendship seem to be with us forever. The seniors' quests will lead them to different places, but the experience of going out from a safe haven to an unknown world is a staple of biography and of literature as varied as Franz Kafka's *Metamorphosis* and Lewis Carroll's *Alice in Wonderland*. They can do some of this reading together in the seminar as well as tend to their separate research and writing projects. One piece of luck is that nearly everything the seniors read or hear about reminds them in some way of themselves. (They are that raw, that self-important.) Seniors who have finished other projects can choose an extra book, use it to inform their fellow seniors on one or another aspect of planning a life, and receive feedback on how to make their arguments more cogent, their example more accessible.

A related topic is the relationship between parents and children on the edge of adulthood. There are examples from all over the world of parents who try to provide extra advantages to their own children. Seniors can discuss the parents' instincts and motives and also the demands of society for equity. Techniques for staying close but also for moving on to new kinds of relationships can be examined. Writing assignments can center around the way in which one's own story differs from that in the novel or memoir.

On the issue of ceding authority, a good play to study is Shakespeare's *King Lear.* It brings up the ambivalence of a parent who knows—or thinks he knows—that it is time to trust his children to handle things for themselves. At the same time, it reveals his children as not entirely trustworthy, so it presents an appropriately nuanced picture. It deals with stereotypes, disappointed expectations, and dozens of other aspects of this difficult situation. The chance to partake in these discussions will act as a kind of therapy for even the least literary.

The seminar can also help seniors deal with the complicated issue of money. On the one hand, money is a very public issue, assumed to be a factor in decision making. People tend to know how much the entry wage is at the local restaurant or how much a car costs or what the tuition is at the college they are considering. They can and will talk about the prices of things. On the other hand, the topic of money is sensitive, one many families have trouble discussing. Income is the hardest thing of all to talk about, probably because it still evokes considerations of self-worth. People may have learned to discuss sex and death, but they remain reticent about these aspects of money.

Given these circumstances and all the emotions that swirl around them, teachers do not want to rush in where angels fear to tread. Their ways of helping will have to be calibrated carefully. Although a teacher may not feel she can tell an individual student he does not really "need" to work to get money for a car, she can lead a discussion in which that point is made. Students can examine the latest studies showing a clear correlation between students' hours at their jobs and their academic records. For most students, the benefits of working—the efficient use of time, the mores of the workplace, the new relationships—outweigh academic costs for the first ten hours worked in a week. In other words, the seniors' conviction that working has actually made them more responsible is true—up to a point. After ten hours, however, the more hours in a job per week, the larger the drop in the quality of their work at school (Steinberg 1996, 169–71). How these studies were designed and carried out as well as their findings are important to analyze as a class. Teachers certainly have the right to expose their students to such information and to ask them to be as open as possible to the joys and benefits of learning, which requires enough sleep and enough time to prepare for class.

Teachers should avoid discussing exactly how much money a family has or how it was obtained. Discussions about the financial factors that affect decision making should be built around hypothetical cases or examples from literature or history. The best material in such cases is specific yet so obviously generic that no one family could possibly recognize itself. If teachers suspect that there are areas of special sensitivity to certain students—the effect of divorce, for example—they can break up the class into smaller groups and distribute the cases carefully. Although the subject may still come up when the small groups report to the whole class, no particular student will have been put on the spot. At the same time, such a student will be aware that he is not alone, that others with his disadvantages have eventually found ways to get most of what they wanted. As we saw in Chapter 3, the gap between the money seniors have and what they expect at times threatens to overwhelm them. By addressing the issue of money in a forthright yet sensitive way, the school can create clear school policies, provide appropriate activities, and offer the counsel of caring adults.

How should the senior seminar handle "crunch time"? Lots of teachers, and I am one, have tried to make up for the turmoil in seniors' lives by keeping their work in class focused on other things. We see Steinbeck or calculus or even the Peloponnesian War as a welcome antidote to what the seniors call "Real Life 101." There are good reasons for diversion, and some of the seniors appreciate it.

Yet there is no getting around the subjects of disappointment and decision during this part of the senior year.

How to get at these topics in a helpful way is a challenge. The biggest temptation will be to talk a lot about the seniors' own experiences, and this will be therapeutic for a while. It's not a good idea for long, however. Some will be so much more willing to talk about themselves than others that the class may become mired in the ongoing sagas of only a few members. A little more abstraction, a little more direction, is needed. The teacher's long-range goal is to help her students handle disappointment so as to recognize it and learn from it but not be overwhelmed by it. This is not done quickly; a teacher is foolish to expect it to be done on her watch, but since she cannot travel the length of the experience with her students, she can at least broaden it somewhat. She can make acknowledging disappointment a safe activity in her classroom. She can help the students who believe they have been lucky see that their sensitivity to others' discouragement is a real and honorable sentiment even though it is also a burden. She can be full of lore about unidentified students who have had similar stories. She can assign reading that considers the experience of disappointment in general: its extra impact when it is unexpected, blaming oneself, blaming others, the ironies involved in getting what one thought one wanted and then being not quite sure. Journal writing about these issues will deepen the dialogue between herself and her students.

This is also a good time to practice the art of oral interviews. Seniors are eager to leave the building and meet new people and try new things; carefully conducting an interview in order to be able to share the information they obtain with others involves skills they can respect. There may well be friends of the high school or of the teacher who would be glad to be interviewed on the topic of disappointment and/or decision making. Part of any life is the ability to handle the setbacks that occur in it. Jobs have been lost; children have moved away; requests have been denied. Those being interviewed do not have to have dramatic personal stories, only the ability to reflect on how they handled the challenges in their lives. For seniors, misery really does seem to love company; a balm can be offered even to the most aching heart by a conversation with someone who has also had his hopes dashed and has learned ways to live with it. Their teachers and parents have told them these things, but strangers may be able to reach them better during this particular spring. This will stress, once again, that one's choice of what is next is not simply another form of ranking, that a student should choose his college or job on the basis of a good match rather than status.

When the interviews are brought back to the classroom, the seniors can identify the factors that seemed to be at play in the decision: money, status, geography, a special program, what others expected. One person may not have cared about status but about geography; another may have had a different set of priorities. If it was money, how much money? If status, how much status? The students may well have grown used to mindless shorthand when explaining their own decisions. "It will look good on the résumé" is a shallow, cynical, and uninformative answer, and yet it has contented them for years. Once they are examining decision making at one remove they can determine what lies under others' but also their own explanations.

Case studies abound in novels, in memoirs, and in the newspaper of the different kinds of decisions that are made by individuals and groups. The seniors—perhaps in groups to take advantage of one another's memories—can review and catalogue the literature they have read earlier in high school to identify the full range of these examples. They can contrast decisions that can be made without too much trouble with the ones that require more serious commitment, that if unmade are likely to cause someone considerable pain. They can compare choices between good and evil with choices that seem to be between two goods. Besides using examples from their own formal curriculum, they can create some hypothetical examples of their own and apply them to their own situation.

Personal counseling may not take place during the seminar, but especially at this time, it is part of a teacher's life—in journals, offices, emails, and the hallways, on street corners, and the phone. It is important to show sympathy and caution rather than efficiency and analysis. Although advice will be ostensibly sought, and sometimes even heeded, teachers need to be very careful to explain the limitations attached to any specific advice they may give. Perhaps they have not taught the student recently. Perhaps they have not been back to their alma mater for years. Undoubtedly, they do not understand the family's finances.

Teachers as counselors are especially valuable to seniors when they ask hard questions in a warm and respectful way. They can insist that before a senior decides where to go next, she or he acknowledge the kind of learner she or he has been. If she learns better from experience than from books, she should choose the most practical education for a while, until her commitment to the field is great enough to sustain the book learning that may also be necessary. If he fears tests and inevitably performs less well on them than he does on papers, he should not expect to learn well in a huge lecture hall with high-stakes tests every couple of months. He will change, but not overnight. How good is he at facing that kind of adversity? How patient are his parents at waiting for grades to improve? Should he go to the kind of college that will teach in the way he learns? How will his choice of college affect the career choices he has been entertaining?

Teachers as counselors are especially valuable to seniors when they ask hard questions in a warm and respectful way. They can insist that before a senior decides where to go next, she or he acknowledge the kind of learner she or he has been.

Growing up is about more than just leaving high school. Seniors are also registering to vote, and the chief thing that discourages them from exercising that right is their sense that they do not know enough, have not followed the news, do not understand the issues. For that reason, a current events component should be built into the seminar. If the seniors themselves can choose the issues to learn about—and especially if they tie it to the projects they are planning to undertake—they will be likely to see the fascinating decisions that lie ahead and make the personal connections necessary to do the serious work of understanding government and becoming a citizen.

* * *

Seniors so often feel alone, sure that no one has ever had it so hard. Those of us who care for and work with them need to understand how much turmoil change has introduced into their relationships, how much emotional energy it takes to keep some sort of balance. These developments and seniors' inability to live up to the expectations they once had contribute to the sense of malaise sometimes referred to as "senioritis." Moving through this period with any kind of master plan or serenity is almost impossible. We should admire such grace as they can assemble and understand why so many try to camouflage their struggle with "cool."

The senior seminar will not solve all the problems associated with transition, but it is a start. Seniors will be grateful for the change of pace, the attention to their deepest concerns, the new research skills and problem-solving techniques they learn, the chance to accomplish something that matters to them. A change like this in their curricular program reminds them that school is relevant, that teachers are sympathetic to the emotional stress and time demands inherent in their situation. A well-designed seminar with sensitive teachers can add much richness to their experience. The seminar's size, shape, and activities are flexible—it must be designed by those who will conduct it—but its purpose is clear: to link the activities inside the classroom with the questions that are dominating the seniors' minds. An effective senior seminar helps seniors confidently accept that the big job of steering themselves intelligently through life is essentially their own.

8 Truth in Advertising

Much of what is difficult and troubling about the senior year stems from decisions made outside the high school. Since placement after high school is selective, millions will want what they can't have and other millions will limit their dreams in order to avoid disappointment. Colleges and employers, not high schools, decide what qualities they are looking for and what instruments they trust to measure those qualities. If they are seeking a uniform standard of previous academic success, class ranking and high standardized-test scores enable quick decisions. If they are seeking variety, however, additional qualities—skills, background, imagination, and enthusiasm, to name only a few—also need to be assessed, in whatever mysterious way the gatekeepers assess them.

Most American colleges use the latter process, and it is fairer and wiser for all parties, for a variety of reasons. Still, it takes time, and often creates considerable uncertainty in the minds of seniors and their advocates. Even when they have been accepted to a college, they don't really know why: was it one of their accomplishments? Two? Three? an attribute they can't take credit for like living in North Dakota or being an alumna's son?

Certainly, the competition and the uncertainty undermine honest presentation and create stress. Too often seniors conclude that what they are is not enough, that they need to resort to manipulation to succeed. This conviction, now an article of faith in the seniors' culture, in turn leads to still more uncertainty, to the warped record, and to the cynicism that has become far too large a part of senior year.

Seniors and their high schools are not the only groups to suffer from these troubling developments. Although colleges and employers look very powerful while they are being wooed so ardently, they will inherit people who have not thought much about their career goals but have instead grown dispirited from "playing the game" and intellectually flabby from lack of exercise. Before real work can be tackled, "senioritis" will need to be cured—and on the colleges' or employers' watch. In too many cases, it is not. Employers do not dare ask their eighteen-year-old entry-level employees to do meaningful work, and colleges are surprised at how many of their entering students require remediation before they can start college-credit courses. The students are surprised too, and taken aback; in too many cases, they drop out in their first few months.

Collaboration

There are changes that will improve this situation, but making them requires the cooperation of all those affected. The first big change needs to start with seniors and their parents. Far more eighteen-year-olds aspire to a selective college than there are places available. This is partly because more seniors want to go to college these days, but also because the frantic air of selectivity combined with the mystery about how one is admitted to a certain college makes them feel they need to apply to even more colleges. Ironically, multiple applications compound the selectivity problem they are intended to address. They also overwhelm college admissions offices, forcing them to resort to hasty and ill-considered methods that only add to the mystery of how they make their choices. At the same time, since every senior will finally choose only one college, colleges are nervous enough to feel they must rely on early decisions.

It's up to parents to understand how illogical and dangerous this cycle has become. A well-known college is not the only place that can provide a stimulating and valuable experience and make possible a bright future. Indeed, it may not be the best place in which to achieve the personal growth that should be the prime goal for college. And less competitive "safety" colleges are not what they once were. A college that a generation ago was full of less ambitious students now enrolls people who did well in high school. The air of seriousness these students bring with them changes the atmosphere even faster than new faculty appointments or a state-of-the-art science building. American seniors are in fact blessed with an abundance of places that offer the opportunity to work, to learn, and to prepare to become accomplished adults. This message is already being disseminated by teachers, counselors, colleges, and even a few newspapers, but the seniors will believe it only if they also hear it from their parents. Once they do, and summon the courage to burst the overapplication "bubble," a number of the dangerous trends of the last few years will start to reverse themselves.

Still, there will always be hurdles to climb in being admitted to a new place, and it is best if they can be seen as worthy ones. Colleges and employers must design an application in which a senior's real strengths can be presented in the way most likely to achieve an informed and appropriate match. There should be many more meetings between high schools and the places seniors are likely to go next. Since the policies adopted by colleges and employers definitely affect what goes on in high schools, all parties need to respect one another's positions and explain what are, after all, common purposes more carefully. High school teachers affect individual admissions, but we do not usually affect admission policy. We should. We could use our knowledge of high school graduates and our imagination to create a better application process and a better twelfth year, but also a better thirteenth.

Colleges and employers must design an application in which a senior's real strengths can be presented in the way most likely to achieve an informed and appropriate match.

We need to stop blaming one another and going behind one another's back. Right now, too many colleges and employers come across as arrogant and dismissive of the academic qualifications of the students whom they are inheriting. They unite with politicians to bully and threaten the high schools. Too many high schools blame their failings on how hard it is to motivate a largely unselected population. They blame the parents and the economy for this lack of motivation. High schools are also hypersensitive to real and imagined slights. Changing these familiar postures is easier said than done, but we will have better success if we work hard to improve our own domain and at the same time tackle the specific problems everyone agrees are problems.

The Application

For seniors, filling out an application opens up a can of worms—which is good. First, the stark fact of selection, that more want something than can possibly have it, is made clear. The probing questions about themselves as individuals and about the present and future communities in which they intend to work have a purpose and deserve the time and attention paid to them. In addition, presenting themselves to life after high school helps them imagine themselves there; from that moment on, most of them are readier to go.

The problem is mostly time. Most seniors' programs don't allow them the time to dig into the application thoroughly. Seniors are stretched so thin by the maximum number of traditional and "hard-sounding" courses that they can't get very far beyond anxiety in their thinking about their future. What's more, the application, however evocative of deep thought, is primarily designed to be easily processed. It is for the convenience of admitting applicants by a deadline. The way the application is written and the qualities it seems to stress convey the message that those considering the seniors' candidacies don't have the time or the money to give them a full chance to show what they *do* know and *can* do. Instead, seniors are asked to provide data *by which they may be kept from achieving* the prize they want. The gatekeepers may not see it that way, but most students do. This perception can be changed, but only by politically difficult means.

Standardized Tests

Since one controversial and often demoralizing aspect of future placement is the reliance on machine-graded testing, we must start by understanding testing's purposes as well as its dangers. We all benefit if at least some of our young people go to jobs, training programs, and colleges away from home, away from where they are known well. To that end, we have to determine what abilities the graduates will need in order to perform well in these places, how to assess these abilities fairly, and how high schools can transfer information about their seniors to distant strangers. But how can the academic "potential" of a woodsman's son in Maine be compared with that of the steelworker's daughter in California? How can the judgment of the new teacher in Pennsylvania be compared with that of the experienced teacher in Idaho? The size and variety of our country seem to cry out for externally set tests.

Even if we teachers could compare one another's judgment in some measurable way, should we trust it? How can teachers be expected even to know what students in other parts of the country are doing? If teachers in the same city or even the same high school are not aware of what academic work their colleagues assign, what they consider "excellent," "good," "fair," and "poor" work—and, lamentably, most of them are not—how can the colleges count on them to communicate the message that students are well prepared? How can colleges or anyone else know what a certain grade means? It takes years to determine a teacher's credibility in these matters, and by then she may have switched schools or left the profession.

Furthermore, are teachers going to be reliable assessors of children whom they have come to love? Most teachers get into this profession because they are better cheerleaders than they are referees. Many believe that the last thing a good teacher *should* be is "objective." Face-to-face with the student, the best teacher will be parochial, loyal, ready to be convinced. Time after time, I have seen students grow (not just bloat, *grow*) on this generous regimen. In the end, teachers give grades that are mostly accepted as fair within their schools, but if "objective" judgment is needed as well, some kind of external assessment must be designed.

The SATs and ACTs, their advocates claim, allow individual students to undertake a common experience—a single set of readings or problems—that can be measured and then compared. The "common" part is probably more useful than the "measurement" part, but as long as the content of the tests in the basic skills are accepted as valid by educators in both high schools and colleges, they will in the long run serve the seniors, their teachers, the colleges, and the nation.

More than content is disputed, however: most high school teachers distrust the extent and importance of testing in college admissions. Good teachers can use both the time and money that external testing takes. We resent having our students limited to a single instrument, one that measures only one or two of Howard Gardner's persuasively identified "multiple intelligences." We fear that students who learn differently, who are more deliberate, or who are outside the mainstream cultural canon may be penalized. We fear homogenization and being forced to endorse a single ideology, whether political or pedagogical.

Skills students need to apply are certainly important, and a test that measured not just the acquisition of knowledge but its application might be helpful. However, at this point too much testing measures the memorization of vast amounts of disconnected data that may have been "covered" years before. The imagination, spontaneity, and flexibility that drew us to the job and that make us good teachers are threatened by an atmosphere that has become dominated by other people's choices.

I have never heard a teacher, even behind a student's back, say that a low number on an external machine-graded test is in itself an accurate measure of that student's academic worth. Although we value much of what is tested, we have a wider definition of learning: we believe we should help our students acquire deep interests, speculate about what cannot be perfectly known, and make connections as well as distinctions among topics. These are the very qualities most teacher-recommendation forms say colleges value as well. Do they mean it? Alas, since these qualities tend to be less measurable than memory, speed, logic, and vocabulary, they will not turn up on the tests, and we may actually harm our students by taking the time to teach them.

We fear the effects of these tests on our students. Test scores are reductionist. They label people at a time in their lives when they need to be understood in all their complexity. After the scores are in, many students think less well of themselves; they begin to describe themselves primarily in other terms—as athletes or photographers or environmentalists—when they could just as well describe themselves as students who have interests in these fields. Even students who have done well do not know what to make of it; they cannot see the results of their talent as they can when they have just written an essay or completed an experiment. It is a number, and the adults seem to be excited about it. "It will improve my candidacy," one senior told me, without finishing the thought. Candidacy for what? He had no idea, beyond the fact of a selective college. No one had told him what it really meant about how his mind worked or even about what he had come to master in the curriculum. Nor had anyone discussed with him the several qualities of mind, such as imagination, that "objective" multiple-choice questions are not designed to evaluate but that are likely to have value in the work he would someday do.

Pitted against external test devisers and others who insist that tests are the only form of "accountability," we teachers are not presenting the reasons for our opposition and are therefore losing the contest. We succumb either because we are told to or because we avoid the subject of testing altogether. Why have we dropped out of this debate? Some may not want to honor the test by learning more about it. Others may fear that knowing our students' test scores will influence our assessment of their real work—the work in our classes. We do not have time to do even the central parts of our jobs well; we certainly don't want to take the time to understand testing, to lend credibility to a flawed, even corrupt, system. Most adults manage to avoid impersonal, machine-graded tests. We would resist having our academic or professional worth judged that way. Whoever got—or kept—a job because of his SAT scores? Who would want to? Why are machine-graded tests such a big part of high school but such a small part of getting ahead in life?

Pitted against external test devisers and others who insist that tests are the only form of "accountability," we teachers are not presenting the reasons for our opposition and are therefore losing the contest.

Most of all, we avoid talking about these tests because we know what a painful subject they are for most high school seniors, who are already a scrappy lot. Because scores on tests are not being treated merely as indicators, because they are introduced into a competitive arena, they are overemphasized. Teachers of seniors feel a considerable amount of pain, every single year, on behalf of one student or another who has been unfairly assessed by this kind of testing, yet we seem resigned to putting our students through it. We denigrate the real value of these tests even as we're lining our students up to take them again, blaming "the system" in a way that must seem hypocritical. We insist that these tests do not really affect their lives, but we know otherwise. The material may not matter, but the number does. Our ambivalence as teachers only adds to the seniors' confusion and adds to their sense of disillusionment.

I too avoided the subject of testing for most of my career, but I now believe that teachers and their allies should become proactive on two fronts.

First, adults and seniors need to take the time to study the tests that are being administered, particularly the more valid ones. Most students, parents, and even teachers see the SATs as monolithic. We allow seniors to carry around their aggregate scores in their head unanalyzed, rarely breaking them down to identify areas in which a student may have done well even though the overall score is not what he hoped. Weaknesses can be acknowledged and tackled better if they are seen against this more complete and positive picture. Moreover, we should determine what piece of information or what skill each item tests for, to see whether there is an important pattern of intellectual strength or weakness that corresponds with their schoolwork.

Becoming familiar with and thinking about these tests reduces their mystery, and that reduces their ability to inspire disabling fear. It keeps students from preparing for these tests in foolish ways. Too many cram vocabulary or math in the week before the tests, building up their memory banks, the better to deplete them on Saturday. The whole concept of "SAT words" belies the worthy goal of an expressive and useful vocabulary and suggests a superficial, short-term scam. Instead, teachers should help their students practice sensible ways of building up sophistication about words and study the ways context influences meaning in words or in sentences. The time, the place, the motivation of the writer, are connections made again and again in English and history classes.

When I was a "transition counselor," I used to tell my students, only half-facetiously, that crossword puzzles are excellent preparation for the SAT, in that every new challenge is totally unconnected to the last challenge. More positively, the clues emphasize close reading and the different meanings so many words have. You see *square* and think *shape,* but after you check out the grid, you realize that you need to think *old-fashioned.* Spelling is also valued, if not downright crucial. So is persistence. All of this is in service to a game, but it is based on fun and cleverness rather than dishonesty and shortcuts.

We can also structure math problems so that the connections and progression between their component parts are identifiable and important. Much should be made of the progress a student makes when she goes from a three-step problem to a four-step problem. This is not teaching to the test; it is good teaching. It will help the students in their SATs but also in their classes—and their lives. When students do not see the connection between their schoolwork and the tests, they do not believe that working harder in school will improve their test performance. But when they do, they may even come to believe that having just finished a Shakespeare play or a geometry problem *will* help them when they come to what one called "sharpening up the old number twos."

This strategy will work, however, only if teachers have, all along, been willing to explain themselves to their students. "Accountability" is the fashionable word among test promoters, but we must seize it back in order to redefine it. We should start by measuring students' progress frequently, carefully, but in a low-stakes way. Assessment should be a natural part of every assignment, since there is no point in moving on until both teacher and student know what has been accomplished. We need to make our students self-conscious as learners, starting well before the senior year and using only those tests that can help them in their diagnoses. We need to give up playing "gotcha," relying on mystery and surprise to keep our students nervous enough to prepare adequately. Students, even if they are not interested in the Civil War, are interested in their own performance. They will learn from teachers who are clear about the different qualities of mind they seek to instill and the ways in which these qualities might be demonstrated and used in a well-led life. Straightforward discussions of assessment will reduce the mystery but need not reduce student preparation.

"Accountability" is the fashionable word among test promoters, but we must seize it back in order to redefine it. We should start by measuring students' progress frequently, carefully, but in a low-stakes way.

Knowing about and dealing with the tests in order to help students is only one aspect of a teacher's work. The other aspect is reform. There is no quick fix for the testing dilemma, and many teachers and parents feel inadequate to such a mighty task, powerless as individuals to bring about changes that will in any case be too late to help the children we are teaching. It's hard to organize to do something that difficult and far away when we already spend so much energy working on behalf of individual children. Still, we are the ones who really know what our students need. So we must gather our data, act as lobbyists for our point of view, organize and express our opinions to those apart from the high school who influence what goes on in it. We must join the movement to reduce testing's importance whenever that testing is clearly harming the students in our care.

In addition, we can practice more authentic assessment and use that experience to produce new ideas and alternative forms of measurement. We can address all aspects of testing—its history, its rationale, its dangers, the qualities it tests, the qualities it doesn't test—and not just with our students but also with our students' parents and others in the community, individually and in groups. Where there are meetings, our purpose should be to inform and explain rather than to defend or attack. Where there is controversy, all sides need to agree to listen to one another. To the extent we conduct test-prep sessions of the "here's how to con the test" variety, they should be minimal, inexpensive, and offered to all.

Further afield, we must join together to pressure the testing companies to replace inexpensive memorization-based multiple-choice questions with more authentic assessment techniques requiring short answers in which students can bring something of themselves to the table. We must insist that solutions be found to aspects of standardized testing that have undermined its reputation: the insistence on speed, the inability to incorporate different cultural backgrounds, and the consistently demonstrated unfortunate effect on the nerves of those who take them. We can also pressure colleges on behalf of portfolio assessment, which would reduce the influence of machine-graded tests.

Who are likely to be our allies in this enormous undertaking? Like-minded colleges willing to pay for more accurate measurements. Like-minded scholars producing research that undermines some forms of testing. Government agencies and private foundations interested in providing a greater variety of options for all students. Parents afraid of watching their bright-eyed children lose confidence and energy as they proceed through a dull, coverage-dominated curriculum. Even a politician or two willing to take the time to understand the complexities of this issue. But the biggest help will be from like-minded teachers tired of the effect the most ill-designed testing is having on their teaching.

The Application Essay

The college essay is another application staple; here too there are benefits as well as a need for reform. Obviously, it's a good idea for the college to receive a sample or samples of the applicant's writing, and colleges could ask for more writing on predictable subjects. However, other kinds of writing may be more revealing than the one-size-fits-all essay. For example, each student could be asked to write about his or her most meaningful recent academic experience. A limited amount of adjunct material—photos, videos, audios—can be permitted. A corrected essay recently written for a class assignment would require no new work and at the same time give the college a look into how the student was being judged and coached by her teacher. It is also an authentic piece of work, as opposed to something cooked up for the express purpose of impressing strangers. The teacher's recommendation might also center around the related project, creating a useful contrast in how the experience was perceived by each of the participants. Two perspectives on a narrower topic would give the admissions readers a fuller picture of the applicant.

Reorganizing the extracurricular section to ask for just a few interests, described carefully, rather than a long, long list would signal that the college honors honesty and depth. Writing like this would easily reveal the superficial and the temporary among a student's interests. The application should also ask about mistakes made and lessons learned, either in schoolwork or in activities, in order to give the seniors permission to be something less than perfect. Those unable to cite examples of any imperfections might well be admissible, but the college would be prepared for a fairly troubled first few months in the new environment!

The epidemic of external "editing" also needs to be addressed. Colleges need to be more forthright in admitting to applicants and their schools that the problem concerns them and make it clearer what they consider an appropriate or inappropriate amount of help. There is no "cheat proof" method, of course, unless all candidates filled out their application at the same time under the same watchful eye. This would make the application process even *more* nerve-wracking, and the logistics would be horrendous! But especially in the extracurricular and discipline sections, the application might ask for more short answers directly on the page, responses that would be less susceptible to vetting by others.

The Interview

In spite of the reservations many seniors have about interviews, quite a few handle them genuinely and well. The physical person is important, no matter how selective a college is, no matter how far away some of its applicants are. Although shy seniors may not show themselves at their best, they can improve with practice. Some seniors are able to be charmingly enthusiastic about what they've seen on their college tour. Others find reserves of self-confidence and warmth they have not been able to project in their essays. Skillfully conducted interviews reveal many important things about the candidates. The chance to ask the candidate questions about her interests and accomplishments is especially valuable; depth can be ascertained and falseness detected more easily face-to-face than on paper. And seniors who feel they have done well in an interview may cut down on multiple applications.

The best interviews take place at the college, but they can also be conducted by alumni who are trained and trusted. When an in-person interview is absolutely impossible, questions answered via email or on videotape can be quite helpful. Most high schools have videotaping equipment, so such a requirement would not be inequitable. As with all other aspects of the application, the interview, whatever the medium, should be conducted during the senior year so that it reflects the quality of the candidate's most recent work.

The very best interviews follow up on the schoolwork and priorities the applicants have indicated are important to them. One student I talked with had her interview right after she'd finished up a week of assistant-teaching a ninth-grade course. She remembered that a question the interviewer asked fed right into this experience. "A little light bulb went off in my head," she exulted, "and I started off on the whole lecture series." She found the words easily because she had just been doing that very work, and the more she talked, the better she sounded. "People tell me that I make a good impression, and I'll go with that! I have to admit it: I blew them away. Maybe they like people who can think on their feet, because I connected theater and environmental science." Does she have some advice for other seniors? How did she do it? "I just had a lot of energy that day."

How can such energy be increased? How can the interview experience be re-designed to be more useful to both the seniors and the people who need to judge them? If a senior's application, and perhaps one of his letters of recommendation, has identified and described a particularly important recent academic experience, the interviewer has a wonderful basis for devising questions. The interview becomes part of a process, an ongoing description of work, and the student gets to have the last word. Linking the essay, the recommendation, and the interview in this way returns the candidate's focus to his own deeper purposes. It makes the interview more memorable and meaningful—it becomes part of the senior's education.

Since seniors had been taught in school, again and again, to learn from their mistakes, many wonder why they are not given a chance to do the interview over when they know it has not gone well. Composure is gained more easily the second time around; a different interviewer may understand a somewhat unusual point; there may be fewer interruptions. This idea is also worth pursuing.

Other Reforms

The overrecruiting of athletes and the distinct advantages given them both before and during college corrupts even the most upright atmospheres and gives the clear impression of people being used to make money and gain prestige for their institutions. College sports are a business, full of implications for adults' livelihoods, a complex arrangement even adults in the colleges cannot understand and justify. High school seniors are swept up in much of that confusion and inequity, which adds to their burden. It is unfair to those who have other qualifications and eventually unfair to the college athletes who receive an inadequate education.

The practice of early admission seems devised to benefit the wealthier, more well-connected seniors and the business aspects of the college. Worse, it unduly hastens decisions and undermines the concept of valuable, important growth during the senior year.

Finally, application fees should increase, with reductions for those applying for scholarships. This would cut back on frivolous applications and reduce the impossible loads of many admissions offices. The raised fees should be used to hire enough people to assess applications that include more writing and speaking by the candidates and fewer lists and numbers. This will reduce the sense of manipulation and cynicism and improve the application process as "truth in advertising"—a worthy educational experience.

Of course, these changes in the application process can only happen if the colleges decide to make them. Still, we as seniors, parents, teachers, alumni of these colleges, and American citizens should press for it.

The High Schools' Contribution

High schools can take the lead in carrying out other reforms.

First, they can help teachers realize and accept that corrected high school essays are going to be used on college applications. Teachers are not used to having their work shared in this way. The stakes are high, and they are afraid to have someone looking over their shoulder. The high school needs to help teachers assign, grade, and correct essays in ways that can be explained to others. Asking writing teachers to look together at student work provides excellent professional development in calibrating standards and helps teachers be clear with their students.

The high school should also take the lead in cutting out what one student described, without apology, as "pumping the stats." Honoring student activities, allowing them a certain amount of independence, and at the same time being aware of what is really going on is a delicate balance. However difficult, it must be kept. We can't look the other way when we see CVs being shamelessly bloated. Rules may or may not help, but a consistent faculty message on this subject will certainly influence both seniors and their parents. Clubs and activities should institute apprenticeship periods that are labeled as such on school transcripts. The first year after a change like this, when the current seniors compare their poor selves with the seniors last year who "got away with it," will undoubtedly be hard, even if the colleges cooperate by inquiring after quality rather than quantity. The next year will be better, and the school must take this longer view.

The school should also support its seniors' applications better. It should send more information about the school to the places its seniors want to go, summarizing its curriculum and the most important characteristics of its faculty, students, and parents and the strengths and weaknesses they bring to the schoolhouse door. If the school has a distinctive educational philosophy that influences both what the candidate and those offering recommendations are likely to write, that philosophy should be summarized. Any recent changes in the school's offerings should be explained. Apparent deficiencies should be explained. For example, a school serving a high-achieving population can make it clear it doesn't need the "honors" courses expected in another kind of school. A school with a diverse population can emphasize the measures it has taken to create a real community. The emphasis should be on putting the school's best foot forward in an honest way.

High schools should also maintain essay portraits of each student that paint a full and true picture of her or his interests, activities, and intellectual growth over the years. A summary of the student's behavior should be included. (One written paragraph is much more useful than a list of infractions.) These essays need to be direct, engaging, and jargon free, the work of people with good writing skills and enough time for the job. The more precise the criteria by which a student progresses in the school, the less necessary inflated grades and social promotion will be, but any such arrangements need to be explained. If admissions officers are knowledgeable about a school, they will be more likely to understand a student's progress in it.

Employers are often criticized for paying too little attention to school records, but this is only somewhat their fault. Until schools put significant resources behind this sensitive and important form of communication, they will produce records that are, in too many instances, unreadable. Yet the employers must also be clear about their expectations of future employees, which skills and experiences are most important to them, so that the schools can ensure that such skills and experiences are offered, measured accurately, and then written about clearly.

School records should also reveal what the student has done to further his or her most longstanding interests both in and outside the school. The senior project, internship, or other important piece of recent work is a helpful way for outside observers to assess a student's match with an academic or work community.

This fuller accounting will not be easy. Both readers and writers will need to spend more time and take more care than they presently do. In this litigious age, lawyers may need to be consulted, at least on the broad guidelines of what is to be included and how it should be handled. Political considerations have contributed to the near-universal blurred record over the years. How honest should the school be in these estimates? How much the student's advocate? A dual purpose is built into the job, and it often becomes problematic. My bent is for honesty, since we are professionals relying on other professionals, and we need to be trusted both now and later. By demonstrating that it is able to produce a full and honest report, a school supports its teachers' professional judgments about what their students know and what they still need to learn.

Everybody Gains

The benefit of all this extra work will be to the school's academic program—and to the seniors. It comes down to this. No one claims that class rankings or test scores are all that is worth knowing about a college candidate. They test what is testable, rank what is measurable, and those of us who stand in front of a real student understand that she is far, far more than the sum of these parts. And we tell her so, again and again. All the gatekeepers in a senior's world owe it to her to find, and build on, a variety of credible forms of assessment, ones that will complement, in moral and intellectual ways, the best work we do in high schools.

Items from a student's real work—research papers, tapes, artwork—are welcome in colleges that are prepared to devote time to examining them seriously. We teachers should talk up those colleges that are prepared to get to know our students, and lobby for change in those that are not. We should join with other teachers who are graduates of the colleges we went to—or our children went to—so that these institutions are aware that our important alumni eyes are upon them and that we have ideas about how they should proceed. If they don't change, we should encourage our students and our children to boycott them. Colleges are businesses, and they will eventually respond if enough of us really believe what we say we believe.

The college or job application won't go away, nor should it. On the contrary, it can and should be a meaningful rite of passage in a culture that has too few of them. On the edge of adulthood, seniors can use it to gain greater insight into themselves: their talents, weaknesses, working style, and accomplishments. Their self-awareness as well as their self-confidence can be enhanced. Their honest description of themselves for a stranger—as one senior put it, "for someone who doesn't have to love you"—and the completion of a task that may once have seemed impossibly hard come together to create an important ritual that strengthens them. A better application that enhances their honesty and their belief in the fairness of the system will be of even more benefit. It lessens the importance of scores, of special categories and contacts, of "edited" essays, and of inflated CVs—the parts of the application process that have dragged down so many seniors. Widening the experience to one they can basically respect will lessen the concentration on competition that has driven so many of them to "play the game."

9 Touching the Future

For seniors, the word *prep* has taken on the unfortunate connotation of short-term cramming for college admission, available only to those who have the money to pay for it. Yet preparation—not only for college but for work, family, citizenship—is exactly what seniors should accomplish with the time they have left in high school. So much time, so much effort, have been spent creating their résumés that once the pieces of paper have been sent off, many seniors wonder what there is left to do. Since there is considerable evidence that the disengagement experienced by so many seniors in the spring semester has a serious effect on their readiness to tackle what's next in their lives, a number of high schools are tackling this problem with a variety of strategies: mostly carrots, some sticks.

These high schools want to do more than just get through senior spring and get their students into college; they want to improve the students' chances of developing broad motivations that will prove sturdy over time. At the same time, their faculties recognize that seniors need to savor the present and that they can best do so by answering questions and engaging in activities that are important to them. Extracurricular activities, senior projects, internships, and exhibitions are designed with lifelong, lofty goals in mind, but they are also an effective antisenioritis strategy. "I only go to school for my senior project," one senior told me in April. I felt bad for her other teachers, but it sure beat the senior prom as the only reason for going to school.

Activities

Students learn most effectively by doing. For that reason, athletic, extracurricular, and service activities are among the most authentic and educational parts of the senior year. Team sports, school plays, the school newspaper, and the yearbook are the most longstanding and widespread examples. The experience of setting goals for themselves and others, the sense of accomplishment that comes from achieving those goals, even the lessons learned in analyzing their mistakes, all hold tremendous value for seniors. They are nourishing their sense of themselves as reliable and imaginative workers, aligning their ambitions to their proficiencies, gaining practice in collaboration, coming to see the value a group can bring to a task, learning about the world, and coming closer to the all-important determination of where they might fit into it. As the oldest students in the school, they are its natural leaders; even shy seniors can experience the many ways leadership can be exercised.

For too many, however, that promise is unrealized. Much needs to be done—and undone. Because sports and other activities have been packaged as a fancy product, their real meaning has taken a back seat. Our best response to this kind of malaise is not to cancel such activities but to enhance them and help the seniors do them well. Each senior should have at least one serious interest other than schoolwork. These interests need not be limited to what's available in school—they can learn to sew or to fly, work for a gas station or the mayor—but the best of them will help them develop skills and habits to be used later in life. What's more, each senior should have an adviser who knows his or her interests and how to talk seriously about them.

Because sports and other activities have been packaged as a fancy product, their real meaning has taken a back seat. Our best response to this kind of malaise is not to cancel such activities but to enhance them and help the seniors do them well. Each senior should have at least one serious interest other than schoolwork.

The dispiriting situation for senior athletes has been in the making for a long time; it has crept up on the school, the teams, and the athletes. Many of its most difficult aspects cannot be helped: they concern talent, growing up, luck, the need to move on. Still, there are a few reforms that the high school's faculty (mostly the coaches) can make. They can reinforce the core value of sports in high school by the structure they set up and by the values they stress in their coaching. They can identify significant leadership opportunities for every senior, mostly centering on guiding a younger player, and revisit leadership values in frequent private talks. They can offer steady counsel to their superstars during the dizzy recruiting season, especially relative to grandstanding, and can help the less talented survive being passed over by league or college coaches.

The school should make sure that all seniors are offered substantial, respected athletic opportunities, either allowing them to play on the junior varsity teams or setting up special all-senior teams that are coached seriously and at least occasionally play teams from other schools. Of course, we all know that spring-term seniors on the varsity team can break the hearts of those who have chosen to rely on them. But what's best for the seniors will finally be best for the coaches. The seniors will continue to contribute; they will keep the name of their high school emblazoned on their chest; they will have seen through a project and kept a promise; they will stay centered; they will have made one part of themselves explainable to another. Keeping connections with the parts of the high school that have been valuable to them will make the final rupture easier, because they will know they have done their best. If we treat them like their best selves, they may surprise us. And even if they don't, that kind of gambling is very much our business.

Leadership

Using the senior seminar as a forum for discussing and writing about the dilemmas seniors face with regard to extracurricular activities carries with it the important message that the faculty honors the learning that comes from these activities. For years the seniors have studied techniques of leadership: thinking ahead, being prepared, standing firm, knowing when to compromise, relating well with others. Now these techniques are needed very close to home, and they can be pulled out of the syllabus and discussed thoroughly.

Examples should be similar to those the students are likely to face. They will probably not relate to tales of Franklin Roosevelt's galvanizing the country to support a war, but they will see similarities between their own challenges and Martin Luther King's efforts to persuade his followers to engage in active but nonviolent protest in the face of unfairness. They will be able to identify with the women's suffragists who made alliances with politicians and others despite substantial differences in viewpoint and remained unified. Whether the suffragists' ends justified their rather unorthodox means is a natural topic for discussion, one pertinent to seniors' concerns. Points of view can be argued, connections made. The point is to take leadership seriously, in all its many guises. These classes and writings will deepen reflection, which in turn will enable seniors to develop emotional stamina in the face of confusion and disappointment—a quality they will call on often in the months and years that lie immediately ahead.

Some schools offer seniors specific and self-conscious help in their role as the oldest students in the school. General lectures on "the better behavior expected of the seniors who are now the school leaders" usually fall on pretty deaf ears. More successful are retreats for some or even all of the senior class. These meetings stress the importance of student leadership to the school, but they can also help seniors anticipate some of the problems that may lie ahead. In one such meeting, some seniors and I came up with sentences that illustrated probable senior-year dilemmas: How do I stand up to the faculty member who is about to grade my history paper? How do I edit the article of the guy I'm hoping will ask me out? How can I be efficient but not overbearing, understanding but not ineffective? How do I ask my friend to do a nasty, time-consuming job when I know how busy she is? How do I inspire others to see things my way, without giving them the impression that I don't respect *their* vision? Then small groups picked one of these dilemmas out of a bowl and wrote a skit putting it into context. The results were revealing, humorous, and poignant. Anticipating these and other problems and discussing alternatives seniors might pursue provide a healthy dose of reality.

Seniors should be involved in the work of the school. Recently, high schools have begun to train peer mediators, peer tutors, peer editors, and peer counselors. Attempts to allow students to offer this kind of leadership face hurdles: some adults believe seniors cannot fill these adultlike roles, and some seniors claim they don't have the time to do what adults are supposed to be doing. However, these new arrangements pay off in several ways. During my career, I've worked with several different approaches to having students participate in discipline decisions. I remember how shocking it seemed to all of us at first, but in school and after school, with time and practice, the students' decisions about punishments turned out to be thoughtful and fair. Staggered terms of service allow the half who have experience to acculturate the half who are new. The benefits for the seniors, the faculty, and most of all for the school in these new initiatives are substantial.

Seniors can also undertake service-learning projects in or outside school and forge fruitful alliances with service providers, their supervisors, and other students. Serious ecologists, "techies," and future teachers will find opportunities for interesting and worthwhile work in these venues. Successful completion of these projects can be documented by mentors' reports, testimonials, and student journals, as reviewed by teachers. Tying extracurricular activities and service-learning projects to graduation requirements gives them and the students who participate in them more credibility. The opportunity for challenge and substantial personal and even professional growth during the senior year should be emphasized.

Seniors who would otherwise fade away as leaders can be helped to stay the course. Teachers need to do more than accept extracurricular activities somewhat grudgingly. They should receive training in being advisers to these kinds of organizations and credit when they perform the function well. Overseeing student-led activities is subtle work. Most of the time, advisers need to hold back, maintain their equilibrium even when the students run into minor problems. At other times they need to offer direct help, perhaps intervene, and then be ready for the awkward conversations that inevitably follow.

Senior leadership is not an absolute value. Situations can grow so chaotic or hurtful that the faculty and administration need to step in. Early and honest reactions may preclude more drastic measures later. But ultimately presses may have to be stopped, shows cancelled, students leaders removed. Yet the faculty needs to continue to believe in student leadership, since 95 percent of the time the students will carry it off, and that's a worthy ratio, well worth the hassle and the risk. Schools are about learning, not perfection, and some of the best learning is in confronting one's own mistakes. No one has much fun doing it, but a genuine sharing of power will produce real growth and will reduce the student suspicion always just under the surface.

The difficulties in setting up a program whereby students can develop in these respects can be fierce. Fostering senior responsibility and leadership is expensive. Setting up retreats, providing training, advising the seniors carefully, sharing power with those who are new to it, are rarely mentioned in teacher-training programs and are not things teachers expect to be doing. These tasks nevertheless take up a lot of a teacher's time, and teachers cannot be expected to put in that many extra hours for nothing. But the challenges and the lack of money are not good enough reasons to avoid these changes. Most teachers would agree that engagement in its most clumsy form is preferable to irresponsibility and cynicism. Moreover, once a serious atmosphere of student leadership is in place, once the service-learning placements are running smoothly, once peer editors are helping out with first drafts, the teachers will see the benefits as well as the costs.

For seniors, the opportunity to exercise leadership is one of the most valuable aspects of the American high school. No matter how small the job, the seniors learn much about themselves and about how to play a positive role in their community. For many, the same kind of chance will not come again. Sensitive and consistent support for this enterprise as a central part of the senior year is well worth the faculty's time. If most of the members of the senior class consider themselves leaders at the end of the year—if they believe they have brought a positive benefit to their high school—then they and their teachers can be proud of a considerable achievement. Even those who have done less well will have learned much

For seniors, the opportunity to exercise leadership is one of the most valuable aspects of the American high school. No matter how small the job, the seniors learn much about themselves and about how to play a positive role in their community.

about a valuable aspect of growing up. Student leadership in a variety of hands-on experiences circles back to crossing the stage, to the conviction, held by almost everyone, that these young people need to be acknowledged as near-adults.

Help for Senioritis

Crossing the stage means giving up the nostalgic look back at one's past as a child and shifting one's focus to the future and an eventual career. But perhaps we need to begin this shift earlier. Senioritis occurs, at least in part, because a student's record is considered "complete" as soon as it is sent in; it is therefore human nature for seniors to cut loose once their applications are in the mail. But do student records *need* to be considered "complete" halfway through the year? What part of the high school's requirements can be reserved for the last months of high school? Even the most talented and hardworking seniors have more to learn. Shouldn't they be given more but *different* work? Shouldn't they keep growing academically as long as they are in an institution designed around that goal? Why should healthy eighteen-year-olds, in the prime of life, be on vacation? If a senior really *has* "outgrown high school," she should graduate and start the next phase of her life somewhere else. But the majority of seniors stay in high school after their records are sent to colleges and employers, even after they are admitted or hired. Therefore, a new academic program must be planned for them, one that is appropriate and challenging. No single group of people will make that happen. High school administrators and faculty, policymakers, employers, colleges, all need to help.

Policymakers need to design and encourage systems of accountability that emphasize what is needed for a successful transition into a responsible working life. They need to abandon the notion that one high-stakes, memorization-heavy test guarantees such a transition—or such a life. They need, instead, to study the schools that have the best record of helping all their students prepare for the future and then promote those practices.

Colleges and employers already dispute the notion that students "need" and "can afford" some time off in senior year (by and large students who are out of the habit of challenging work do *not* jump in again with renewed energy), but they should do so even more widely. They complain that students arrive unprepared to do serious work in either place, but they need to let high schools know what skills are required to do well both in the short and longer term. Both venues need young people who are able and willing to apply the "hard" (reading, math) and "soft" (imagination, collaboration) skills day after day (Murnane and Levy 1996). Some employers (along with the K–16 initiatives in some states) are attempting to erase the gaps between high school and postsecondary options by establishing clear basic-skills prerequisites, thereby motivating students and reducing the time and energy wasted in transition (National Commission on the High School Senior Year 2001b).

The number of high school seniors who are accepted by colleges is rising—which is considered good news, because it indicates ambitiousness and hope—but so is the number who, once they arrive, do not have the skills to be offered places in entry-level courses. All but a few highly selective colleges have been forced to set up special remedial courses, which range in quality and effectiveness and use up money better spent in the high school or on regular college work. Even selective colleges that enroll talented, well-educated, motivated students ask that students who take a term or a year off pursue some type of constructive activity during that time.

If employers and colleges ask that seniors' plans for the spring be part of their application and monitor the progress of those whom they have accepted for employment or admission, the widespread assumption that a senior slump will be tolerated and is even expected will be discredited. If they insist that those whose plans change drastically or whose records turn worrisome provide an adequate explanation and withdraw their acceptance of those who cannot do so, they will counter the seniors' claim that "they can't really get us." In the long run, this policy ensures the match both the seniors and the colleges want and mirrors the accountability of life.

However, only the bravest and most principled colleges and employers will insist on a better performance from the spring-term seniors they have admitted or hired, because the policy would initially create chaos in the marketplace. Employers have told other applicants there is no longer a job. Colleges have elaborately built their class, arranged their scholarship packages, set aside the space, hired the teachers. Rejecting young people they have accepted earlier reduces their numbers. Going too far down their waiting list, however sensible the reason, may be seen as a sign of weakness.

Nearly every letter of admission or offer of employment counsels the senior to keep working, but the seniors don't think colleges and employers really mean it, because they don't enforce it. Cases in which a student's offer of admission or employment has been rescinded usually involve a serious disciplinary problem rather than declining grades. High schools, for their part, are also unwilling to report news that might harm the chances of individual seniors. Seniors rightly conclude that colleges and employers are counting on the high schools, despite their dwindling authority, to keep the lid on their seniors during these last few months. But high schools can do better than that.

The Senior Project

A senior project can help students focus their energies on the future rather than the past and at the same time combat senioritis. However, students who have not achieved the basic skills in high school should not undertake a time-consuming new challenge like this. Their senior project is to graduate. All through senior year, and preferably earlier, imaginative teachers and administrators should reorganize classes to help these students meet their old challenges in a new way. High school teachers should work with their colleagues in the workplace or college remediation courses to get new ideas and to persuade their students that this work is important. The most effective last-chance efforts involve devoting more time to fewer subjects: clear programs offering instant feedback and multiple explanations taught by outstanding teachers. Each of these seniors should have his or her own program and timetable geared to his or her particular weaknesses.

For the rest of the seniors, we must look for projects wherever we can. Some schools have less senioritis than others, so it is to them we can turn for ideas.

The teachers in technical schools, especially the "shops," seem to have convinced most of their students that there is important material to be learned right up to the end. In some cases, local employers reinforce that idea, stating exactly what they expect from entry-level employees. New machinery needs to be mastered while it is available, when the "boss" is a good explainer and mentor and beginners' errors can be tolerated. New techniques are not taught until the old ones are mastered, and some of the most challenging and important are saved until the last few weeks. New methods of collaboration are not only demonstrated but practiced. These connections are not abstract: they are based on individual conversations and shared information about each senior and his or her plans. Since the skills acquired in technical school make a material difference in the workplace, students have a lot of incentive to work hard.

In regular high schools, the senior project and the resulting exhibition can transform the experience of the senior spring. The project provides novelty—an important commodity at this point—and replaces other courses such as the senior seminar, although it is supervised by a teacher. A project has a beginning, middle, and end, and some aspects of it are determined by the student. The senior project should be interdisciplinary, to reinforce the idea that the boundaries that seem so fixed during high school are going to be much more fluid later on. And the senior project should be of use to a wider community. Sometimes this wider community is the school itself. For example, seniors often choose to give the school something they feel was lacking in their own experience: a soccer video that can be used in training sessions on rainy days, a style handbook for the school newspaper, an obstacle course for the athletic department. Other times the usefulness is even broader: testing and cleaning up the water in a local river, helping out at a local elementary school.

When service learning has a strong base in the school, seniors have little trouble deciding what to do. After months of summing up what they have achieved and emphasizing a common standard, seniors enjoy the chance to tread new—even risky—ground. Being able to choose the topic and the mode of study and presentation is a chance to demonstrate real interests and talents.

When service learning has a strong base in the school, seniors have little trouble deciding what to do. After months of summing up what they have achieved and emphasizing a common standard, seniors enjoy the chance to tread new—even risky—ground.

Transcripts, graduation programs, and yearbooks often include the titles of senior projects as an important piece of information about not only each senior but also the school. Some schools reinforce commitment to the senior project by establishing a fund to which students can apply to offset expenses.

The most successful senior projects fall into three categories.

The first is creative: constructing a harpsichord, creating a video, choreographing a new performance. These should each involve work and explanations in a number of areas. The maker of a musical instrument, for example, should explain the physics behind the sounds the instrument makes, the history of the instrument, the artistic considerations that dictate the way the instrument looks. The director of a theater performance should describe how she made artistic decisions and got past personal squabbles to create a group effort.

The second kind of project is an investigation, alone or with others, of an area that holds great interest. This could involve the geological, cultural, and historical aspects of one's own part of the world—the border region between California and Mexico, the Adirondack Mountains, the Upper Peninsula of Michigan—including the reproduction of artifacts. The emphasis is on what's most important about the region, to others but also to oneself. The project might end with a tour, in person or on a video. These same techniques can be used with investigations of French cooking or Chinese cinema.

The third category, the one most likely to allow the senior to "touch the future," is closely tied to a student's anticipated career choice. The student does research, interviews members of the profession, perhaps observes or participates in the workplace. Activities may also center around acquiring relevant skills: drafting for future architects, lab work for future scientists, writing for future journalists, tutoring or a teaching assistantship for future teachers.

These projects are not just passing time; they are shown and described to others orally and in writing, deeply and individually. The presentation or artifact in which these projects culminate is the first entry in a "career portfolio": a substantial record of what activities seem most worthwhile and why.

Senior projects require planning. If the intention is for the senior seminar to turn into a senior project and/or internship at some point during the year, it might be sensible to organize the seminar around fields of interest: health, business, education, the arts, the environment. The advantage here is that the students will be working on career goals as well as defining and then pursuing their most immediate inclinations. They can save time by working with others who are pursuing similar interests. In the health group, one member can check out the hospitals in the area, another the nursing homes. One member can look for lab work, another can work in a clinic.

Organizing a seminar this way reinforces several important skills. Teachers are trying to persuade their charges that they can undertake complicated projects and yet do them thoroughly. For one thing, students can pool—and discuss—their findings. Taking the process a step further and writing about it will bring even more clarity to the undertaking. The students are not writing just to keep themselves busy; they are writing to deepen their own thoughts and to inform others. Working closely with other students like this, with the outcome for all resting on the efforts of individuals, is an excellent way to reinforce responsibility. Sources must be checked carefully. Deadlines must be met. Procrastination becomes not just a personal failing but a hurdle in using class time together, and class time, once lost, has to be rescheduled outside school. Each week, each exercise brings the group closer to a successful final project. If they can see their place on that continuum, they will feel that their time and their efforts are respected, and they are likely to dig in. Once the environment is changed to resemble the working world, many work habits take on a new meaning.

Organizing the senior seminar around fields of interest has some disadvantages, too. The seminar curriculum suggested in Chapter 7 may have to be curtailed. Some groups may get too narrow. Clustering around a field of interest such as business or the arts may mean that the same kids are hanging out together, and the benefits of heterogeneity in their last year in high school will be lost. Each high school needs to solve this problem differently, depending on its size, the opportunities in the local area, and the specific attributes of its faculty and its seniors.

Whatever the form of organization, the research skills that students have developed in their search for jobs, colleges, and training programs can be applied to finding worthwhile projects and/or internships. This avoids the problem of either letting adults do all the finding or getting an internship through some kind of personal or family contact in which the student's real needs—to get substantial experience doing the kind of work adults do in a field he or she finds interesting—are not adequately understood or met. It's a sensitive balancing act: the match must be made carefully, and by students too inexperienced to know how to do it. The teachers must become coaches, presenting the students with a variety of resources on how to decide which experiences are the most useful and what strategies to use in going after them, reacting to the students' plans and ideas instead of presenting their own.

Designing a senior project depends entirely on the experience and maturity of the individual student. After casting about vaguely for a while, the senior starts reeling in a number of likely ideas. The necessary focus for a successful project will materialize if each senior asks a burning question capable of being answered after a few months of work. Thus the question *Is there any justice in the world?* may have to be recast as *What are the ways in which gender and/or racial equity are being assured in South Africa?* The history of South Africa will then have to be researched, the laws that pertain understood. The project might involve preparing a pamphlet, report, website, or other instrument to disseminate information that has been lacking or misunderstood.

Topics will of course vary. In one school I visited, there were two senior projects, one each semester. In the fall, the seniors were asked to research an aspect of their city that could be used in a brochure luring new businesses. This was quite a challenge for an age group that could "hardly wait," as one of them put it, "to get out of town. This is the last place I would want to research. And I was supposed to think up reasons why workers would actually want to live here!" The project was popular nevertheless, because it involved activities and developed skills the seniors respected. They were interviewing local leaders and researching local history, sociology, and economics; their resources were challenging yet accessible; and they were able to present their findings with the help of graphics, photography, computers, multimedia presentations, and public speaking. They were working collaboratively in a style similar to that in the "real world." The assignment was authentic; its pertinence in a city wrestling with a decline in manufacturing was clear. Still, these seniors were looking forward to the spring, when they would design their own projects.

In most schools, senior projects are individual, and in some they can be undertaken only by the more successful students. Though broad requirements are drawn up by the faculty, the specifics of each project depend on the particular student's time and interest. The final outcome of the project also varies: a written paper, a poster, a piece of artwork, a video, a speech, a website.

Seniors' descriptions of their projects reflect their increasing self-consciousness as learners and workers. "Our senior seminar," one senior reported, "teaches self-discipline. We're learning to work on our own because we don't always have to come to class. That's nice because it gives us some of the freedom we want as seniors, and only seniors are allowed to take that class." Some take advantage of the broad requirements and do the minimum amount of work, but others surprise themselves by the level of their engagement. "The senior project was the best work I did in high school. I worked so hard I couldn't believe it," one said. "It was so beyond requirement it wasn't even funny! I wondered if the rest of my life is going to be like this."

Senior projects are notorious for the teacher time they require: investigating local opportunities, mentoring, encouraging, and cajoling students. This kind of work, often unfamiliar, sometimes drives teachers crazy, although it may also be a welcome change in their workload. But most are happy to help the seniors with their projects and proud of the outcome, often the most rewarding one they've ever experienced. But for projects to be successful, the high school must be prepared to assign each adviser only a small number of projects to oversee and reduce her other responsibilities.

Internships

Many high schools are eager enough to send their seniors elsewhere during the spring, but on a get-them-out-of-here basis: work in a law firm, but empty wastebaskets. No questions to be answered, no journals to write, no exhibitions at the end of the semester. Other high school seniors already work outside school, but in jobs unconnected with their future, jobs in which they do not need to apply the skills they have been learning. This is one reason they undervalue school.

An unpaid internship or similar arrangement that involves challenging, authentic work is something else entirely and is likely to be of long-term benefit. "It's time for me to think about what I want to get out of life," so many seniors declare. They also mean what they want to *give to life*, and work is a large part of that. In internships, the seniors experience what it's like to work, but without closing off options; instead, they are *exploring realistic options*, finding out what feels compelling to them, what they might be able to do. Seniors see their eventual working lives as a natural extension of this kind of worthy work—although with more knowledge and skill and, therefore, with pay.

Barbara Schneider and David Stevenson, in *The Ambitious Generation: America's Teenagers, Motivated but Directionless* (1995), write about the value of internships for students in high school. Drawing from a recent, exhaustive study, they declare that the overwhelming majority of students, while ambitious in one sense—they expect to go to college and pursue careers—are ignorant of the demands of those careers and of whether their own talents and habits will match up. Their hopes for the future, therefore, are not as likely to be achieved, because their ambitions are focused on how selective a college they can go to rather than on what they want to study and eventually do later in their lives. Senior projects and internships that are constructed around a senior's interests and career goals help align his or her ambitions in the light of realistic experience. Experiencing these future activities can bring new hope as well as purpose into the senior spring.

The best internships are thoughtfully arranged and coordinated with other curriculum so that the last weeks in school are kept as coherent as possible. Keeping a journal and talking frequently with one's mentor on the job and one's adviser at school help the senior reflect carefully on the experience. Learning from experience is a truism: easy to say but harder to do, especially for those who are familiar with a different kind of learning, where topics have been laid out carefully by others. But if the primary aim is to keep the seniors working, thinking, and growing, learning from experience is necessary.

Some schools encourage their seniors to work out in the world, but not as individuals investigating possible careers. Instead, they arrange for the whole class to provide a community service together—rehabilitate a building, for example. The skills the students learn may be less relevant to their particular interests, but the sense of doing something together for others reinforces a relationship with the larger community. It also gives the seniors a sense of accomplishment and tightens their sense of themselves as a distinctive class. Years later, passing by the house or the community garden on which they have worked, the seniors remember this experience with as much pleasure as their senior pranks. In fact, the best part of an experience like this is similar to the best parts of a "good" senior prank.

The Exhibition

More and more high schools end the senior year with an exhibition, a new form of accountability when grades in the old sense "don't matter." The students demonstrate not only what they have achieved but also how well they can describe it. It is a serious, even reverent process, designed to show seniors at their best, judged by their teachers but also by their peers, by teachers from other schools, and by people invited from the community. Exhibitions can take different forms.

One is a graduation portfolio. The school's standards in different areas of learning are held up against a student's own work in various forms: written essays and math tests, videos and live presentations, artistic expressions. The emphasis is on the way the student does this work most skillfully—not the usual "gotcha" that characterizes comprehensive tests—but all bases are covered. They include the student's best academic work from each year, with special emphasis on the work in senior year. They may also include letters from parents, employers, and the senior on recent observed academic or personal growth.

In a portfolio the seniors' self-consciousness is put to good use. One teacher asked his students, in essays due weekly for the last seven weeks of school, to describe seven different aspects of themselves: as mathematician, athlete, brother, etc. In a number of schools, students are expected to produce an essay discussing their hopes and plans for their future lives: its professional, emotional, even athletic aspects. These essays are not meant to be binding, of course, but they are an opportunity for the student to write down what he or she is already thinking and then think some more.

Another form of exhibition is an oral exam in which a panel of faculty and a few invited outsiders put the seniors through their paces, conducting a comprehensive evaluation of their progress. The questions usually follow a student's portfolio carefully, allowing him to clarify areas of interest. Depending on the questions and the answers given, these can be grueling sessions, and some need to be repeated by seniors who have not prepared carefully. The personal nature of the requirement and the time adults are willing to take to prepare them for it help the seniors withstand and respect what is a substantial hurdle.

Other kinds of oral exhibitions are reports on a more limited area of the senior's work, such as the senior project. In schools that take this requirement most seriously, there is a "practice exhibition" in which serious criticism is expected and offered and necessary improvements are outlined, and the senior is then given the time to do the necessary work. The responses can range from the most informal to the most formal, the most open to the most private, the most minor to the most fundamental. Observers may fill out forms, with or without their names, that solicit comments and questions. All this feedback is of great help to the senior and her adviser as they consider the suggestions. Decisions about graduation depend on how well the student responds to and meets these expectations in preparing the final product.

As graduation approaches, many high schools display their seniors' work, be it in a concert, an art show, an exhibition night. These are celebrations: competitions without the prizes, with everyone meant to be a winner, with a clear and joyful demonstration of the new standards that the seniors are able—and willing—to meet. The best exhibitions are not just retrospectives but include a new piece of music, a new drawing, a new piece of research. It is very exciting to visit high schools during senior exhibition night. Inviting the parents and the community into a school to see the exhibitions is a big motivator for the seniors to do their best. The relief of a challenge met is palpable, and the congratulations from siblings, grandparents, parents, and family friends heartfelt and deserved. The seniors' pride in what they have accomplished is obvious. Forgotten for now is the cynicism, the "cool," even the list of college acceptances.

Though exhibitions require much preparation from students, mentors, and faculty, they are worth it, because they give the senior a chance to reflect about what she or he has done. They also emphasize academic accomplishment in an environment that is otherwise rapidly turning into a circus. The cultural imperatives of senioritis and beach week are diluted while the seniors strut a different sort of "stuff."

Successful completion of the exhibition should be an important graduation requirement. No matter how many courses have been passed, how many credits collected, how many external examinations taken, how many portfolios prepared, this is a final important hurdle set by a loving and self-respecting institution. Some seniors' graduations end up having to be delayed. When the diplomas are finally earned, however, they will have real meaning for all the participants.

* * *

How can seniors be persuaded to engage meaningfully with the new standards and challenges of projects, internships, graduation portfolios, and exhibitions? The answer is, with difficulty. Seniors will complain that in other high schools, graduation depends only on credits earned years before, not on proficiencies that continually need to be applied and tested. Most of all, they may not be willing to give up their "senior spring," however unsatisfying it eventually turns out to be for so many of them. To counter these criticisms—which in some schools amount to short-term rebellions—the faculty must give as well as get. The projects must be individual, designed over several months, and be interesting as well as challenging. The process of reflection on the seniors' new work must be helpful and deep. The kind of exhibition (or exhibitions) undertaken must match the student's learning style. Much flexibility must be shown, except in relation to whether the student is expected to work hard and make measurable personal academic progress during the senior year.

Any high school's process of moving to meaningful new graduation requirements will be slower than some would like. These first conversations around change are often difficult ones. Each faculty group will want to understand and then address senioritis according to its own terms and methods. Some may have advantages or constraints that don't apply to others, so the idea of change requires imagination as well as determination. Some will be more comfortable with a senior project that resembles a term paper; others will be more determined to pursue career plans; still others will carefully negotiate a separate path with each senior. Some teachers will want to ask seniors to do better work in the same way instead of a new kind of work in a new kind of way—work that, in the beginning, is inevitably less impressive. Others will insist that this is the very time for the seniors to take those first steps in a new direction.

The standards—and the stakes—will have to be lifted gradually. Some seniors will find ways to protest and malinger, which always lends fuel to a reform's critics. Even in schools that have a successful first round of projects and exhibitions, loopholes will need to be identified and plugged. This all takes vigilance and toughness as well as inspiration and persuasion on the leaders' parts. Much work will have to be reallocated. It will hardly be neat. Teachers who are good advisers for projects may not be the same teachers with the time to do so. The process will have to be handled with sensitivity and care.

The seniors eventually buy in. Projects carry importance, excitement. Those who have been dreading the "slipping away and slipping down" aspect of senioritis are grateful that there is more to do. Others have always wished that school provided a chance for them to pursue their interests and their career plans. One young woman's project involved working in a clinic treating the medical problems of immigrants. The research she did in sociology, cultural mores, and medical ethics as well as the tasks she was assigned in the clinic demonstrated her interests, her initiative, and her growth during her senior year. She had substantial experience in a number of areas that could become a college major and a career. This, even more than the colleges that accepted her, was how she measured her sense of her own worth. "It was a lot of work, but I know that I really made something of my senior year." She had used an important time well. And it was *her* senior year.

Another senior admitted that he never would have done his senior project or presented it at the school exhibition if it hadn't been a graduation requirement. "Still, it's real learning because it

> "Still, it's real learning because it makes you think about things. The exhibition is a challenge. Some kids are even transferring to another high school to avoid it, but I think it's something I will need to do in real life."

makes you think about things. The exhibition is a challenge. Some kids are even transferring to another high school to avoid it, but I think it's something I will need to do in real life. I am learning all about taxes: why we have them, where they go. And how to fill out the tax form. It's something that I need to know how to do." His project lent a breadth and a solidity to his experience that helped him set goals, both for now and for later, to work with a broader range of people and to assess the value of his studies.

For another student, the work he had done paid off in two ways. First, he got himself off a college's waiting list by sending in his senior project, a substantial and credible essay with accompanying graphics and a computer program—an excellent piece of work that reflected his growth during his senior year. The late-in-the-year deadline for the project kept him on target. "I didn't think I wanted to work any more, so I'm amazed at what I still could do." He appreciated the variety and the chance to end the year with a sense of triumph rather than drift. And second, all this gave him confidence for his exhibition. "I think it's easier for seniors to realize that presenting our work is an important part of our life now," he said. "There are people that are doing dentist things and people that are doing stock market stuff. It makes you think about what you want to do in life. I'm excited to move on and see what's going to happen with me. The exhibition helped with that." His excitement about and commitment to his own future were a far cry from the seniors who "weren't there any more."

It is so important for seniors to stay connected with their hopes for their lives. The last few weeks of high school can remain relevant. The seniors and their teachers can get past letters and numbers—sent somewhere else—as the only motivator for or measurement of learning. When the whole community has a chance to concentrate on a substantial piece of each senior's real work, the high school's standards and its people can again be seen in a proud and generous light.

Epilogue: Walking Away Forever

In the last weeks of her senior year Maria was experiencing a strange state of excitement, nostalgia, and regret. It was "finally time to leave," but she wasn't quite ready. "I need to go around the school one more time, to see the room where I took algebra and the hall where I used to hang out sophomore year." The past needed to be revisited, the future faced. Passionately anticipated and yet somehow inconceivable, graduation would bring an end to her formal affiliation with high school. The most momentous year in her life was over. The vacuum left in its wake varied; her friends felt it positively and negatively, but each one of them felt it at least a little.

Maria felt it a lot. She admitted to a fear of change. "When they put up the senior countdown, and I see how many days there are left, it makes me sad. I always thought I would be so ready to leave; just, I'm out of here, I'm going. But I'm not, because I'm going to miss everything. I mean, it'll be fun next year, and I'm really excited, but I'm nervous. To tell you the truth, I'm scared to death. My friends tell me I'm crazy, but I think they are scared too. I guess being scared is all part of it. It's refreshing, I guess, to be scared. It keeps me awake and alert to the changing world, and I like that." She and her friends were recording their feelings, trying to come to some understanding and then resolution. "Every time you move on, it means you have to leave something in the past. I never thought about it until lately, but when you've been somewhere your whole life and you have

"Every time you move on, it means you have to leave something in the past. I never thought about it until lately, but when you've been somewhere your whole life and you have never dealt with a major change, you don't know how hard it is. This is my high school. These walls are my comfort zones. It's kind of sad accepting that."

never dealt with a major change, you don't know how hard it is. This is my high school. These walls are my comfort zones. It's kind of sad accepting that."

Maria also felt the school still needed her. "It's so strange to think that we are not going to be around in the fall. I feel like we have to fine-tune some of the stuff we started senior year. What are they going to do without us?" But *would* they be missed? "My teacher said, 'In twenty-nine days you guys are going to be pushed out into the world. You're going to be out of here.' All of a sudden, I saw that was true. That's when my time started to feel limited. I'm not sure I'll ever be part of a class again."

Torn by conflicting impressions, Maria watched herself, eager to believe that she could handle the transition gracefully. "You never would think that you would be homesick for a high school, but I know I'm going to be," she said wistfully. "Graduation really dominates your senior year. You do things that you wouldn't normally do. You do things with your friends more often. You go back to see the teachers that you liked. I just went back to my elementary school and saw my old elementary school teachers. You want to make sure that everyone that has been in your life who's been good to you understands the influence they had on you before you move on."

After graduation Maria would never again be required to return to this building. High school wouldn't be part of her day anymore; instead, it would be memories in her head. If she came back, it would be because she wanted to. That reality made a huge difference, and yet the emotions surrounding it were mixed. "Senior privileges were great in October," she remembered, "when I just walked away from school during a study hall, and the others had to stay there. I felt wonderful. I felt like I was cheating even though I wasn't, and it was quite a rush. But now I am walking away forever, and that's different. The next time I come back here, I will need a visitor's pass."

Moving on is hard to do. It matters how well the seniors have accomplished their last year in high school, for there is another arduous journey just ahead.

References

Bok, Sissela. 1999. *Lying: Moral Choice in Public and Private Life.* New York: Vintage Books.

Csikszentmihalyi, Mihaly, and Barbara Schneider. 2000. *Becoming Adult: How Teenagers Prepare for the World of Work.* New York: Basic Books.

Gardner, Howard. 1983. *Frames of Mind: The Theory of Multiple Intelligences.* New York: Basic Books.

Hine, Thomas. 1999. *The Rise and Fall of the American Teenager.* New York: Avon.

Murnane, Richard J., and Frank Levy. 1996. *Teaching the New Basic Skills: Principles for Educating Children to Thrive in a Changing Economy.* New York: Free Press.

National Commission on the High School Senior Year. 2001a. *The Lost Opportunity of Senior Year: Finding a Better Way.* Princeton, NJ: The Woodrow Wilson National Fellowship Foundation.

———. 2001b. *Raising Our Sights: No High School Senior Left Behind.* Princeton, NJ: The Woodrow Wilson National Fellowship Foundation.

Perkins, David. 1992. *Smart Schools: From Training Memories to Educating Minds.* New York: Free Press.

Quindlen, Anna. 1998. *One True Thing.* New York: Dell Books.

Schneider, Barbara, and David Stevenson. 1995. *The Ambitious Generation: America's Teenagers, Motivated but Directionless.* New Haven, CT: Yale University Press.

Steen, R. E. 2001. *Opportunities Missed: Reflections on Transitions from High School.* St. Louis, MO: Fleishman Hillard Research.

Steinberg, Laurence, with Bradford Brown and Sanford Dornbusch. 1996. *Beyond the Classroom: Why School Reform Has Failed and What Parents Need to Do.* New York: Simon and Schuster.

Tyack, David, and Larry Cuban. 1995. *Tinkering Toward Utopia: A Century of School Reform.* Cambridge, MA: Harvard University Press.

Index